ISLAM & EUROPE
Crises are Challenges

Forum A. & A. Leysen for Intercultural Relations

ISLAM & EUROPE
Crises are Challenges

Edited by
Marie-Claire FOBLETS
Jean-Yves CARLIER

Contributions by
Ahmed ABOUTALEB
Durre S. AHMED
Abdullahi AHMED AN-NA`IM
Shaheen SARDAR ALI
Mohammed BENZAKOUR
Jean-Yves CARLIER
Marie-Claire FOBLETS
Ziba MIR-HOSSEINI
Fouad LAROUI
Bettina LEYSEN
Rashida MANJOO
Bhikhu PAREKH
Mathias ROHE
Cedric RYNGAERT
Prakash SHAH

UPL in Context

© 2010 Leuven University Press / Presses Universitaires de Louvain / Universitaire Pers Leuven

All rights reserved. Except in those cases expressly determined by law, no part of this publication may be multiplied, saved in an automated datafile or made public in any way whatsoever without the express prior written consent of the publishers.

ISBN 978 90 5867 739 6
D / 2010 / 1869 / 22
NUR: 741 / 717

Cover design: Jurgen Leemans
Typesetting: Friedemann Vervoort (Friedemann BVBA)

Table of Contents

Foreword and Acknowledgements:
Islam and the Requirements of Liberal Democratic Principles
Marie-Claire Foblets   7

Part I - The Islamic Challenge: Faith, Gender and Politics

Introductionary Speech
Ahmed Aboutaleb   15

Islam and Politics: Towards Post-Islamism?
Fouad Laroui   25

Human Rights and Islam
Bhikhu Parekh   39

Penetrations: A Psycho–Cultural view of Modernity,
Fundamentalisms and Islam
Durre S. Ahmed   53

Part II - The Islamic Challenge: Islam and the Secular State

Acknowledgments
Bettina Leysen   73

An-Na`im and His Work Toward an Islamic Reformation:
A Short Introduction
Jean-Yves Carlier   75

'European Islam or Islamic Europe':
The Secular State for Negotiating Pluralism
Abdullahi Ahmed An-Na`im   85

The 'Secularization' of Shari'a in Iran
Ziba Mir-Hosseini   109

Resurrecting Siyar *Through* Fatwas*? (Re)constructing
'Islamic International Law' in a Post–(Iraq) Invasion World*
Shaheen Sardar Ali   *117*

The Indian Dimension of An-Na`im's Islam and the Secular State
Prakash Shah   *153*

European Foreign Policy and the Universality of Human Rights
Cedric Ryngaert   *167*

*Compromising of Gender Equality Rights – Through the
Recognition of Muslim Marriages in South Africa*
Rashida Manjoo   *201*

*Islam and the Democratic State under the Rule of Law
– and Never the Twain Shall Meet?*
Mathias Rohe   *215*

Toward the Triumph of Reason
Mohammed Benzakour   *237*

List of Contributors   *243*

Foreword and Acknowledgements
Islam and the Requirements of Liberal Democratic Principles

We were privileged and pleased to have been given the opportunity, within the framework of the A. & A. Leysen Forum, to invite an illustrious roster of scholars of Islam whose essays are collected here, to Leuven, in 2008 and 2009. From the outset, we, therefore, wish to express our deepest thanks to them and special appreciation for their sustaining support that made the Forum and this work possible. This is the second book in the series of the Leysen Forum. Informed by their several contributions collected in the first book[1], this volume continues in the same vein and seeks to provide an objective and open forum in which experts from both within and outside the Muslim world come together to show how, in their views, convergences between Islam and the West, with a focus on Europe, can be achieved and compromises justified.

In the introduction to the book *Muslims in Western Politics*[2], Abdulkader H. Sinno recently expressed the following concern: *"Many Western Muslims, particularly Europeans, continue to feel that they live in the midst of Western societies without belonging to them [...]. And clashes of cultures and violent attacks have made many in non-Muslim Western publics wary of Muslim minorities. Western States and their rapidly growing Muslim populations are adjusting to each other under the constant pressure of exogenous shocks such as transnational terrorism and wars in the Middle East that involve Western militaries or produce intense interest among Westerners, Muslims and non-Muslims. The way they manage the process will deeply affect the future of Western polities and their relations with the Muslim world, which constitutes a fifth of humanity"*.[3] The risk in his view is that, against such background, Muslims in Europe become embittered, in particular the younger generations, and would grow into an irreconcilable fragment of society, driven by confrontational activism and seeking support from those who wish to make the case that the West in an enemy of Islam. He in particular refers to the situation in France and Belgium.

---

[1] M.-C. Foblets (ed.), *Islam & Europe. Challenges and Opportunities*, Leuven University Press, 2008.
[2] A.H. Sinno (ed.), *Muslims in Western Politics*, Bloomington & Indianapolis, Indiana University Press, 2009.
[3] *Ibid.*, 5.

The risk A. Sinno is referring to is undoubtedly real, to some extent it has already become reality. Unfortunately, some advocate positions that touch on separatism and/or justify the use of violence. This book, therefore, argues for an adequate understanding of how growing Western Muslim communities in Europe experience their minority position in Europe and what needs to be done to improve their participation in society. Its goals is to address some of the challenges in comparative context and to explain variation among different countries in facing the question how much room secular democracy should ensure for this relatively new religious subgroup in contemporary European history, and when it does, whether it should do so as a matter of normative principle or instead a compromise of principles?

The grossly unequal and biased focus on robust incompatibilities between the ideals of Western democracies and Islam, engendering feelings of xenophobia or threat, does blatant injustice to Western Muslims in many cases. Through a broad range of arguments and perspectives, the papers in this work imaginatively advocate in support of the kind of pluralism that approaches Islam as a living, breathing and rich civilization, characterized by extreme (internal) diversity, and embraces this diversity. This volume thus is concerned with the appreciation of difference(s). All authors agree on the importance of scrupulously exploring the practices and policies that can establish a sustainable balance between the claims for participation expressed by Muslims and the requirements of liberal democratic principles.

The authors explore several interrelated questions: how much diversity is permissible within the constitutional framework of a liberal pluralistic democratic society? How strong are the implications of citizenship for how Western Muslims can be expected to arrange their lives, conceptualise gender identity, comply with domestic human rights frameworks and contribute to it? What are equitable accommodations of contested practices? How can misunderstandings around these issues be prevented? The papers explore resources from political theories, ethnography, gender studies, also from psychology, as well as comparative legal analysis. The authors include a majority of legal scholars, but also political theorists, social scientists and psychologists.

Yet a number of papers in this volume revolve around the work of Abdullahi Ahmed An-Na'im who also has made a contribution to this work. The reason for that is the fact that A. An-Na'im was awarded an honorary doctorate 2009 from the Catholic University of Leuven. For the honorary doctorates of 2009, the themes of *Multiculturalism, intercultural relations and diversity* had been selected. In the invitation letter by the rectors of the UCL and the K.U. Leuven, this choice was explained as follows: *"mutual understanding between nations, races, cultures and philosophical ideas, among others... but also the desire to explore differences in a dynamic and open manner."* The choice of An-Na`im was, for reasons we elaborate below, an obvious one. Thanks to the support of the Leysen Forum we were in the position to organise a two day international conference in his honor in Leuven. The papers presented at this conference are grouped in the second part of this book.

Today An-Na`im is recognized the world over as a leading expert in the area of religion and law, and as a human rights activist. As Jean-Yves Carlier explains in his paper in this volume, he may serve as an outstanding example of a thinker who for several decades has restlessly endeavored to build up viable relations between Islam and Western democracies.

An-Na`im's starting point is a humanistic interpretation of the Qur'an. The basic principle is that the foundation of human rights is firmly embedded in the Qur'an, provided that the accent is placed on the *universal* values contained in that text. In this regard, An-Na`im takes a stand against cultural relativism. But his reasoning does not stop there, in his view discussions about Islam and human rights are best conducted in the context of a secular State: for the State must create the (pre)conditions for groups to be able to find clarity, on their own, without external pressure, about a number of key questions of faith; the neutral, secular State is best placed to guarantee these conditions. In his work, *Islam and the Secular State: Negotiating the Future of Shari'ah* he states, *"It is critically important to maintain the religious neutrality of the State, precisely because human beings tend to favor their own views, including their religious beliefs, over the views of others"* [4] He therefore vigorously argues that freedom of religion, also in the case of Islam, is best protected under secular law and therefore proposes returning to a clear separation between the coercive authority of the (secular) State and the normative system of Islam.

An-Na`im enjoys much credit and gratitude among those who, with him, look for ways to reconcile Islam with the principles of constitutionalism and democracy. His work offers an outstanding example of an understanding of the relationship between Shari'a, as a religious normative system, and State Law, that emphasizes the need

---

[4] A.A. An-Na`im, *Islam and the Secular State: Negotiating the Future of Shari'ah*, Cambridge, Mass., Harvard University Press, 2008, 85

for a secular State administration. State law should in his view not be part of Islam, but the expression of the democratic will of a society. An-Na`im goes unusually far in his conviction that Islam and universal human rights are compatible and seeks to build bridges between what, wrongly in his view, is regarded by some as contradictory positions on the (political and legal) organisation of human societies. He goes so far as to argue that the positions of women and of non-Muslims may be subject to review within Islam. He even sees it as the duty of Muslims to review their standpoints critically on these matters and to adapt them to the new historical context in which the religion of Islam is lived out today. This renewal cannot be imposed from above, but must grow from internal discussions of such questions among Muslims themselves. An-Na`im is convinced that in this way, Islam and human rights can be reconciled. For what is true of religious affairs is also true of human rights: An-Na`im's starting point is that human rights cannot be imposed from above by means of laws and formal legislation unless they are also supported from within by the social groups concerned.

On the occasion of An-Na`im's award in Leuven a number of colleagues joined forces at a meeting/conference in his name, and with this volume, not only with a view to show by so doing their great appreciation for his work, but also to discuss with him the views of the relationships between Islam and human rights. The second part of this volume is a collection of papers written in his honor. It was no easy task to decide on a list of participants. The contributors who make up the second part of this volume were invited ultimately for their acquaintance with An-Na`im's positions and for the reason that, like him, they commit their academic work to the view that the fundamental values expressed in human rights are not a disavowal of the aspirations of Islam. They too regard the reconciliation of Islam and universal human rights as of crucial importance. Their work falls first and foremost within the legal sphere, but it touches also very closely on politics, culture and ethics.

In his more recent pieces, An-Na`im has started also to be concerned with the position of Western Muslims, living in secular, pluralistic societies. He has the kind of intellectual distance necessary to be able to write on this sensitive topic with vision, but at the same time he exhibits the necessary, militant engagement to go beyond mere non-committal statements. It is probably this combination of international academic renown and activism that makes An-Na`im such an inspiring scholar on the question of how to shape, in contemporary setting, the interactions between Muslim minorities in Western societies and the State legal system(s) and how to benefit from the input these minorities may have in preparing the future. An-Na`im's position as a Muslim and a human rights advocate, his intelligible criticism of relativism and his constant appeal for universal human rights, and his commitment to multiculturalism, have all combined to give his positions the necessary legitimacy. Discussion of matters of Islamic faith would not be accepted coming from any person who is an outsider to Islam; similarly, people would not believe that an intellectual who is not a trained jurist could understand what is meant by the universal claims of human rights, or what can be expected within a secular democratic framework with regard to the safeguarding of pluralism and protection of minorities. An-Na`im's work addresses several audiences: he offers an alternative to the orthodox interpretation of Islam, and expects human rights activists to be more critical of their own prejudices towards Islam. In the work and personality of A. An-Na`im these several, at first sight incongruent positions, harmoniously merge.

The editors and the authors owe a large debt to Anne and André Leysen, and their children, who by their visionary approach to European society made it possible for the Leysen Forum to be created and, by so doing, indirectly prompted the series of lectures that were the inspiration for this book. They have the vision that pluralism enriches human experience and that, therefore, we have to pursue that path by all means. The Leysen Forum began with a conversation between the sponsors, the Leysen children acting for their parents, and Prof. em. Roger Dillemans, then director of the Senate Leuven. The latter supported us with his legendary warmhearted generosity that no equivalent experience can bring. In his own unique way he infused the whole process. The sponsors generously provided us with the necessary finances that enabled us to convince some of the best scholars in the field of Islam to come to Leuven, and share their experiences with us. They indeed generously sponsored the preparation of the series of lectures and they also supported all events, including this publication. But they also assisted us with a deeply rooted faith in the ultimate power of balanced arguments and respectful dialogue between cultures in preparing the future of Europe, and this is probably the most solid support one can give to an initiative that is set up to address multicultural challenges in contemporary society. The way they have accompanied the project, from the start to the production of this second book, has been no less than superb. We acknowledge therefore their generous sponsorship, both the financial assistance and their moral support.

Undoubtedly, striving for harmonious relations between Islam and the West is one of the most important challenges of our time.

Marie-Claire Foblets

The problem is of burning political importance. Reflecting on possible solutions to this question raises high scientific expectations, presupposing in particular a thorough knowledge of the worldviews and cultures involved. On the latter point, all authors who agreed to publish in this work, endeavor to address issues linked to Islam and the position of Muslims in the West with much intellectual integrity. Not only in terms of content - as should become clear from the contributions - but also through the position they adopt as scholars with a cosmopolitan commitment. They share the spirit that inspired the Leysen Forum. In Leuven, the memories of the Leysen Forum will undoubtedly remain an enduring symbol of this dedication to humanity and the promotion of diversity in Western democracies, including Islam.

We thank all the contributors to this volume for providing their excellent essays and for the true pleasure the collaboration with them within the framework of the Leysen Forum gave us. We also wish to express our special appreciation to the colleagues who have no written contribution in this book but who accepted to respond to the speakers. Thanks to the care with which each of them prepared their responses to the speaker they were 'assigned' to, they introduced - each in his or her own way - vivid and high quality discussions, with the speakers and with their audience: Paul Lemmens, Tariq Modood, Nadia Fadil and Helge Daniels.

We acknowledge Mrs. Isabel Penne among administrators and the indispensible and very outstanding members of her staff. They helped us navigate complicated financial and other practical logistics, providing technical support and being of continuous assistance. Betty Vanden Bavière meticulously assisted us with formatting the manuscript, and Claire Riley with editing several pieces.

We finally recognize our publisher, in particular Mrs. Schipper, and her staff for their helpfulness and patience.

Marie-Claire Foblets,
October 2009

Part I
The Islamic Challenge:
Faith, Gender and Politics

INTRODUCTIONARY SPEECH

Ahmed Aboutaleb

Ladies and Gentlemen,
 It is an honour and a pleasure to have the opportunity to speak with you for nearly a whole evening on matters that are close to my heart as a Dutch politician.
 I would like once again to thank you for this invitation.
 The organisers have asked me to address the question of what integration means in (Dutch) society - with the word 'Dutch' in parentheses. Therefore I may speak of Belgian society as well. But if you don't mind, I will limit myself to my own, with an occasional brief excursus across the border.
 Perhaps, in light of increasing globalisation, we will all soon be talking about our society. But that will take a while yet. Though you never know, human beings need to have something to dream about...
 I want to acknowledge from the outset: I don't have a ready-made answer to your question. I struggle with the concept of integration. I would like you to share in that struggle this evening. To take part in my struggle to discover how to bring population groups closer to each other. A process that is accompanied by a great many personal considerations. In the end, the political is also personal. Telling each other the truth is far from easy. And yet I choose to tell you my truth. For there can be no shine without friction. I hope that are prepared to think along with me.
 The title of this lecture series, on which I have the privilege of occupying the first spot, 'Crises are challenges', is one that I can identify with. But as I said: I struggle with it. As a true Dutchman, my motto, like that of Zeeland, is 'Luctor et emergo'. I struggle and rise to the top.
 Ladies and Gentlemen. For over a year now I have been Secretary of State for Social Affairs and Employment in a centre-left cabinet, that of Balkenende/Bos. A cabinet consisting of Labour (PvdA), Christian Democrats (CDA) and Christian Socialists (ChristenUnie). My political/governmental career began when I was a city councillor in Amsterdam, where I gained the necessary political experience in the areas of education, youth, employment, income and urban policy. As a secretary of state, my aim is during the time I have to help more people find employment. At the same time, I would like to combat poverty and see fewer people require social assistance.

Social assistance – I believe you call that 'minimum income' in the context of social services. My goal is to do both those things simultaneously and jointly, together with what in the Netherlands we call all stakeholders in the employment and income chain in the region.

Integration is not itself my core business, although you might say that for people of immigrant backgrounds, participation in the labour market may well be the best road to integration. Paid work is one of the scarcest resources a society can offer. In the Netherlands we have opted for a separate minister of Integration, linked to Housing and Communities. The underlying idea is that housing, the home environment are the basis for individual and social development and thus for integration and settlement.

Concretely, this means that we intend within ten years to transform some forty problem neighbourhoods into vital residential, working and living environments where people enjoy living and working and are involved in society. And I hope to be able to make my own modest contribution to this plan in the area of paid employment. But I am the first to admit that the degree of integration cannot be measured solely by hard indicators such as housing and participation in education and work. That is indeed the basis, and I will come back to that shortly, but it is much more than that.

For instance, there is the question of whether migrants are prepared to immerse themselves in the Dutch language and culture, history and rule of law. In these areas as well there is a long road ahead. But indispensable for a successful integration.

And here we come to one part of my struggle. Back to the title 'Crises are challenges'. To make a challenge out of a crisis demands daring and flexibility of mind. The fact is that migration and integration leaves no one indifferent. In our country, as in yours, the issue has been occupying our minds for many years. Everywhere, in meeting rooms large and small, it has been and is being talked about. Problems are identified and discussed, sometimes resulting in vehement emotions. Over time, a laborious quest for effective solutions has been undertaken. In migrant circles, people were asked to think about their own contribution to the rise of fear and a sense of unease in society. Some feel that they have been backed into a corner, see themselves as victims and turn their backs on society.

Efforts by people of good will to reverse the growing alienation often have but a limited effect. That is nothing new - it has been going on for quite some time. But come what may, we must not allow that alienation to grow.

On the other hand, you still see in the Netherlands a group that is inclined to relativise these fears. They point out, among other things, that our country has only a short history of migration, and consider that in the course of time attitudes toward each other will naturally take a positive turn. Behind this line of reasoning lies the tendency to try to rationalise away feelings of unease. Therefore I find this the wrong reflex. The opposite is just as much a mistaken reflex, that of rousing feelings of unease by telling people that everything would be better if immigration were halted. Or that it is time to force minority cultures to embrace the majority culture. Forced marriages do not usually succeed. And so this in turn sharpens my struggle.

What is striking is that many people in the Netherlands have a negative view of integration, cultural diversity and Islam. Many Dutch people are afraid of losing their jobs and their identity. They see in the current debate a confirmation of their notion that the arrival of immigrants in the Netherlands is more of a threat than an enrichment.

The attack on the WTC in New York, the murders of Pim Fortuyn and Theo Van Gogh, threats to politicians and others, attacks in many other countries, the over-representation of persons of immigrant origin in criminal activity, and the riots in Utrecht and Amsterdam have led to even more distancing between native-born Dutch people and those of immigrant background.

Moreover, there is the fact that a significant part of this sense of unease in the Netherlands has come about because debate about immigrants and newcomers is linked to Islam. That muddies the waters of the discussion. The Islamisation of the public debate about integration does not make the climate any easier. I think that it should not be about religion but about human beings. Not about Islam but about Muslims. It may seem a subtle distinction, but the first is about religious conviction and the second about the behaviour that people derive from those convictions. The reasoning should not be: there are some extreme Muslims and therefore Islam is extreme. That reasoning is just as flawed as when you say: there are extremist Christians who kill doctors who perform abortions, and therefore Christianity is wrong.

So much, then, on my observations about the climate. Now the question is: what do we do about it? I have already said that I am struggling, but what lies between denying the problem and arousing unease is, as far as I am concerned, a relatively untrodden path. That is, the path of listening *to* and truly recognising our feelings of unease. Back and forth. I believe, and I call this a progressive insight, that we cannot simply take on the populist elements in politics, such as the PVV party led by Wilders, with a businesslike, policy-oriented approach. Rather, it is precisely by engaging the debate with an honest account. And above all: by having the courage of one's convictions.

Politicians must show that we truly feel the pain of our citizens. Even if you must admit that you don't have ready-made solutions to offer on all issues. That, too, is important.

Even without having drawn up a concrete policy, you can rank high in the opinion polls; this is true even if you stand for proposals that are clearly not feasible. There can be no other conclusion, therefore, than that you can gain adherents in society independently of any concrete policy. Apparently this depends on the whether you make a personal commitment and are prepared sometimes to take unconventional stances. That provides clarity. Citizens find the construction of hospitals, the availability of electric power, clean drinking water, etc., to be 'ordinary' things that a government must provide.

In addition, people want to know whether politicians will provide leadership in social change in a way that meets their concerns. Migration is one of these difficult areas. Citizens expect us to take a clear position on this matter.

Engage in the discussion, always and everywhere. Name the pain. That is what citizens want to hear. Without being populist, but precisely by remaining realistic. In any case do not forbid things, don't deny them. Politicians and government officials still tend to think far too often that general policy can influence a particular climate. Established politicians are too ready to believe that clever policy and a lot of money can make a difference. That is but half of the truth. Citizens think that governing, in the sense of doing things, is just normal. You can make a difference if you name the pain felt in society. But politicians have no idea what to do with people's feelings. Populists, political populists, do.

However important government measures may be, they are not enough to improve the position of migrants. In addition to the efforts by the government, it is migrants themselves who must recognise that they need to take their future into their own hands. That is something I have noticed during my many official visits throughout the country. Migrants and their social ties can and want to contribute to assuaging feelings of unease. It is primarily a matter of strengthening mutual trust. But there remains a gap between wanting and doing.

I have learned a lesson, personally, in this regard. I referred to it before as progressive insight. It began after the death of Theo Van Gogh. He was murdered during the period when I was a city councillor in Amsterdam. During a meeting at a mosque, I said at one point: "We want to create a we-society in Amsterdam. One that everyone belongs to. But anyone who wants to remain outside society, rejecting all that the Netherlands has to offer in terms of values, culture, freedom, etc., would do well to decide not to belong among us and to leave the Netherlands." And I added: "And there are airplanes taking off every minute."

I did not yet realise it then, but afterwards these words seemed to have been of crucial significance for managing the tensions in the capital at the time. People later said that my words gave them the sense that they were being heard in their pain.

With this message, I went into communities, mosques, schools, tea houses. I saw my task as being to provide the text and an explanation of my stance. The reactions in Amsterdam, as well as in the rest of the country, gave me the conviction that there is fertile ground in the Netherlands for such words, which do not trivialise the problems as perceived by many Dutch people.

By giving a signal that you see and recognise the problems and want to do everything is possible, you draw attention to your positive account, from native Dutch people, immigrants and of course from Muslims as well. There lies the key, as far as I'm concerned, to solving the problem. Speaking honestly and courageously. To both sides: longstanding Dutch people as well as Dutch people of immigrant origin.

Integration consists, effectively, of two components: Adaptation and Acceptance. I find that we must be honest both to the original Dutch population and to newcomers. To the original population, we must say: That's right, migration and globalisation have a shadow side as well. It is true, diversity leads to friction between cultures. Your concerns to preserve your own hearth and home are legitimate. We see your problems and feel your pain. And we find that the pain and concerns belong on our political agenda. But we need your help. We have to search together for a new equilibrium. This struggle is something we must undertake together.

The fact that there is so much hatred of Muslims ought to give Muslims themselves cause for reflection, instead of immediately jumping to the defence. Call it a quest within yourself. How can this be? What role do we Muslims ourselves play in the image of us that is out there? Instead of simply seeing the words of Wilders as unacceptable, reprehensible and ill-intentioned solely in order to gain political capital. For even though that is all true, the fact is that the 500,000 people in the Netherlands who voted for Wilders likely share his sentiments. And that is something to bear in mind. For me, that is important.

Migrants thus have their work cut out for them. A great responsibility rests on the shoulders of Muslims, given the current fear of the adherents of Islam. Only they can allay that fear.

Muslims can take steps within their own community to ensure that radical elements are not regarded as heroes. The ethnic and religious solidarity that is now being recognised is one step along the road to Muslims' own emancipation. Moreover, this wrongly gives the impression that Muslims are indifferent to the radical elements in their own circles.

The vanguard among Muslims is remarkably quiet. It is precisely from this group that one would expect a strong involvement in the public debate. They can serve as an engine to steer public debate in a favourable direction. That is also true for the much vaunted moderate religious leaders. From them as well I expect a position with regard to the radicals.

We are standing at a crossroads: there is the threat of further alienation, but ultimately this also threatens our stability. Merely sticking it out is no solution either. So what to do?

The present alienation can and must be stopped. This is, moreover, necessary because it presents a danger to the stability of society. The danger that we will have a society in which migrants form a new underclass instead of giving these new Dutch residents a full and appropriate place in society.

Sharpening the discussion is appropriate in the transition period in which we currently find ourselves. The 1970s and 80s were years of a certain social stability - call it the 'getting acquainted' phase. We are now going through a phase of which the endpoint is unknown. As far as I am concerned, the *transitional phase* is one of clear oppositions. A *conflict phase*, if you will. It is an apparent opposition. Clear opposition is sometimes necessary in order to enable us to see where we stand and to be able to build a bridge to the future.

A conflict stage can have a salutary effect. By vigorous polishing, a shine can emerge, as I have already said. But be careful lest too strenuous polishing become painful. It is hard to find a delicate balance. And if this reasoning is characterised as polarisation, then I say there is nothing wrong with polarisation!

The reality today is that many migrants feel that they are victims. They evoke discrimination as the reason why they remain stuck at the bottom of the social ladder. I am constantly pointing out that inadequate language skills and low educational levels are also obstacles to social improvement. These are issues on which migrants themselves must work, with support from our institutions. No one can do it for them.

Only with a great deal of effort on their part can they improve their social position. I call upon them first and foremost to have confidence in their own ability.

Thus in the final analysis it is strange that we need a law on integration in order to compel migrants to learn Dutch and familiarise themselves with the Netherlands. It is strange because these are people who freely chose to make their home in the Netherlands. You might expect that they would voluntarily wish to do what the integration law requires. That we need a law for this attests to a lack of curiosity for their new country. And that is unacceptable!

I don't mean to say that migrants must burn all their bridges when they come to the Netherlands, or that there is no room for their own cultural expressions, speaking the language of their country of origin or practising their religion. That would not only be unreasonable but also contrary to the international conventions on the rights of minorities.

There are fortunately many signs of hope. For instance, we see that many migrants are beginning, through education and employment, to ascend the social ladder. Increasing numbers of immigrants are very successful: in education, on the labour market, in the media, the medical world, politics. That inspires hope. I too have come a long way. Literally and figuratively. Via a lower-level technical training to an MTS (technical high school) and then to an HTS (higher technical school). I worked my way up until I became what I now am: Secretary of State for Social Affairs and Employment.

Unemployment among immigrant youth has been falling considerably in recent times. That is a good trend. Moreover, we in the Netherlands are not alone in this. I saw a report on the decrease in the number of unemployed Moroccan and Turkish youths in 13 cities here in Flanders. Unemployment among immigrant youth with low educational levels seems to have fallen by at least 38 per cent. The report mentioned the 'miracle of Limburg mining communities and of Mechelen'. Now I don't begrudge you all the miracles of the world, but I have compared the figures with those from our country, and it appears that in the Netherlands as well, the percentage of unemployed immigrant youth between the age of 15 and 25 has fallen from 26% at the end of 2005 to 16.4% at the end of 2008. And doing the figures, I come to a decrease of 37% in our country. The percentage of unemployment among all immigrants in the same period fell in the Netherlands from 15.8% to 8.7% in the final quarter of last year. That is a 50% decrease, and thus even more spectacular in our country than in Flanders.

That things are getting better is not only an economic fact resulting from the labour shortage. We also see that there is an increase in the level of education among the second generation of people of immigrant origin. The rise has begun at the higher educational levels and so, too, has the social advancement of this group. With as an interim result a cabinet in which for the first time in Dutch history there are two members of government from an immigrant background.

In absolute figures, however, we are still speaking of small groups. The majority is still hanging on to the lowest rungs of society, and there are still too many people who depend on benefit payments. That is cause for concern and weakens opportunities for migrants.

Mixed schooling is one part of the solution to reducing the gap, but that may well take another thirty years. What is needed is that neighbourhoods where there are such schools should be mixed. Social advancement in education and in societies takes generations. A cabinet that thinks that with a strong educational policy it will in four years be able to influence the social climate in this regard is very much mistaken. The Dutch government realises this. But this does not mean that nothing should be done. The recognition that social advancement by migrants takes generations is no excuse to let the current situation alone, in the hope that time will eventually turn the tide.

At the same time, we know that the capacity of many migrants – and of Muslims in particular – to meet all these demands is slender.

Therefore, the governments, and the communities in particular, must assume the task of support by word and deed those groups of good will that are willing to join us in building the great we-society.

A 'wish list' directed solely at migrants is not sufficient. If we expect migrants to join our society fully and together with us build a safe society, then we must recognise that 'joining' in the Netherlands can only happen successfully if the native Dutch population is prepared to surrender their indifference. And to transform that indifference into a first step towards trust and hope. We are right to expect a good deal from newcomers.

But if we do not convey a sense that they are welcome, and if we continue to regard them as foreigners instead of full-fledged fellow residents, then the integration process will not succeed. If we do not want migrants to become an underclass, we must give them a true chance to access scarce resources: education, employment and housing.

What has also struck me is that we in the Netherlands are focussing increasingly on that which makes us Dutch. Attentiveness to one's identity is very important. I need only remind you of the controversy that arose last year in the Netherlands regarding my dual citizenship. But that is not all. It is also evident that the discussions around national identity are slowly beginning to influence our view of Europe.

We must all endorse the fact that European identity, the European market have brought us a good deal of prosperity and stability. What the American financial crisis could have meant for the European exchange rates if we had not had the euro doesn't bear thinking about. But that is all evidently of limited importance to many citizens, compared with the sense of their own identity and of being threatened in their own cultural values. That is an important signal, but also a contradictory signal.

The fear of losing one's own identity is, to my mind, the cause of the contradiction in our migration policy and in the attitude, both of politicians and of citizens, towards newcomers. On the one hand, they want to stop admitting new migrants, but on the other hand from a socio-economic point of view we need them.

We are seeing labour shortages in the Netherlands in a large number of sectors. At the same time, many people recoil when it comes to whether or not to admit new Europeans. Remarkably, the fact that progressive parties such as the Socialist Party take a very conservative stance on this point: opposing the admission of Polish workers because they may take jobs away from Dutch people.

The facts speak for themselves: large parts of Europe are aging and lacking in workforce. Additional workers from other regions are necessary in order to keep up economic growth. And here, too, the fear of the unknown plays an important role. Many European citizens see immigration as one of the most important issues (read: threats) facing them.

More than half of European citizens fear that immigrants will take their jobs. Or threaten their culture. Politicians should not negate this paradox. For this lies at the heart of the fears of many people.

From a macro-perspective, there is an enormous need for new workers. And Europe makes that possible with its open borders. But from the micro-perspective of the street, the neighbourhood or the city, we see an aversion to newcomers. Citizens are telling ups: Stop!

This is the paradox of 'welcome and resistance', something that in the Netherlands we have long refused to admit. Yet it is the task of politicians to manage that paradox!

Ladies and gentlemen, I have taken you along on my struggle to determine what integration means in Dutch society and what may be expected from citizens and politicians. I have no ready-made answer, but I would like to stop and take stock of a new type of effort that we must make. I have argued that we must listen to and feel the pain and concerns caused by migration. But also that we need political courage to place that pain and those cares on our agenda. A new sort of leadership is necessary in order to manage feelings of unease. In this way we can put an end to the polemical struggle over words with populist politicians. And begin truly to take seriously the important feelings of a broad segment of society.

Crises are challenges. That is simply the case.

But take them on with honest, courageous words.

The Netherlands can regain its much vaunted tolerance if everyone contributes in some way to mutual trust. If everyone works at building a society in which there is room for everyone who is legally resident here and identifies with the Netherlands. I am curious, as well, to see what this account would be like if you substituted Belgium for each time I mentioned the Netherlands. I don't think there would be much difference. For both you and I want a society of proud people who stand up for each other and do not accept that some should be left behind.

That is the reason why I went into politics.

It is for these very people that I struggle.

Thank you very much.

Islam and Politics: Towards Post-Islamism?

Fouad Laroui

It is difficult to talk about a topic such as 'Islam and Politics' without first taking a look back through history. For the ideas, convictions and prejudices of today are the results of historical development.

What History Teaches Us

Muhammad, the Prophet of Islam, died in 632. We do not know whether he left his followers any instructions. According to the Shiis, he designated his nephew Ali, but this is contradicted by other currents within Islam. Be that as it may, his father-in-law, Abu Bakr, was chosen by the first believers to 'succeed' Muhammad.

But... in what capacity can one 'succeed' a Prophet? All Muslims are agreed that the death of Muhammad also marked the end of Revelation. In other words, as of Muhammad's death in 632, the religious and the political constituted two distinct spheres. The one who succeeded him, Abu Bakr, did so *in the political sphere*: he was the leader of a community at a specific time and place. Therefore there is no harm in stopping to think for a while about the widespread idea that in Islam there is no separation between politics and religion: since the death of Muhammad, there are two spheres that are *de facto* separate from each other. Perhaps a clarification of this point can somewhat facilitate the discussion of Islam in Europe.

This position also has consequences for the status of *sharia*, or 'Islamic law'. Contrary to what certain people believe, the *sharia* was not written down by the time of the Prophet's death. What is more, it didn't even exist yet! The *sharia* as we know it today only came about in the course of the centuries after the death of Muhammad, and is the work of several authors. The *sharia* is thus not holy writ: it is the work of human beings. As such, it is something that can be discussed, criticised and, if necessary, opposed, here and now, in Europe and thus also in the Netherlands.

When Abu Bakr died, in 634, he was succeeded by Umar, his 'commander-in-chief'. In no time at all, Umar had conquered Palestine,

Mesopotamia, Egypt and Persia. Though his rule lasted less than ten years, he succeeded in laying the basis for a new empire. In November 644 Umar was stabbed to death at the mosque of Medina by a Persian Christian slave. (Another version has it that it was a group of Persian warriors who had been reduced to the rank of slaves.) Before dying of his wounds, Umar appointed a council of six people from amongst whom the third caliph was to be chosen. The choice fell on Uthman (644-656). The new candidate came from a rich family from Mecca, the Umayyads, a dynasty that would play an important *political* role in the course of history. On 17 June 656, Caliph Uthman was assassinated in Medina by a crowd of disgruntled Muslims.

The death of this old man of over 80 years old led to the most serious crisis within Islam, the so-called 'Great Fitna', during which Muslims broke up into various factions, of which the best known today are the Sunnis and the Shiis. Ali, the son-in-law of the Prophet, succeeded Uthman to become the third caliph (656-661). The period of his 'rule' was characterised by vehement conflicts. In January 661 Ali was in turn assassinated outside the mosque in Kufa (present-day Iraq) by Kharijites, former allies who had turned against him.

The first four caliphs, who brought unity among the Muslims, are usually referred to as the '*rashidun*', that is, 'the rightly-guided'. But how can one reconcile 'right guidance', which appears to have God's blessing, with this sorry laundry list: 644, Umar is murdered; 656, Uthman is murdered; 661, Ali is murdered? Yet that is precisely what our modern *salafists* are doing when they talk about the Golden Age to which we ought to return. Theirs is clearly an idealised reconstruction of the past. They are not really to be taken seriously when they try to tell us how, based on their utopias (or 'u-chronicles'), the modern world could be improved.

The opposition between Sunnis and Shiis dates back to that era. What was referred to as the Shi'a-Ali (the party of Ali), later abbreviated to 'shia' (our present-day Shiism) began as a group linking all those who had opposed the choice of the first successor to Muhammad. These first 'Shiis' wanted to see Ali, rather than Abu Bakr, succeed the Prophet and lay the foundations of Islam. They did not, however, have a specific religious doctrine or theological interpretation. This fact lends further support to what we said above: the religious had split off from the political very early on, for the most serious conflicts between the first Muslims had nothing to do with religion. What was at stake was simply power, politics, personal ambitions or the honour of the clan.

After the four 'good leader' caliphs there came the Umayyads, a dynasty of caliphs who between 661 and 750 would rule the Muslim community from Damascus. As noted above, the Umayyads were connected with the third caliph, Uthman. When the latter was murdered by opponents who wished to bring Ali, the nephew and son-in-law of Muhammad, to power, the partisans of Uthman, and in particular the Umayyad Muawiyah, cried for vengeance. After a great deal of strife, Ali was deposed and Muawiyah was appointed caliph by the Syrians (661). That same year, Ali was assassinated.

Let us now stop for a moment and consider an important conclusion from all that has been said: from the first years of Islam's existence there has been not only a separation between the political and the religious, but *it was politics that prevailed*. And that would remain the case for the next thousand years… To this day, the problem in Europe and in the Netherlands is not due so much to Islam but to those who wish to instrumentalise Islam *for political aims*: history repeats itself.

Let us now move on. When Muawiyah died, the supporters of Imam Husayn, Muhammad's grandson and the second son of Ali, wishes to elevate him to the throne. The throne: the function of caliph began closely to resemble that of a king. Husayn's supporters suffered a crushing defeat at the battle of Karbala by the army of the new Umayyad caliph, Yazid I. Tradition has it that Husayn was beheaded and his body mutilated. Since that fateful day, Shiis commemorate the death of Husayn on the tenth day of the Islamic month of Muharram.

At the risk of being repetitive, it should be pointed out that it is always about politics. What does the story of men who keep on killing each other in order to become caliph/king have to do with God? It is a fact that the Shiis – in their various forms – have in the course of the subsequent thousand years developed such an original religious outlook that it sometimes seems as if the two main strands of Islam (Shii and Sunni) constitute two different religions. But we must not forget that from the very beginning, the differences between them were political in nature.

The subsequent history is even more chaotic. In 683 a prominent member of the Koreish clan led a revolt in the two holy cities, Mecca and Medina, and extended his power as far as Basra. At the same time, another revolt broke out in Kufa in the name of one of the sons of Ali. At the same time, other factions were causing unrest in southern Arabia, Central Iran, Upper Mesopotamia, etc. Stability was restored with the arrival of the Abbasids, who in 750 formed a new dynasty after having deposed the Umayyads. We know the Abbasids, and in particular

Haroun al-Rashid, mainly from the Thousand-and-one Nights. Haroun, the caliph of Baghdad, held sway over all Muslims except those in Spain. For a prince of the Umayyads, Abd al-Rahman, had managed to flee to Spain and establish a new dynasty there. One of his descendants, Emir Abd al-Rahman III, had himself named caliph in 929, thereby declaring Cordoba fully independent. God now had two vicars on earth. If only we kept to the fiction that all this was a religious issue. But of course it was in fact all political, and it is not at all strange that in Baghdad there was one prince and in Cordoba another who sat on the throne. Personal ambition is the most evenly distributed good in the world.

The new dynasty, the Abbasids, held the caliphate until the sixteenth century, but these gentlemen held the actual reins of power for only short periods. Their power was quickly attacked, particularly by the presence of Turkish mercenaries in the army as well as among the caliph's bodyguards. The caliphs' authority weakened at the borders of the empire. Tunisia and Tripolitania declared themselves independent, under the leadership of a new dynasty, the Aghlabids. Other territories were eventually given other caliphs. Ultimately, only the symbolic function of Amir al-Muminin, 'Commander of the faithful', remained; and the actual political power came into the hands of non-Arab dynasties that only maintained an Arabian caliph for the purposes of certain religious claims.

The Ottoman sultans, whose authority extended across the entire Arab world as far as Morocco, arrogated the title of caliph to themselves. Mustafa Kemal Atatürk put an end to the caliphate on 3 March 1924, two years after he had abolished the sultanate. The last caliph, Abdul Magid, died in exile in Paris, at his home on the boulevard Suchet, in 1944.

Colonialism and Political Islam

It is essential to try to find an explanation of the role played by colonialism in the question we are discussing here. That is to say, modern Islamism arose in reaction to colonialism and, more generally, from contacts with the West. The beginning of this common history coincides with the landing of Bonaparte in Egypt in 1798. The Corsican general found there a weakened country, a civilisation that had been slumbering for five centuries, and a people who did not understand what was happening to them. How is it possible? Westerners have conquered our land? This is the world turned upside down, for isn't it always the Muslims that conquer other people, in the name of God and his Prophet? Around the end of the nineteenth century, some people believed they had discovered the reason for the success of the English, French, Dutch and even Russian and Italian colonialism and at the same time to have found an answer to the above question: the fact that the Islamic countries could be defeated so easily was due to the fact that Muslims had drifted away from the example of their virtues forefathers: *as-salaf as-salih* (the word *salafist* derives from this term). The answer is thus clear: we must return to the virtues and the mentality of that Golden Age.

It should be noted that Salafism has two distinct periods. For the first great leader of Salafism, Muhammad Abduh (1849-1905), a return to the original teachings of Islam was the obvious answer, since in his opinion this did not stand in the way of modernism. On the contrary: rationalism and scientific positivism would be able to develop precisely within Islam, which, according to Abduh, gave pride of place to human reason. According to him and those who shared his views, 'true' Islam could put an end to the superstition and intellectual backwardness that had led to the decline of the Muslim world and had delivered it up defenceless to the Western desire for conquest.

Unfortunately, however, 'progressive' Salafism (of which the great Moroccan nationalist leader Allal al-Fassi was an illustrious example: he did not consider it in any way against his principles to send his children to a French school) had to give way in the course of the twentieth century to a 'reactionary' Salafism that was initiated by one of Abduh's own students, the Syrian Rashid Rida (1865-1935). He and his followers conceived of the return to the past in literal terms: *the political-religious unity* of the early days of Islam had to be re-established again and in concrete form, for this unity was considered to be perfect. This utopianism transformed itself almost automatically into a form of extremism, which found that whatever did not fit in with the Golden Age was bad and had to be destroyed.

This is also the radical and reactionary thinking of the founders and intellectual leaders of the organisation of the Muslim Brotherhood, established in 1928 by Hasan al-Banna and of which Sayyid Qutb (1906-1966) was the ideologue. It is therefore not surprising that someone like Tariq Ramadan (the grandson of Hasan al-Banna) could, only recently, write a hymn of praise of the prophet Muhammad without any basis in scientific argument: not a word of the hundreds of academic studies in which the majority of the hagiographic traditions regarding the first centuries of Islam have been called into question. Muhammad and his era are presented in Ramadan's work as a model of perfection that must be followed, period; the utopia of the Golden Age is alive and well in the thought of those who are nonetheless known as 'European Muslims'. But in order to gain an idea of the essence of European Islam, one need not necessarily give priority to their backward worldviews over the ideas of someone like Abduh and his modern followers.

The Next Caliph

Some Islamists call today for a restoration of the caliphate. Others, tired of waiting for the end times, have already restored it. The caliphate of Cologne was set up in 1984 by a Turkish imam named Metin Kaplan and his father, Cemaliddin Kaplan, who died prematurely in 1995 - prematurely, because he did not live to see the realisation of his dream: that of the whole world united under the enlightened leadership of one man, the caliph. The caliphate of Cologne is a sort of Vatican of Islam, without territory but with a Constitution comprising fifteen articles taking their inspiration directly from the Qur'an (so they say). What do you think of Article 7, which specifies that "no agreement is possible with unbelievers and with political regimes that represent them"? Doesn't Kaplan pay his municipal taxes? Does he perhaps pay his phone bills with flowery words, or sometimes drive in the left lane? These sorts of questions give them a taste of their own medicine, if they bring their odd ideas to the discussion that is currently under way in Europe and the Netherlands.

Even more odd: in December 2005, a few Muslim youths gathered behind closed doors in a high school classroom in the centre of Copenhagen, the Vestre-Borgerdyd lyceum. On their agenda: the restoration of the caliphate and other urgent issues… When the principal was informed, he expelled the leader of the group from school: let him go restore it somewhere else.

Of course the Caliphate of Cologne and the Islamist 'club of five' in Copenhagen are grotesque. Yet they provide a glimpse of the desire that has been alive in certain Islamist circles for nearly a century. Examples abound. At the beginning of the last century, Al-Marâghî, who would later be the rector of Cairo's Al-Azhar university, launched the struggle to restore the caliphate on behalf of the rulers of Egypt. He assured everyone that Islamic law could provide for all human needs, anywhere and at anytime.

We could, of course, go much further back in time. Hasan Sabbah, the renowned 'Old man of the mountain', chose the career he did – fanaticism, murder, terrorism – for the sake of the caliphate. At the time there was still a caliph, but Hasan Sabbah was unhappy about the situation, since the caliph was just a puppet in the hands of the true rulers, the Seljuk Turks, who were Sunnis. Hasan entered into a pact with Nizar, the eldest son of the caliph. Upon the caliph's death, Nizar was to lead the Shii armies of Egypt and conquer Persia, which had fallen into the hands of the Seljuks. The plan failed, but that is another story. The astonishing tale of Hasan Sabbah shows once again that it was all about the lust for power and not about religion. It also shows us one of the most revolting aspects – but alas, one that seems all too familiar even today – of the abuse of religion by politics, namely the *takfir*, or banishment on grounds of apostasy. This is a method popular among Islamists: they claim that their opponent is not a true Muslim. That means you can fight him and even, if necessary, kill him. It was in this way that Islamists, invoking the *takfir*, murdered Egyptian president Anwar Sadat in 1981, despite the fact that he was a devout Muslim.

The *takfir* was more or less the 'invention' of the Kharijites, the sect we have referred to above and that no longer exists as such in the present day. Over the course of history it was once again put in a place of honour - for purely political reasons - by Ibn Taymiyya (1263-1328): the issue at the time was how to justify the war that his superiors, the Mameluks, were waging against the Mongols. But how is that possible, you might ask; how can one launch a holy war, a *jihad*, against your fellow Muslims? The Mongols had, after all, converted to Islam? Very simple: you declare that they are simply unbelievers... It goes without saying that groups which nowadays make use of the *takfir* have no place in a modern democracy. For them, there is no room in a State governed by the rule of law, much the less within a European Islam. And yet they are running around by the dozens in Europe. One of these days someone will have to put a stop to them...

Within our own era, Rashid Rida was one of the most fiery advocates of the restoration of the caliphate. He proposed that the caliph be chosen from amongst religious dignitaries and that he be given the power to issue laws based on the interpretation of religious law. The caliph's government should be at the head of what Rida called an 'Islamic State'. This was a true turning point, or even the birth of an Islamist way of thinking, in which a notion of the State also became evident. The concept of an Islamic State was taken up by political groupings founded in the period between the two world wars, among which is the Muslim Brotherhood already mentioned.

The Muslim Brotherhood in Egypt tells a different story. They no longer talk about a 'totalitarian' Islamic State; even the restoration of the caliphate seems no longer to be on the agenda. You can interpret this change in strategy in two different ways: either they have adopted the modern concept of the rule of law and are interested only in what happens in Egypt. Or it is pure pretence. The voters and the Western financial supporters should under no circumstances be frightened. Once in power, then we'll see. It is important to know that the influence of the Muslim Brothers on young Muslims in Europe in growing, whether that be direct or indirect influence via charismatic (or telegenic) 'leaders' who themselves live in Europe.

But even if the Brothers have somewhat watered down their demands, most movements of political Islam that do not have to worry too much about voters, such as the Hizb ut-Tahrir, include in their political platform the demand that the caliphate be restored. In the Hizb's own presentation, we read in the first sentence that the goal is "to appoint a caliph and swear loyalty to him, which means listen to him and obey him, on condition that he rule in accordance with the rules of the Holy Book and the Tradition (*sunnah*) of his Messenger".

What is striking is the theoretical poverty of such a programme. Who appoints whom? And how? And who is competent to confirm that the lucky chosen one is ruling in accordance with the rules of the Holy Book and the Tradition of his Messenger? And what happens if there is disagreement on the latter point? Plus: how can one make sure that questions regarding the person, the nationality, and even the ethnic group or tribe do not immediately lead to new discord? Will Iranians accept a Saudi caliph, or will Turks swear fealty to a Tunisian? In the Netherlands, there is not a Sunni – whether Moroccan or Turkish – who will agree to sit at the same table with an Ahmedi from Pakistan…

You can see behind the idea of a 'worldwide caliphate' the outmoded delusions of fanatics; but you can also regard it as something that arises from the rage that many Muslims feel at finding themselves among the ranks of the defeated for at least a century: think of the Palestinian-Israeli conflict. In other words, this question will not disappear on its own, as long as resentment remains the point that attracts the most adherents among Arabs and Muslims.

The most remarkable element of this story is, however, that the question was settled once and for all in 1925 by a Muslim theologian of considerable stature, a student of Abduh: Ali Abderraziq.

Islam Without Politics, Politics Without Islam

In 1925, Ali Abderraziq, a judge and theologian educated at Al-Azhar, wrote a book entitled *Al-islam wa usal al-hukm* (Islam and the Fundamentals of Government), that landed like a bombshell. The book immediately provoked enormous debate and even led to a governmental crisis in Egypt. It represented a major shift in twentieth-century Islamic thought. Abderraziq subjected the theological foundations of the caliphate to fresh scrutiny. He began with an analysis of the word 'caliphate' itself: from a linguistic point of view, it means no more than 'successor'. (Even on this fairly insignificant point, our *qadi* based himself on a verse of the Qur'an (43, 50) in order to establish the meaning of the term, thereby indicating his respect for the sources). After citing a number of writers, he levelled the following charge against them: "Given that they attribute such power, elevated dignity and broad competencies to the caliphate, these authors should have pointed to the origin of this power and these competencies. How did the caliph come to have these powers? Who granted them to him? That is a line of inquiry they did not, however, follow." So Abderraziq does it for them. He concludes that Muslims have developed two different theories on this question.

The first asserts that the caliph received his authority and power directly from God. (Abderraziq comments at the end of the chapter that "this conception is close to the ideas of Hobbes"). He then cites theologians and poets who have given further clarification to this conception and in some cases have gone quite far, to the boundary of blasphemy: "This conception expanded so greatly that poets placed the caliphs nearly on the same level as the Almighty, or very nearly". A serious accusation when one considers that in Islam there is but one mortal sin, the *shirk*, which means to set someone on an equal footing with God.

The second theory states that the caliph received his power from the community of believers, the *umma*, which appoints him and grants him his privileges. The caliphate in this account is thus simply an agreement and the community in fact continues to hold the reins of power in its own hands. Abderraziq notes that "this concept agrees more or less with that of the philosopher Locke". In terms that are closer to those of the Enlightenment, one could also say that "sovereignty rests with the people".

For the purposes of this study, it is pointless to go on. For we have but one question to put to the Islamists of today: My good sirs, when it comes to Hobbes or Locke, where do you stand? Or perhaps I could put it another way: When it comes to Abu Ja'far al-Mansur, who claimed 'to embody the power of God on earth', and for whom 'the caliph is a representative of the community', where do you stand?

A dilemma. In the first instance they become guilty of *shirk* and place themselves entirely beyond the pale. In the second case: why should this temporary transfer of political power, which is fully consistent with the ideas of the Enlightenment and the modern conception of democracy, have suddenly to transform itself as if by magic into a religious authority? Is that not contrary to the Qur'an and the *sunnah*? Do the latter not emphasise the direct, immediate relationship between God and each believer? Do we need a religious authority on earth?

Abderraziq concludes that religious and political matters must be kept apart. He explains that the *umma* is not a State, and that the Qur'an makes no mention of the caliphate as a political institution. The Prophet was not sent to found a State, and no Islamic State ever existed in his lifetime. Islam has nothing to do with the form of State that has emerged in the Islamic world as a result of historical circumstances. As a result, there is no need for this form to be re-established today. The type of government that believers choose is entirely up to them; the caliphate is not an obligation.

Let us suppose, however, that Islamists, despite all that has just been said, continue to seek a caliph to lead the *umma* with the Qur'an in his hand. The question then arises: is such a thing possible? Can a State really be governed in this way?

You Cannot Govern a Country With the Qur'an

Some Islamists wave the Qur'an about as if it was the Islamic Constitution for which they so ardently long. But the holy book is completely unsuited for such a role: the Qur'an provides at most a hundred or so rules, many fewer than the 610 in the Old Testament (according to Talmudic commentary) or the 2414 in Roman canon law. This suggests that as regards the organisation of society, Islam gives free rein to citizens and legislators.

As regards the economy, for example, one finds in the Qur'an only one relevant verse (2, 275: "God permits commerce and prohibits usury"). How can one speak, therefore, of an 'Islamic' economy? In practice, people have to muddle along one way or another. In Morocco, for instance, there is not a single statute that mentions the Qur'an or

Islam in its text. This indicates that a country that is Muslim through and through can manage very well with putting a mention of Islam solely in the recital of the Constitution and then proceeding to regulate society on the basis of practical rules and regulations that are appropriate to the time and place.

The Tunisian Constitution likewise specifies in its first article that Tunisia is a Muslim country, a sort of sociological observation, but nowhere does it say that the source of the law is *sharia*. Nowhere does it say that Islamic law should serve as the source of explanation for judges or legislators. What is more: Article 5 emphasises the principle of freedom of conscience. It is thanks to that assertion that Tunisian Muslims can freely profess their religion in a thriving country where the laws are suited to the demands of a modern State.

The examples of Morocco and Tunisia should give food for thought to all those who find it self-evident that a European Islam should on its own initiative apply *sharia*. This reflection also applies to those who think that wherever Muslims form a majority, there *sharia* must be applied. Tunisia has a population that is 99% Muslim, and yet has no *sharia*!

We can see, therefore, that over fifteen centuries, not so very much has changed. Politics and religion are separate everywhere in the Muslim world, but politics, which always plays an important role, occasionally uses and even abuses religion for its own purposes

On the matter of the economy, which is of course essential for the governance of a modern country with today's complex industrial or post-industrial organisations, what does the Qur'an have to say? Nothing, unless we point once again to Sura 2,275: "God permits commerce and prohibits usury". That principle is not original (the ban on usury, and indeed on any sort of interest rate, is a Christian principle as well – even if it has fallen into disuse). Moreover, this principle causes more problems in a modern society than it resolves. How can one imagine a world without banking today? There are, of course, banks and other financial institutions that may be described as 'Islamic'. Lending at interest (*riba*), which is deemed equivalent to usury, is banned. In the place of interest, there is a sharing formula, agreed in advance, based on a so-called sharing of risks and returns among the saver, the bank and the productive capital. The difference between this system and interest is not great, and indeed seems to have become largely a play on words.

In order to finance commercial contracts, the way it works is that when A sells B something via an Islamic bank, the merchandise must actually be delivered first to the bank before it can be sold on to B. The basic principle is that the profit earned by the bank is justified by the commercial and not by the financial nature of the transaction (purchase and resale must really take place, and may not be fictitious). Here, too, one may speak of wordplay: for merchandise is never actually stored in the bank's vaults.

Other than *riba*, there is but one other economic concept in the Qur'an, *zakat*, which is generally translated as 'purification tax' or 'statutory alms'. According to the *sharia*, the percentage of the *zakat* is fixed and payable in cash or in kind. In an Islamic economy, one could also apply the term *zakat* to the portion of taxes held by the State (which all States in the world collect) and used to pay for support and social security for people who have nothing. But did that not already exist? And what has the filling out of a tax return, a thankless and eminently worldly matter, have to do with God?

It is not only taxes that concern chiefly profane matters, but all of politics – whether at the local, regional or national level. A few examples: public roads, municipal taxes, new technologies, rubbish removal in big cities, opening hours of shops, the rights of trade unions, the need to subsidise railways, moving to daylight savings time, etc. What has all this to do with religion, or with God? Nothing. Absolutely nothing.

To conclude these considerations, I refer to something that will surprise the Islamists greatly: politics is of no importance whatsoever in Islam. For Muhammad – like Paul before him – was convinced that the end of the world was near (perhaps that is also the reason why he did not appoint a successor, as we have seen above). As a result, the idea of regulating the organisation of future societies down to the most minute detail would have been contrary to his idea of the approaching end. The 'Constitution' of Medina was only drawn up for 'here and now' – that 'now' was some fourteen centuries ago…

Conclusion: Towards a Post-Islamism?

Since there are a million Muslims in Europe, and because there is a 'Muslim community' in the Netherlands, the relationship between Islam and politics is gradually becoming an important question. But if one subjects the historical dimension of this question to closer scrutiny, one quickly comes to the following conclusions:
1. Islam and politics are not necessarily linked. In fact, after the death of Muhammad they came to be separate.

Islam and Politics: Towards Post-Islamism?

2. Since that time, politics has always and everywhere taken the lead. The clergy have almost always upheld the political *status quo* without seeking to make any changes to it.
3. Islamism, or political Islam, is a recent phenomenon that was a reaction to colonial conquests in the nineteenth century and that flourished anew in the 1970s primarily for pragmatic rather than religious reasons: the Israeli-Palestinian conflict, the influence of the Iranian revolution, the democratic deficit in the countries in question, etc.
4. Many young Europeans of the second generation – sons and daughters of immigrants – are proud to consider themselves Muslims. That is their right. But they should consider carefully the three conclusions outlined above, for they must develop their own, individual Islam, a private Islam that does not put itself at the service of political ambitions and that stays far away from politics in general. It is only once they all do so that the era of post-Islamism will begin in Europe.

HUMAN RIGHTS AND ISLAM

Bhikhu Parekh

Most Muslim societies lack a well established regime of human rights, and the more religious they are, the weaker is that regime. This needs to be explained. The explanation is to be found at various levels, such as the history of these societies, their level of economic development, their inequalities and injustices, their colonial history, contemporary international context, and the critical resources of Islam. In this essay, I critically examine the simple minded but widely held view that the problem lies within Islam itself in the sense that its theology and view of human life are inherently incompatible with human rights and indeed with democratic ideas and institutions themselves. Since the concept of human rights is far more problematic than is sometimes appreciated, I analyse it in some detail. I then explore how Muslim writers have responded to it, and the kinds of problems they face when they seek to reconcile human rights with the central tenets of their religion.

Human Rights

The idea of human rights represents a great historical achievement. For the first time in human history it provides a universally accessible moral and political language in which to articulate our shared concerns. Violations of human rights in any part of the world are widely denounced, vigorously investigated by journalists, and used to embarrass and shame governments including those that systematically ignore them in practice and do not even see their point. For their part oppressed and marginalized groups invoke human rights in the firm belief that this is the most effective way to draw attention to their grievances and seek their redress. The language of human rights builds moral bonds between human beings in different parts of the world, and helps create an awareness of our shared humanity. Since human rights reflect our beliefs concerning how human beings should treat each other and lay down in reasonably clear terms the moral minimum to which they are deemed to be entitled, they give moral and political life a clear focus and have a great evocative and inspirational power.

Since the doctrine of human rights is a precious and fragile achievement, we need to protect it against its overzealous advocates and cynical detractors lest they should in their own different ways discredit, weaken, or undermine it. While its enemies are easy to identify and the harm they do is obvious, the unwitting damage done by its overenthusiastic champions is often too subtle to detect, and hence more worrying. It is therefore of utmost importance to be clear on what we mean by human rights and what particular rights meet that description.

Basically human rights refer to those rights that human beings need in order to lead a minimally decent or worthwhile life.[1] Two related but separate ideas lie at the heart of the concept of human rights. First, certain liberties, opportunities, forms of treatment, etc. are central to human dignity and well-being in the sense that in their absence, human beings cannot lead minimally worthwhile lives. As self-determining agents they obviously entertain and organize their lives around different conceptions of the good life. However these basic liberties, opportunities etc. are central to them all and no form of good life can be lived without them. They are obviously not the only ones needed for a worthwhile life. But they are basic and indispensable, and constitute fundamental human interests. Since they are required by human beings *qua* human beings, they must be available to them all. The ideas of fundamental importance and universality are crucial to human rights, and are conveyed by calling them 'human'.

Second, human beings should enjoy these essential constituents of their well-being as a matter of right, not as a matter of others' contingent goodwill or individual and collective charity. To call them rights is to say that they entail claims on and impose correlative duties on others. In pre-modern societies the idea of rights played no or limited role. Certain things were no doubt considered due to human beings, but these were to be done or given as a matter of duty, which was enforced by a complex set of social, moral and religious sanctions. The desired outcome was obtained without introducing the idea of rights. The idea of human rights represents a different approach in the sense that it makes rights rather than duties a primary category. It has several advantages over the pre-modern approach. It affirms and institutionalises human agency and dignity. It ensures that human brings are not passively dependent on or

---

[1] For valuable discussions of the questions relating to meaning and basis of human rights, See J. Waldron (ed.), *Nonsense upon Stilts: Bentham, Burke and Marx on the Right of Man,* London, Methuen, 1987; R. Plant, *Modern Political Thought*, Oxford, Blackwell, 1991; and P. Jones, *Rights*, Basingstoke, Macmillan, 1995.

objects of others' goodwill but independent sources of mutual claims.. Furthermore, in large, impersonal, atomized and often secular modern societies, the moral, social, religious and other sanctions are necessarily weak, and cannot be replied upon to enforce a regime of duties. We are therefore led to rely on legal sanctions and the institutions of the state, where the language of rights is most appropriate. Making fundamental human interests a matter of right is also a more effective way of sharpening our appreciation of them and ensuring their promotion than making them a matter of duty, at least in modern industrialized and individualist societies.

Views as to what rights qualify as human rights vary greatly. The seventeenth-century theorists of natural rights, the intellectual godfathers of the contemporary discourse on human rights, were content to stress three, namely life, liberty, and property, to which the United States later added the pursuit of happiness. The French Declaration of the Rights of Man and Citizen added about a dozen civil and political rights, seeing the latter sometimes as rights of the citizen and at other times as those of man. The Universal Declaration of Human Rights over a century and a half later replaced the philosophically freighted language of 'natural' rights with a less problematic language of human rights, and introduced an even longer list of over twenty human rights. Subsequent declarations and international covenants have added economic, social, and cultural rights and, more recently, environmental and developmental rights. Authors of these declarations seem to have realized that the rights they listed were not all of equal importance, which is why they called some of them 'fundamental', meaning that they carried much greater moral weight. Since they also called other, evidently non-fundamental, rights 'human rights', they implied that the term 'human rights' did not necessarily refer only to fundamental human interests, and included almost all desirable rights.

This tendency to widen the usage has continued unabated in recent years. The European Court has interpreted the European Convention on Human rights and Fundamental Freedoms to generate a litany of rights, all of which are called human rights. These include freedom of competition and trade, free movement of goods, the right to confidentiality of business information, and the rights of the elderly, the disabled, the mentally ill, adolescents in remand homes, prisoners and others to be treated in decent ways and to receive certain levels of services. The Court has also ruled that detaining a person before a court hearing for more than four days, denying transsexuals the right to acquire a new civic identity, and corporal punishment in schools that exceeds certain limits are all violations of the human rights of those involved. Not only has the list of human rights been expanded to cover all desirable rights, their scope too has increased. They are extended to public and private organizations including business corporations, schools, hospitals and universities, and used to demand certain kinds of service and forms of relationship. They are even extended to interpersonal relations, including those between married couples and parents and their children.

Such an indiscriminate expansion of human rights deprives them of their moral force and focus. Human rights have the power to evoke strong moral feelings and to mobilize our moral energies for and against certain kinds of actions, because we consider them crucial to out humanity and believe that to deny or violate them is to treat the relevant individuals and groups as if they belonged to an inferior species. We assign different moral status to different rights depending on their moral importance, which we in turn determine on the basis of their relation to our conception of their fundamental interests. This is why we call some rights human rights, and make a further distinction between fundamental rights, which are give a constitutional status and placed beyond normal politics, and ordinary rights which can be altered with relative ease.

When all or almost all rights become human rights, we lose this sense of moral discrimination. Human right properly so called lose their unique moral authority, and other rights acquire exaggerated importance. The right not to be enslaved, tortured, or disposed of by murder squads is of a different order from the right not to be detained without a trial for more than four days or to receive prompt and adequate medical attention. At a different level a prisoner's or a patient's right not to be subjected to degrading treatment is quite different from their right to hot meals and comfortable beds. Human rights require countless specific rights either as a means to their realization or as conditions of their exercise. Since the latter are derivative and instrumental in nature, are contingent in the sense that the relevant human rights might also be realized through other rights, are specific to particular societies and cultures, and are dependent on the availability of resources, they are not and should not be called human rights. They are valuable and ought to be guaranteed, but they should not be confused or equated with others of far greater importance John Rawls was right to suggest that the language of human rights badly needs a conceptual quality control.

As I argued earlier, human rights should be limited to those rights that are of fundamental importance or central to human dignity and well-being and can be claimed by all human beings including immigrants and refugees. Rights to life, liberty, basic necessities of life, freedom from slavery and degrading treatment, freedom of conscience, fair trial, freedom of expression, equality of treatment, personal property, etc. eminently qualify as human rights. Rights to freedom of trade and competition, business confidentiality, to stand for elected offices and to education in one's mother tongue do not. This does not mean that human rights are fixed for ever. As we acquire deeper insights into how human dignity is sustained and human well-being promoted, as new threats to them emerge, as unexpected historical experiences such as the Holocaust highlight the need to stress certain rights, or as we appreciate that certain important interests are best protected by making them a matter of human rights, we may rightly expand and even contract the conventional list of human rights. However we should not do so indiscriminately, inadvertently, lazily, or for political convenience. We should have compelling reasons, and any right we classify as a human right should satisfy the basic criteria mentioned earlier.

Human rights are normative statements about what human beings in our view require to lead worthwhile lives, and which they may legitimately claim as of right. They are not natural or inherent in human nature but social in origin in the sense that they are a matter of human judgment and collective decision. They are not self-evident either, but arrived at by a slow process of collective deliberation and negotiation. And nor are they inscribed in the structure of the universe and apprehended by a rational intuition; rather they are norms of conduct, a moral practice, which we think we have good reasons to adopt.

Justifying human rights, that is, showing why certain rights should be given the status of human rights, involves giving good reasons why we think that certain liberties, opportunities, etc. are central to any form of good life and constitute fundamental human interests. The reasons must be general in nature, that is, not derived from or tied to a particular conception of the good life, and universal in their scope. They are of several different kinds. Some involve an appeal those basic capacities without which human beings cannot lead meaningful lives, such as the capacity to make choices, order their conflicting desires, form and revise their ideas on how they should live, impose a measure of self-discipline, engage in self-reflection, and to acquire a sense of agency.

The justifying reasons for human rights also involve well-established and universally common empirical facts about human beings, such as that they possess a limited knowledge of themselves and others, suffer at the loss of their loved ones, are fallible, and given to mistaking the familiar for the natural. Human beings require a rich world of social relations, develop different degrees of mutual attachment, and care more for those they love than for total strangers. They also need a stable and loving environment in order to develop normal human sensibilities, a relatively inviolate private space to nurture their sense of individuality, a climate of mutual respect to develop their sense of self-respect and agency, and so on.

Other kinds of reasons for human rights are based on human experience, and involve what earlier writers called maxims of prudence or practical wisdom. They are reflective distillations of the past and present experiences of different societies and the lessons that can be drawn from them. They tell us what is or is not practicable, what is likely to have what long-term consequences, and how different social institutions and practices are related. We can, for example, show by appropriate historical and contemporary examples that the identification of State and religion corrupts both and undermines human dignity and freedom; that absolute power corrupts not only in the mundane sense of creating vested interests but also in the deeper sense of breeding self-righteousness and intolerance of disagreement; that the self-evident moral truths of one age turn out to be falsehoods in another and that we should be wary of all such claims; and that institutionalized criticism is the best way to guard against the all too common human tendency to claim infallibility. We can also show that inequalities beyond a certain point corrupt all involved, that degrading groups of human beings exacts a heavy emotional and moral price from its alleged beneficiaries as well as its victims, and that human freedom is best protected by setting up appropriate institutions and practices rather that by trusting the wisdom and good sense of the powerful.

These and other kinds of reasons used to justify human rights are intersubjectively accessible and assessable. They do not invoke a privileged cognitive capacity or intuition that is available only to a gifted few. They do not appeal to an authority whose deliverances must be accepted on blind faith. They do not presuppose and are not made within the framework of a particular substantive vision of the good life. They are subject to critical public discussion, and it is open to others to expose such cultural and other biases as they might contain. Based on these and other kinds of reasons, we arrive at a broad consensus on human rights.

Although this is generally enough, it is not so for those who are committed to a particular comprehensive vision of the human life and are determined to organize their lives in terms of it. This is generally the case with religious people, though it is not limited to them. They aim to be good Christians, Buddhists or Muslims, and define their identity and self-worth in terms of their ability to live by their religious beliefs. They seek to relate human rights to their religious beliefs in order to reassure themselves that the two cohere, and that their subscription to human rights does not compromise their deepest beliefs and generates a divided moral loyalty or a sense of guilt. It is only because they do so that the question arises whether Islam, Christianity, Buddhism or some other religion is compatible with human rights. Not all religious persons look for such coherence. Some might accept human rights for the kinds of general reasons mentioned earlier, and feel no need to relate them to their religious beliefs because they see the two as belonging to different areas of life, do not place much value on coherence, see human life as inherently ambiguous and marked by tension, or for some other reason. Since such persons raise no questions, I shall ignore them and concentrate on those for whom coherence is of utmost importance.

Their search for coherence can take several forms. They might be attracted to but entertain some doubts about the validity of human rights, and wish to assure themselves that the rights are compatible with and find support in their religious beliefs. Or they might be convinced of the value and importance of human rights on independent grounds, but seek additional justification to give their conviction a religious depth, to strengthen their commitment to it, and to generate an additional powerful motive. Or they might be 'true believers' who consider human reason fallible, corruptible, inherently untrustworthy, and only do what their religion dictates. For them it is not enough that human rights are compatible with their religion, for that implies that the rights have an external origin and even perhaps an independent validity. Rather they want to be sure that their religion entails and enjoins human rights, and that the latter are not an alien import that somehow happens to be consistent with their religion.

As the idea of human rights first emerged in Europe at a time when Christianity was still a dominant cultural and even religious force, the debate on the relation between the two first occurred among Christian thinkers. As the idea spread to other societies, the debate occurred within other religious traditions as well and took different forms in each of them. I shall concentrate on how human rights are currently debated within Islam.

Current Debates in Islam

One detects several stands of thought in the current Islamic debate on human rights, of which three are most influential.[2] First, for some the idea of human rights is alien to Islam. It is individualist whereas Islam is communitarian; it stress rights whereas Islam stresses justice and duties; it is anthropocentric whereas Islam is theocentric; it derives rights from human agreement and consensus whereas Islam recognizes only the authority of the *Qur'an* and the Prophet's life and thought. Second, some advance the opposite view that Islam is fully at ease with human rights, that in fact it entails and enjoins them on its followers, and even assert with pride that it is the only religion to do so.[3] Third, some take the view that although Islam arrives at the idea of human rights differently and is aware of it limits, it is in principle sympathetic to it and that, though it is critical of some of them, it is sympathetic to the most important of them.[4]

The first view is deeply flawed. As its critics have pointed out, some of the important elements in the idea of the human rights are to be found in Islam. Although Islam talks of the unity of the *umma*, it takes individuals as the basic units of moral and religious life and cherishes their dignity, independence and unique personal responsibility. Human beings are Allah's unique creations, and have an intrinsic value. Each of them is a distinct individual and responsible for the way he or she conducts his life on earth. As the *Qur'an* says, 'Each soul will be paid for just what it has earned". And again, 'every soul will be confronted with all the good it has done and all the evil it has done". Islam also insists on human equality. As the Prophet said in his final sermon: "Oh people! You have one Lord and one forefather; all of you are from Adam and Adam is from dust. No Arab is superior to non-Arab, and no non-Arab to Arab; no white man is superior to black man, and black man to a white, save by virtue of their fear of God"

---

[2] For a useful summary of these views, see J. Esposito, *Islam and Democracy*, Oxford, Oxford University Press, 1996; T. Ramadan, *Western Muslims and the Future of Islam*, Oxford, Oxford University Press, 2004, and B. Tibi, *Islam between Culture and Politics*, 2nd ed., Basingstoke, Palgrave Macmillan, 2005. For their discussion in the context of contemporary Iran, see A. Bayat, *Social Movements and the Post-Islamic Turn*, Stanford, Stanford University Press, 2007. For a rich study of the various strands within the Arab debate, see K. Dwyer, *Arab voices: The Human Rights Debate in the Middle East*, London, Routledge, 1991.

[3] This is asserted in, among others, the Universal Islamic Declaration of Human Rights. This view is analysed by A. Mayer, *Islam and Human Rights*, London, Westview, 1991.

[4] A.A. An-Na`im, *Towards an Islamic Reformation: Civil Liberties, Human Rights and International Law*, Syracuse, NY, Syracuse University Press, 1990.

Islam sees human life as God's great gift, and contains strong injunctions against taking it. The idea of justice is central to Islam and imposes justice derived obligations (*takalif*) to help others secure those things without which they cannot lead worthwhile lives, and to fight against the injustices to which they might be subject.. Islam sees relations between the ruler and the ruled in contractual terms, and requires that the former should act justly and respect the legitimate claims of his subjects. Islam also requires that no one should be punished unless he or she is found guilty according to established procedures.

All this shows that Islam is solicitous of fundamental human interests, and that its view of the latter is not at odds with that underlying the doctrine of human rights. It is, of course, true that it seeks to promote fundamental human interests by emphasizing duties enforced by means of social, religious and legal sanctions and does not much talk of claiming them as of right. However the latter is not wholly absent and can he read into various verses that deal with the sanctity of the individual and the basic demands of his nature. More importantly, in so far as Islam recognizes fundamental human interests and seeks to promote them, which is what human rights are largely about, they are not at all alien to it.

The second view, which represents the opposite end of the spectrum and sees no tension between Islam and the doctrine of human rights, is also flawed. As I argued earlier, the idea of rights is uniquely modern and part of a particular way of looking at human beings. It is not to be found in its fully developed modern form in Islam, Christianity, or any other religion. Even Christianity, which claims to be a friend of human rights, long resisted them and had to be radically reinterpreted before feeling comfortable with them. Islam is no different. Furthermore, while Islam respects many of the human rights, it is not hospitable to some others, such as the Muslim's right to change his religion or openly to criticize it, the rights of the non-Muslim minorities to equal citizenship, the rights of gays, gender equality and the right to public protest.

The third view has much to be said for it. Although not hospitable to the idea of human rights in its modern individualist form, Islam recognizes the dignity of the human person and sees him as a source of moral claims on others. As for the substance of human rights, it is or can be so interpreted as to be compatible with many, though not all, of them. Islam rules out coercion in religious matters and allows minorities the right to profess and practice their religion, though not the right to propagate it. It respects the right to fair trial and rules out retrospective punishment and punishing the innocent. It insists on *shura* and the ruler's obligation to consult his subjects. When properly interpreted, this makes room for popular participation. The Prophet did not claim infallibility and allowed disagreement. This could be interpreted to mean that if even the Prophet allowed freedom of expression and dissent, there is a greater obligation on the civil ruler to allow freedom of expression and criticism. During his rule in Medina, the Prophet permitted minorities (*dhimmis*) to follow their traditional ways of life and respected their customs. The civil ruler should do the same and respect minority practices and allow freedom of association.

To avoid misunderstanding, our concern is not to Islamicise human rights, that is, to start with a check list of human rights as found in several Universal Declarations and look for some support for them in Islam. Rather it involves a dialectical interplay, a creative dialogue between the two, reading each in the light of the other, and exploring areas of convergence and divergence. When one reads Islam in the light of, and with the moral sensibility developed by, the idea of human rights, one approaches it in a new spirit and is likely to notice things one had not seen before or to discover new meanings in familiar verses and *hadiths*. Conversely when one examines human rights from the Islamic perspective, one is likely to gain new insights into and expand and deepen our understanding of them. Islam might throw new light on them, reveal their unsuspected ambiguities, and suggest new rights, and in so doing make its distinct contribution to the global debate on the subject.

Interpreting Islam

Interpretation of a religious text is never simple and uncontroversial. In a religion with a text of over 6000 verses and hundreds of *hadiths*, it is as easy to support one view as its opposite. Although an interpretation based on one verse or *hadith* is valid, it is not and cannot be conclusive because another verse or *hadith* may point in a different direction. The interpreter therefore cannot remain content to point to a supporting piece of evidence; he needs to go further and critically examine the counterevidence. This involves complex hermeneutic techniques. He could argue that the word in question does not mean what it is taken to mean, that the relevant verse needs to be located in its textual or historical context, that the Mecca revelations are less context bound than those of Medina and should carry a greater religious weight, that the text should be read in the light of the Prophet's life, and so on. In some cases this settles the matter. In others it at least plants a doubt, and keeps open a vitally necessary space for critical discussion and dissent.[5]

In some cases an interpretation of the *Qur'an* and *hadiths* is not enough, and we need to look at their context and the history of Islam. This is, for example, how Muslim feminists such as Naawal al-Saadawi and Falima Mernissi have made a case for gender equality. Khadija, the Prophet's wife, was a powerful figure and greatly respected by him. Ayisha, his young and independent-minded wife, had her views on various subjects and debated them with him. She enjoyed considerable authority even after his death, Invoking the practice of *Shura*, she invited the Prophet's leading companions to select and appoint her father Abu Bakra as a Caliph. When she lost ground after the death of Uthmen, the third Caliph, she raised an army to wage an unsuccessful fight against the fourth Caliph. In the long history of Islam, several women have enjoyed considerable power, and some even ruled over the faithfuls. Muslim feminists have also argued the although the *Qur'an* did not grant women full equality with men, no other religion of the time did either, and that Islam's treatment was comparatively better. As a progressive religion, they think that it should therefore constantly reconsider its treatment of women, and ensure that it is better than the current practice. The kind of hermeneutic strategy adopted by the feminists and others can also be employed and indeed is being employed to justify other human rights, such as giving equal rights to non-Muslim minorities, freedom of conscience including the Muslim's right to change his or her religion, rights of homosexuals, and the civil and political rights of ordinary Muslims.

In these and other cases we need to be clear about what we are doing. Sometimes we replace distorted and biased interpretations with what we can show to be the correct ones. In some other cases we exploit the text's silence and ambiguities. In yet others we read our ideas into the text and subtly change and amend it. Sometimes we do it unknowingly, at other times half-knowingly or deliberately and in full knowledge of what we are doing. The last move obviously involves an element of intellectual disingenuity as we stealthily amend the text while pretending to be doing nothing of the kind. Although such a strategy is open to obvious objections, it is necessary and excusable, partly because it is intended to save the religion by exploiting its emancipatory resources and making it historically relevant, and partly because this is often the only way to

---

[5] For a discussion of the various ways of reading a religious text and a critique of its literalist interpretation, see ch. 7 in my *A New Politics of Identity*, Basingstoke, Palgrave Macmillan, 2009.

counter similar moves by those reading the text in a manner that serves dominant interests. It is a rationalist fallacy to think that scholarship can ever be 'pure', and hermeneutics free from political considerations. This is not unique to Islam or religion in general. It is how the U.S. Constitution has been profoundly transformed and brought into harmony with new moral values and historical reality by the Supreme Court. While convinced of the permanent validity of certain basic principles, the architects of the Constitution could not possibly foresee how their country would evolve, what new challenges it would face, and what new constitutional problems these will throw up. The Supreme Court not only interpreted its various provisions in a culturally and historically sensitive manner but subtly redefined its own role as the guardian of the Constitution. Since amendment is a highly cumbersome process and politically often impossible, the Supreme Court chose to reinterpret the Constitution in a manner that addressed contemporary concerns but did not involve too radical a departure from its spirit and guiding principles. In the case of the *Qur'an*, even the possibility of amendment is ruled out, and there is no equivalent of the Supreme Court. The need for its creative reinterpretation is therefore even greater. The responsibility to do so lies with its religious and intellectual leaders, and ultimately with the ordinary Muslims who are its historical bearers and whose precious possession it is.

No religious text is ever read in a political and cultural vacuum. One brings to it certain assumptions, anxieties, and concerns, asks it questions that worry one, and hopes that the answers will be broadly of a particular kind. This is why every religion is interpreted differently in different historical epochs and societies, and by different groups within the same society. A remark that in one age or society is given only a passing attention, ignored, or left as an unresolved puzzle becomes an obsession in another. Its qualifications are ignored in one age but highlighted in another, and its ambiguities are resolved in different ways. When people are frightened and feel helpless and confused, they tend to be obsessive about their religion and take a rigid and dogmatic view of it. By contrast when they feel confident and think that they are in charge of their destiny, they take a relaxed view of their religion, locate it within the framework of their other identities, and moderate its demands by theirs.

In their current phase, vast masses of Muslims the world over feel besieged and deeply disoriented. They feel put upon and manipulated by Western powers. Within their own societies they are often at the mercy of despotic rulers, who stifle debate and use their vast funds and officially patronized clerics to propagate an ideologically convenient reading of Islam. This has generated an intellectual climate in which a creative and culturally attuned reading of Islam has proved exceedingly difficult. If this climate is to improve, profound changes are needed within Muslim societies and in their relations with the West. These changes cannot be brought about without democratic struggles including demands for human rights. However these struggles are unlikely to be mounted and gather popular support unless the deeply religious Muslim masses feel convinced that their demands and struggles have a basis in their religion.

Theological and political struggles are dialectically related, and each depends on the other for its success. A creative interpretation of Islam, which aims to show that human rights and democratic institutions are or can be made compatible with it, is at once both a scholarly and a political activity, and its ultimate objective is to restore both the religion and the levers of power to the people, their rightful claimants. Islam has as rich a history of internal debates and creative interpretations as any other religion. Muslim champions of human rights today have a better chance of success if they link up with the critical strand within their tradition and draw from it an interpretive legitimacy that exceeds or at least rivals that of its conservative and self-appointed guardians.

PENETRATIONS:
A PSYCHO–CULTURAL VIEW OF MODERNITY, FUNDAMENTALISMS AND ISLAM

Durre S. Ahmed

Abstract

Despite billions of dollars spent on (defunct) 'Soviet Studies', academia was unable to predict the collapse of the Soviet Union. The emphasis was on 'hard' data, security, economics, geopolitics, not on 'soft' concerns of culture. A similar blindness is occurring in the west's study of Islam. Drawing from feminism and (post)Jungian psychology, the blindness is traced to the Cartesianist–Christianist world view dominating modernity. It's conception of the human self mono–maniacally denies its own dark 'shadow'. Globally internalized, it precludes a western (or Muslim) understanding of various fundamentalisms.

Soon after the collapse of the Soviet Union, leading academic journals began reflecting on a process summed up by an article in The American Scholar titled 'Why Were We Surprised?' (Spring 1991). That is, in spite of billions of dollars spent by academia, think tanks and security agencies on (now defunct) 'Soviet Studies', not a single scholar/ institution could predict what would happen, when, and how. One main reason was that most analysts had focused overwhelmingly on relations between leaders, economics, geopolitics and security concerns. Largely ignored were "the passions (…) appeal of ethnic loyalty and nationalism, demands for freedom of religious practice and cultural expression". These areas were considered 'soft', 'unscientific' and academically 'weak'.

I experience a sense of déjà vu and apprehension regarding the West's current interest in Islam. The ghost of 'Soviet Studies' is evident in scholarship and public perceptions: Once again, geopolitics, economics and security concerns dominate the flow of analyses at the expense of 'soft' concerns such as women and culture. Similarly, the emphasis on fundamentalism focuses mostly on legalist theology and political Islamism, rather than Islam as it has existed, and continues to exist, in the lived psycho–cultural realities of the vast majority of its adherents.

Durre S. Ahmed

Modernity and the Self

Religious fundamentalism today is not restricted to Islam but is a powerful presence in all religions across the globe. In the Judaeo–Christian world, its rank and file comprise well–educated individuals living in, what are in many ways, post modern societies. Reflecting what is today part of a growing critique pointing to a 'cultural crisis' in and about modernity, one way or another, fundamentalism, as Habermas says, is 'an exclusively modern phenomenon' (2001). As such, modernity can be linked to a certain 'mind set' about how we think about self, others and the world at large. The idea of the self has been a long standing and ongoing concern in feminism, which has extensively critiqued the construction of the self in western moral and political philosophy in the 20th century. Even outside of academic philosophy, the self is a crucial concept since it ultimately concerns our notions of human nature, you and I. How each of us responds to this conception will impact our understanding of religion generally and Islam specifically.

Existing (neo–Kantian) dominant notions of the self identify it primarily with abstract rationality. Similarly, economic behaviour is seen as the application of reason to prioritize desires and devising means for their satisfaction. Thus, the self is either *homo rationalis* (rational man) or *homo economicus* (economic man). For decades, western feminism has challenged this idealized and narrow conception of the self, claiming that western philosophy and popular culture is derived from the experience of predominantly white, heterosexual, economically advantaged men who have wielded social, economic and political power, dominating the arts, literature, media and scholarship. Cast as a lesser form of the masculine individual, woman is the Other and thus, the non–person, non–agent, non–subject (Myers: 2004). In short, "In western culture, the mind and reason are coded masculine, whereas the body and emotion are coded feminine (...) to identify the self with the rational mind is to privilege a narrow idea of reason and to masculinize the self." (Llyod, 1992) This split between an emotional, nonverbal, 'feminine' body and a rational 'masculine' mind is simultaneously a critique of the Cartesian dic(k)tum about the self: I *think*, therefore I am, leading to what Susan Bordo called 'the Cartesian masculinization of thought' and what feminists in different disciplines call the 'logo–centric', 'phallocratic', 'disembodied' mind in Western cultural and intellectual consciousness. Now this mind seeks to understand Islam and Muslims.

Examining the rise of fundamentalism in Judaism, Christianity and Islam, Karen Armstrong differentiates between two ways of thinking, mythos and logos (2000). Logos concerns the rational, pragmatic and scientific, enabling functioning at a practical level. Mythos has to do with meaning, 'making sense' of the complex, emotional experiences called 'life'. Mythical stories were never meant to be taken literally, but rather symbolically. They are metaphors, symbols for situations and experiences that we all encounter and which have a strong impact on us. In the west this dimension of mythos has been overwhelmed by overvaluing of logos, precipitating a crisis of meaning.

Armstrong is the most recent in a long line of authors who similarly diagnosed a malaise afflicting the west as linked to its loss of mythos. They include Paul Ricoeur, Ernst Cassirer, Mircea Eliade, Gilbert Durand, James Hillman, Joseph Campbell to name a few. One refers to them, as a means of moving to Carl Jung, who more than 50 years ago, alerted the west to the psychosocial dangers implicit to what he called the loss of the 'symbolic life', and the resulting havoc this has created in the western individual and collective psyche. So my dilemma is this: How can I explain that there is a malaise within the world of Muslims, in a context where my (western) audience itself has been repeatedly diagnosed by its own 'doctors' as severely handicapped when it comes to understanding religion generally, including its own? My existential situation demands that I begin with 'you'. With a Muslim audience it would the other way around. Sickness implies being [a] patient. So, before discussing Islam, let us understand what afflicts, by now, not only the western self but many others.

Cartesianism and Loss of the Symbolic

Everyone agrees that religious fundamentalists take scriptures literally, but what about the non–believer?

Science functions on the law of non–contradiction, applying Cartesianist logic to the world of material facts. To take things literally is to take them as facts, which, by definition, can have only one meaning. For example, water will always be two parts of hydrogen and one part of oxygen and there are no two ways about this. But what 'water' *means* to each of us has to do with our varied *experiences* of it: drinking it, swimming, or walking in the rain, we don't think of it as 'H_2O', but rather in terms of feelings/emotions and we explain these not via quantities but different qualities, experiences which are subjective, multiple, symbolic, and *cannot* be meaningfully communicated in any other way. Confronted with the subjective world of mythos, the logocentric mind responds in Cartesian terms and is unable to deal with the multiple meaning and metaphoric ambiguity. Thus, the meaning(s) of religion must also be singular, either right/wrong true/false. In the post–Enlightenment west, this eventually led to the notion that 'those who think cannot believe and those who believe cannot think'. The 20th century discipline of psychology (logos–of–psyche) further entrenched this notion with the ideas of Freud, in which the 'ego'(self) functioned on reason and willpower which are considered the hallmark of a mentally healthy person. Religion was labelled an opiate, 'infantile neurosis', an illusion without a future. Clearly this has not happened. Perhaps the ideas of Carl Jung need re–viewing.

Beyond their historical significance, Jung and Freud represent two distinct epistemological premises underpinning all contemporary psychotherapeutics of the self. Bear in mind that their quarrel was over religion which Jung insisted was a vital aspect of the psyche and should be taken seriously. The fact remains that people kill as much in the name of God as they kill *without it.* In the 20th century, between the 'death' of God, the two world wars, the Gulag, Hiroshima and Nagasaki, more than 300 million people died violent deaths for reasons that had *nothing* to do with religion All this occurred either in Europe or originated in the modern 'secular' west. Till very recently, there have been no non–western equivalents to Stalinism, Fascism, the Holocaust, apartheid, or the inventions of chemical, nuclear and biological weapons. Overall, the sheer scale of the genocides in the previous century (the Holocaust, the Indian partition, Rwanda, Cambodia, the Balkans), not to mention the Oklahoma bombings and periodic massacres of school kids in Europe and the US, indicate that there is something inherently self destructive within the modern self. Fanaticism lurks deep within the human psyche.

Humans need meaning(s) and traditionally mythos provided this. The ancient pantheons were simultaneously a reflection–projection of the psyche's inherent diversity and (understanding) the transcendent realm. Mythic forms/names/stories provided emotional containers which could receive the varied, intense, at times unbearable or inexpressible experiences of life, pointing not necessarily to a single 'truth' but to a 'way' of being in the world. Thus, both the self and the Divine were/are multifaceted, polyvalent and there was no permanent ruling 'god'. In this psycho–theological context, male and female divinities represent diverse *psychological* (symbolic) *perspectives*/capacities within both men and women—and the Divine. Mythos speaks of the eternal and immutable and we remain meaning seeking creatures, albeit now, more literal than ever. From the Jungian perspective, over two thousand years, this symbolic diversity has been obliterated in western psychological and theological consciousness, particularly the loss of the 'feminine' aspects of the psyche and the Divine. The original gender– diverse Greek pantheon was steadily over whelmed by the Age of the Heroes and eventually Zeus gave way to the God–Father of Christianity. Eventually, the vestiges of the Divine Feminine of Marian Catholicism were erased with Protestant Christianity and its materialist ethic. In short, the mythic Hero dominates, literally.

With the advent of psychology, the Freudian self (ego) is similarly 'heroic', modelled on Apollo and other youthful gods representing reason and determination. 'Theos' in Greek means god, as in mono–theism and theo–logy (a logos–of–god). But 'theos' also constitutes 'theory' and the intellectual/academic endeavour of *theo*rizing, constructing a framework of meaning. As such, there is a god behind any construction of theory/meaning and manifests as an *attitudinal perspective*, a way of life. Non–religious ideologies can exercise a psychological power similar to religion, witness the last century. As a perspective, rational logic can also psychologically become god, functioning as a sort of religious conviction. Jung was referring to this when he said that the west's "true religion is a monotheism of consciousness"(13:51) whereby the Freudian/Cartesian ego–self has made its self a god of reason and will power. Whether in the Divine or self, the dominance of this psycho–theological male–god has implications for women.

Given the intertwined roots of psychology and religion in western cultural history, much of what we call psychopathology can be seen as a secularization of 'heretical' tendencies, which in western/Christian public imagination is represented by Joan of Arc and the witches of the Inquisition. Today women still bear the brunt psychologically. Even as multibillion dollar global psycho–pharmaceuticals promote a masculine 'mind' as a model, worldwide more women suffer from depression than any other illness. Almost everywhere women are given more pills than men having the *same* condition. In short, women are either bad or mad.

The West's loss of symbolic consciousness, is thus, loss of psychological and spiritual diversity. It is not only a devaluation of the many feminine aspects of human consciousness, but also other styles of masculinity different from the dominant adolescent heroic model. The heroic ego of reason and power is just one important aspect of the self. In light of the reality of many diverse inner selves and their steady obliteration/relegation to pathologies today, Jung's view of mental illness is simply a 'one–sidedness in the presence of many' — which is another way of describing fundamentalism.

By now there is a huge body of work from within different disciplines that place these ego–attitudes at the heart of modernity and its psycho–cultural condition. Deep ecology, critiques of science, feminist spirituality and eco–feminism particularly, have analyzed how these attitudes underpin the environmental crisis. They suggest how woman/body/nature are, from the view of the Cartesian ego, psychologically synonymous, regarding as this ego does, both women and nature as objects to be tamed, owned, mastered and manipulated at will. The mythic element remains but literalized. Thus, from this feminist–Jungian perspective the logocentric worldview of modernity is a heroic, confrontational, patriarchal, fundamentalist machismo that permeates our ideas ranging from politics and health, to science, development, progress, religion.

Cartesian–Christianism

Jung's statement about the west's true religion being a 'monotheism of consciousness' has nothing to do with religious belief but about a particular dominant psychological *attitude* and *style* of thinking. A religious Hindu can be termed a psychological MONO–theist if he believes his is the only 'correct' religion, as would a secular Hindu if he insists that the only 'correct' view is to see Hinduism as irrational or false. In both instances, there is the conviction of an exclusivist, singular truth cut off from diverse inner realities.

Exceedingly critical of particularly Protestant Christianity, Jung saw how Cartesianism reinforced the dogmatic foundations of Christianity, turning it into Christianism. Both emphasize the singular and literal. For example, Christianity is the only religion which has tried to establish the 'fact' of Christ through sciences such as archaeology, carbon dating etc (but not applied to the devil). Thus, Christ had been totally literalized into an exclusivist idea of a male person–as–God. By simply accepting this literal 'fact', my salvation is assured. Evil cannot touch me because of this essentially *mental belief* (credo). This splitting of faith and reason, good and evil, is in synchrony with the Cartesian mind–body split. Hillman (1983:78) also points to this, and how "the Christian mind splits the negative and projects in onto the enemy" (the heathens, Jews, Catholics, terrorists). Accordingly, the

Christian heritage is constantly at work " invisibly inside our feelings and reactions and ideas, preventing us from seeing ourselves and our world ... you and me, too, we cant help but be Christian" (84).

The psycho–theological ruptures in the modern self have created a moral sickness in the western psyche leading to a world view which can be called Cartesian Christianism. This is the tendency to split phenomenon, literalize and morally reduce them into irreconcilable opposites. Thus, Jung urged the 'white man in general' to recognize the evil *within* the self, the 'shadow', and its universality in the human psyche. Honestly speaking, there is much about us that is neither rational, heroic nor free of evil. Christianist dogma makes what is basically one's own evil, into a metaphysical principle of the devil, which is then endlessly mulled over philosophically as the 'Problem of Evil'. Denied psychologically within the self, through a process of moral reductionism, it is projected onto others. "Christianity has made the antinomy of good and evil into a world problem and by formulating the conflict dogmatically raised it into an absolute principle" (Jung,12:16).

Between an unconscious Cartesianism which claims the 'light' of reason and insists on singularity of meaning, and a similar unconscious Christianism based on theological exclusivity and absolves one of the darkness within, evil is seen in others, outside of the self. Any MONO–theos is morally reductionist, seeing all issues in terms of good/bad, either/or. This heroic masculinism is evident today in globally popular films such as Harry Potter and Lord of the Rings. Reflecting a literalist, reductionist, adolescent view of both God and human, these narratives rely on techno–magical weapons of destruction not philosophical wisdom. The view of the world is a decisive battle between good and evil. The goal of victory is destruction, extermination, annihilation (Warner: 2001). Even though, many myths/religions speak of options such as deliberation, negotiation, redemption, reconciliation, not to mention Christian ideals of love and forgiveness. A decade before 9/11, Hillman's observations on Christianism and the modern person remain relevant, pointing out how " terrorism and nihilism are inherent to the (modern) western world view and system of thinking" which is rooted in the west's "religious unconsciousness". The world conquering force of Christianity was not inspired by Christian love but by successfully mobilizing "the will, which needs fundamentalism or it does not know what to do...there (has to be)only *one* meaning, one reading of the text, for instance, the one meaning of Christ's suffering" (81–82).

To sum up: the modern mind, irrespective of religion, is over-whelmingly Cartesian, masculine, literalist, positivistic, Appollonic,

Protestant–Christianist, heroic, adolescent and morally reductionist. It is unable to deal with, and reacts with violence to that which is considered different from itself, including the feminine, other modes of masculinity, the intermediate, ambiguous and the symbolic/metaphorical(82). From a psychological perspective, fundamentalism may be expressed in a religious or non–religious idiom but is imbued with Cartesianist–Christianist principles. To reiterate, this is not to contest Christianity as a religion, so it is best to let Jung speak: "I do not combat Christian truth. I am only arguing with the modern mind"(Post, 234). This 'mind' has made 'God' a wholly notional truth reached by the critical intellect and thus, has itself de–meaned the life nourishing symbol central to the profound Christic *mythos* by literalizing it.

All religions encompass notions of good and evil and other dialectical opposites. However, these are not (to be) seen literally, or existing separately in warring conflict, but rather, as symbolic, interconnected, contrasting, *mutually defining* complementary qualities. Similarly, all sacred texts are less about 'true' mental 'beliefs' and more about how to cope daily with this beautiful, painful, paradoxical, frequently confusing and difficult business called 'life. Every religion urges humans to try and live (and die) according to two core, related principles: do unto others as you would have others do unto you, which automatically leads to the idea of compassion. These are the challenges of religion and they have been marginalized today by Cartesian–Christianist dogma and geopolitics. The 'dark epiphanies of the 20th century' reveal that secular humanism does not automatically evoke compassion and nor does religious belief per se. For Jung, it was not that westerners are more evil than their ancestors, rather, given the distortions and internalization of Cartesian–Christianism, their moral capacities have not evolved in proportion to their modern ability to destroy on an unprecedented scale. "That is the great problem before us today. *Reason alone no longer suffices*" (10:574). These failures tell us that the problem is not with any religion but with human nature. Thus, it is imperative to be aware of how we conceive of and understand the human self and its relationship with religion.

Promoted and internalized via the universally 'civilizing' projects of colonialism, modernization/globalization, the nature of 'secular' fundamentalisms today exhibit similar Cartesian–Christianist features in which the world of 'facts' dominates at the expense of meaning(s): excessive literalism, an exclusivist attitude, singularity of meaning and a reliance on history–as–'fact'. This historicism bears directly on our individual and collective consciousness which today believes that historical 'facts' determine us to the exclusion of everything else. It ranges from evolutionary psychology to genetics, to the 'case history' project of psychotherapy/psychiatry's reduction of the meaning(s) of life to chemicals or what happened in childhood; to rigid ethno–religious ideas of identity and the creation of nation states based on the politics of nationalism and literalized spiritual geographies. Similarly, it is evident that even apart from the Muslim world, it is the literalist–historical view of religious and political identity that dominates. Thus, Hindu fundamentalists also relied on archaeology to destroy the Ayodhya Mosque and there is similar psychology at work in Jerusalem.

Internalised today by millions belonging to different religions, or not to any (that is, Cartesian Christianism), the insistence on psychological singularity is an implicit, mythical ideology, supplying images and appropriate feelings about self and other, creating a fantasy of what it means to be 'a people'. Every concept is MONO–theised, whether as a one–dimensional theo–logic–al god or a 'secular' (Cartesian–Christianist) political ideal. For instance, One God(mine) is accompanied by One Faith (orthodoxy/modern secularism). There should be One Law (sharia/WTO), One State (darul–Islam/ globalization), served by One body of the faithful. A perfect evocation of a totalitarian, paranoid society. This literalized unity requires a Hero who can lead/fight dangerous dragons: Thus, the Communists and Capitalist west required each other and now the Muslims, who in turn, require the Great Satan and their own heretics(minorities and women). In order to function, *logos* requires 'problems' which it can 'solve', an attitude which eventually leads to Final Solutions.

Thanks to modernity, Hinduism today is increasingly Cartesian–Christianist–Hinduism. Similarly, we have Cartesian–Christianist–Judaism or Buddhism, and of course Cartesian–Christianist–Islamism. Religious or secular, these fundamentalisms are misogynist, hegemonic, hypermasculine expressions which psychologically and theologically artificially negate psycho spiritual tendencies in favour of logocentric supremacist thought. As such, the terrorism of political Islam is one side of the symmetrical psychodynamics underlying (post)modernity where there is only ONE choice, 'your either with us or against us'. In the absence of the feminine, it is a mirror image response to various masculinist 'penetrations': psychologically, of western Cartesianist–Christianist modernity, and literally, the penetration of a homophobic, homoerotic dialogue/battle violence into a language of war.

It should not be forgotten that the primary 'image' heralding the colonial project was of white men carrying weapons accompanied by a priest/missionary. Additionally, it was most of the Islamic world which was colonized. Which is not to say that everything wrong with the Muslim world has to do with Cartesian Christianism. The point here is to identify certain psycho–religious dynamics within modernity which are coming from the fusion of a distorted vision of Christianity and an instrumentalist–weaponized vision of reason, and their internalization in the colonized/modernized psyche. The psychology of the rational–warrior–priest fuels all sorts of extremism, including the way we relate to self, society and *any* religion. Religious or 'secular' (Cartesian–Christianist), as participants in a global modernity, we are all influenced by what Hillman calls 'this extraordinary religion, the religion that we are all in no matter how hard we try to deny it or escape it'(143). We are all in the same boat.

In the process, our psychological relationship with *spiritual* heroes, the prophets, saints and sages of *mythos*, and especially Christ's message of love and compassion, all have been forgotten in favour of the scientist/inventor/warrior/ politician/economist in the mythic quest of 'progress'. Without the capacity to comprehend the symbolic; its moral and ethical transformative potential remains dormant. The price for 'progress' is self evident, not just in the massive and growing psychopharmacological industry, but most vividly in the natural environment which symbolically reflects the ravaged human psychological condition in a demythologized world. The pathologizing and erasing of inner diversity is reflected in the steady extinction of different species and is symptomatic of a global environ–*mental* crisis.

(Cartesian–Christianist) Islamism

The 'secular' concept of culture as separate from religion stems from the modern Christianist idea of religion being primarily a *mental* belief/creed and a system of worship. This leads to questions of whether Muslims can be assimilated in Europe. A prominent scholar on Islam states: "… for Muslims the word 'religion' does not have the same connotations as it has for Christians … for Muslims, Islam is not simply a system of faith and worship … {it}concerns the whole complex fabric of life" (Lewis:25). This is entirely correct. But what is not mentioned in these debates about Islam in the west, and as vast numbers of even nominal Hindus, Buddhists, Sikhs will tell you, actually *every* religion concerns the "whole, complex fabric of life". Except, by Lewis' own admission, Christianity. Nevertheless, this exception has been the decisive norm for studying *all* religions. Only now are leading scholars admitting that prior to the Enlightenment, it was impossible to distinguish religion from culture in the west. Additionally, that it was an enormous mistake to have considered Protestantism as the paradigm of religion, indicating that the entire edifice of the academic study of religion merits serious reconsideration. (Lincoln 2002:3–4).

One of Islam's greatest strength has been its ability to adapt to different cultures. Beyond the unifying centrality of the prophet, and the simple liturgical prayer and Quran in Arabic, there is really nothing else that 'holds' it together other than a symbol (Kaaba) which essentially serves as a signifier for 'direction'. Within a 100 years of its inception, Islam had *settled* in dispersed regions spanning continents and widely divergent societies/cultures. If this inherent adaptivity to other cultures was not part of its *raison d'être*, Islam could not have given rise to five great civilizations – the Mughal, Ottoman, Persian, Moorish and Spanish. Each was a distinct civilization of the highest order and at the same time uniquely Islamic.

As part of the Indian subcontinent, Pakistani culture and hence its Islam, is primarily Indo–Persian Islam which subsumes the rich *mythos* of two ancient civilizations, not to mention the multi layered world of *mythos* which is the Quran. I was raised in an environment in which the Arabic Quran, the Persian poetry of Rumi (13th century) and the Punjabi poetry of Bulleh Shah (16th century) and others, were intermingled in conversations on religion (not to mention Bach and Handel). Apart from literature, this intermeshing of culture and religion, in particular of Persian/Central Asian Islam and Hinduism, is fully visible in the exquisite beauty of Mughal architecture and in the classical music and performing arts of India even today. In short, it is important to remember that what is today called 'Sufism' was, as Armstrong points out, the *normative* form of Islam until the end of the Nineteenth Century (2005: 101). As such, people did not see themselves as 'Sufis' but simply Muslims living in what was/is a vast, multilayered canvas of numerous indigenous Islams. Edward Said is correct in saying that there are actually innumerable Islams (2002). The countless civilizational–cultural manifestations provide the best evidence for its inherently pluralistic and inclusivist worldview.

Jung called Sufism the secret backbone of Islam because it is indistinguishable from culture. Today, this backbone has been severely damaged. The reasons are numerous: the colonial, modernization/globalization projects, 20th century geopolitics, dick–tatorial regimes 'officializing' Islam by 'Islamizing' societies, and the world wide promotion of Saudi 'money–theism' and a MONO–cultural Salafi vision which has resulted in cultural vandalism across the Muslim world. It is one of the most deadly assaults on Islam(s). The *logos* centred analytic gaze of the west on a logocentric Cartesian–Christianist–Islamism, neglects the dimension of cultural history, perhaps because of its own cultural amnesia. In any case, today all cultures are also under seige from a MONO–cultural globalization which, according to also Derrida, remains at heart Christianist/Latinist (2002:63)

A major problem with the present discourses around Islam, including among Muslims themselves, is the constant conflation between the psychological and the socio–political with the latter dominant. While all religions teach us how to live with others, most importantly all address the mystery of death. This is something that all of us will experience and know nothing about. Death is a uniquely individual experience. It is one area having no 'experts' and has to be faced alone. Thus, the psychological primacy of religion is paramount. So my concern here is the psychological dimension. Of not only the Islamic conception of God but also how its variations resonate within the Muslim psyche as mediated by modernity.

Unlike Christianity, God in Islam is beyond gender. The 'He' is more of a linguistic constraint rather than a theological imperative and there is no such notion as 'Father' or (Mother). However, for centuries, numerous commentaries on the (more than) 99 Names of God have categorized them as Names of Majesty/Power and Names of Beauty/ Compassion, that is, they can be seen as symbolically 'Masculine' and 'Feminine'. This 'gendering' is similar to Taoism's *Yin* and *Yang* which *together* make for the Great Absolute. Life is both male and female.

Seen from this perspective all religious fundamentalisms can be understood as hypermasculine approaches to text, interpretation, meaning(s) and expression which negates and devalues the Divine Feminine (Ahmed:2002). Psycho–theological hypermasculinism, past and present, also explains why heresy and the violence directed at it, frequently concerns a more feminist/feminine vision of a given religion, hence the witches. In Greek, the word 'heresy' actually means to 'choose for one self'.

Broadly speaking there are two types of (Cartesian–Christianist) Islamists. The first are economically successful and well educated, frequently in modern sciences such as engineering and medicine. They constitute the leadership of groups such as Al–Qaida. They can be termed 'high' Islamists and are the ideologues of movements which draw their strength from less educated and less well to do 'low' or mass islamists. Thoroughly modern and present in many Muslim societies, Muslim feminists had noted two decades ago how many 'high' Islamists were well educated in modern disciplines. If today they are globally present, North and South, it is because there is a unity of a modern literalist, logocentric 'mind'. The fact that Islam has never had an official clergy or 'Church', no 'Rome' or 'Canterbury', has been true for 1500 years. But within roughly just the past four decades, Saudi *money*-theism has successfully first created a clergy (the 'high' Islamists), and then will follow the inevitable central 'Church'. This of course will be encouraged by the west since it is in resonance with its own centralized (Christianist) religious institutions. It is also intellectually easier to 'deal' with a handful of 'officials' rather than a cacophony of innumerable voices and languages all claiming to be Muslims.

Between Cartesian–Christianist modernity and the Saudi–Salafi theo–cultural bulldozer, the psycho–spiritual (cultural) diversity of Islam is being steadily obliterated. This is a disaster for any natural phenomenon, and religion is no exception. All religions are languages of the soul, and like languages, have numerous dialects and accents. Today, there is increasing pressure that all Muslims must 'speak' with just one accent, in one dialect, namely Salafi Islam. Even though 85 percent of more than a *billion* Muslims are not Arabs. If the west indiscriminately encourages this direction towards insitutionalized, 'official', mono–polist representatives and institutions, it will be assisting in the eventual extinction of 85% of the Islamic spiritual/cultural rainbow, replacing it with the monolithic monochromatic bigotry of Wahabi/Salafism and other hypermasculine expressions.

For Jung, the west had basically destroyed its own religion and via the modernity project threatened the world not just physically but also psychologically and spiritually. "No wonder the western world feels uneasy, for it does not know what it has lost through the destruction of its numinosities (symbols). It has lost its moral and spiritual values to a very dangerous degree. Its moral and spiritual tradition has collapsed, and has left a world wide disorientation ... The great religions of the world suffer from increasing anaemia ..." (18:254). Such disorientation and collapse is evident in the denigration of the feminine dimension of the psyche *and* theology in all religions. It is telescoped by the situation in Algeria during the 80's and 90's in which Islamists threatened to kill the unveiled woman and 'secularists' the veiled one.

From whichever angle I see the situation, past, present, future, Islam and the west are connected. The distant past is well known: the Crusades, Spain and the transmission of the intellectual legacy of the

Greeks and colonialism. However, the genesis of the Taliban, it should not be forgotten, was the Cold War and eventually a real but 'proxy' war between basically the Soviet Union and the U.S/west in which the Pakistanis and Afghans were footsoldiers. That war in Afghanistan lasted over almost two decades during which tens of thousands died and many children lost one or both parents. Vast numbers were put into segregated orphanages run by semi–literate 'low' islamists, mostly in Pakistan. Thousands of young males had literally NO experience of woman — as mother, aunt, sister, grandmother etc. This absence of psychological experience of the feminine was reinforced by the indoctrination of a hypermasculine, patriarchal interpretation of Islam which only emphasizes the Names linked to God's Power, Vengeance etc, not the *dominant* ones of Love, Mercy, Compassion and Beauty, to name a few. In sum, the feminine, Divine or human, has been rendered wholly 'Other', obliterated in the psychological and theological consciousness of the Taliban (and many other Muslims). Once this sort of mutation occurs, it takes generations to reverse.

Self and Other

The human sensorium functions on the physiological principle of contrast (difference). As such, no perception or knowledge is possible without contrast. The Quran is quite clear that humanity was never meant to be religiously, or otherwise, uniform and identical. It speaks of human racial, linguistic and ethnic diversity as one of the "signs" of God, so we may "recognize/know each other" (49:13). Also, "if God had so willed He might have made you one community but He wishes to show your perfection (the capacities and capabilities) that He has endowed you with. Therefore compete with each other in pursuing the good" (5:48).

Thus, we are not (meant to be) the same because of the varied nature of "capacities and capabilities" we have been (potentially) endowed with. The idea is to improve/perfect these and they can only emerge/develop when we encounter difference, the "other", hence 'compete with each other in pursuing the good'. So, we must first recognize that what we *share* most strongly with the 'other' are our weaknesses and limitations, our flaws and failures. Only then can we know what sets us *apart* and makes us distinct(ive) and different, for it is through our positive capacities, our successes, that we 'distinguish' ourselves from others. In short, the 'other' serves as a mirror in which I can glimpse foremost my *own* darkness, the shadow, and the evil potential in *all* of us. By way of explanation, let me bring the body into the picture and put it bluntly: while outwardly we may be different, when it comes to our shit, we all smell the same.

It is not easy to acknowledge to oneself, leave alone to others, certain aspects to us which can only be termed shitty. Lust, vengeance, greed, rage, ambition, envy, violence, perversions, fetishes, treachery, betrayal, the list is endless. Believer or not, this inner world of demons will not go away however much we 'think', avoid or deny it. As a natural phenomenon, shit shadows us as long as we live. But it is also a vital part in the regeneration of life and the best natural fertilizer, expressed in the more scientific word 'humus'. Which is also linked to 'humility' and 'human'. So to be aware of one's shit, is to remain grounded, down to earth, humble. The catalyst for this regeneration is the 'other'. S/he provides both a mirror which keeps me grounded in humility and a foil against whom I can assess and develop my specific capacities in "pursuit of the good"— a different type of 'progress'.

Individual or collective, if the shadow remains unconscious, it will continue to be projected. During the Cold War, Jung wrote how "a peculiar feeling of helplessness was creeping over western consciousness", the need to take extreme defensive measures and the failure to see the west's own shadow "glowering" at it through the Iron Curtain. He urged self awareness, the futility of thinking that it is only "*they* who are morally and philosophically wrong", and to recognize that "we are doing the practically the same things as *they* are, only with the additional disadvantage that we neither see nor want to understand what we are doing under the cloak of good manners" (18:245). These observations remain valid today for the west (and Muslims). However, "what makes matters worse (is that) the enlightenend European is of the opinion that religion and such things are good enough for the masses and for women, but of little consequence compared with immediate economic and political questions"(10:185).

- - -

If I have been critical of the west and modernity, it has not been for the sake of west bashing, nor to sentimentally suggest a return to some utopian past of 'tradition'. As a closer look at modernity reveals, the world really does not become better but simply different. For every gain there is a corresponding loss. Modernity also includes feminisms, some of which continue to inspire women everywhere. Educated by missionaries, I received many gifts of learning including familiarity with the Bible and am convinced that part of the present problem(s) with Muslims has to do with their ignorance of it. Similarly, much of what I have said is based on western sources, acknowledged and wise voices existing on the margins of western intellectual consciousness. Whereas an insatiable appetite for knowledge is one of the west's most distinguished aspects, it has unfortunately literalized the profound idea that 'knowledge is power'. That is, power for the sake of power, an end in itself, frequently exercised through arrogance and brute material force.

The motto of the Pakistani University I studied at, is taken from Kant: 'Courage to Know' *Sapere aude!* It sums up the spirit of the Enlightenment and still holds true, implying that it takes courage to think independently about self, religion, politics, or anything else. If 'ignorance is bliss', then knowledge is also a burden requiring ethical responsibility. Today, I don't think the bliss factor is an option for most of us here. Christ carried his own cross, and his last words had to do with humans not *knowing* what they do. Knowing oneself first as *connected* to the other, may be more productive than the present, repetitive "dialogue" between the deaf.

As the counterpart to *logos*, *mythos*, above all, is the domain of the Feminine. The rational intellect as *logos* has a higher dimension, wisdom, which is associated with age, experience, maturity, not youthful adolescence. In western culture it is represented by Sophia or then Sapientia, the patron of this University. Demographic projections indicate that as my part of the world becomes increasingly driven by the raging energy of testosterone driven young males, in about 20 years, Europe will be primarily a continent of old women. I leave you to contemplate the symbolic implications inherent in the juxtaposition of these two images: a young male and an old woman. One can only hope that by that time, the dominant vision of the human self will be neither *homo rationalis* nor *homo economicus* but rather, *homo sapiens*: the (hu)man of wisdom.

References

Ahmed, D., *Gendering the Spirit: Women, Religion and the Postcolonial Response*, London, Zed Books, 2002.
Armstrong, K., *The Battle for God*, New York, Knopf, 2000.
Armstrong, K., *A Short History of Myth*. London, Penguin, 2005.
Derrida, J., *Acts of Religion,* New York, Routledge, 2002.
Habermas, J., *Faith and Knowledge ... an Opening*, Acceptance Speech for Peace Prize of German Publishers Association, Frankfurt, 14.01.2001
Hillman, J., *Inter–Views*, New York, Harper and Row, 1983.
Jung, C.G. *The Collected Works of C.G Jung*, London, Routledge/ Princeton, N.J., Princeton University Press.
Lewis, B., *Islam and the West*, Oxford, Oxford University Press, 1993.
Lincoln, B., *Holy Terrors: Thinking About Religion After September Eleven,* Chicago, Chicago University Press, 2003.
Lloyd, G., "Madness, Metaphor and the 'Crisis of Reason'", in L. Antony and C. Witt, *A Mind of Ones Own"*, Boulder, Westview Press, 1992.
Myers, D., "Feminist Perspectives on the Self", *Stanford Encyclopedia of Philosophy*, 2004.
Post, L., *Jung and the Story of Our Times*, London, Penguin, 1978.
Said, E., "Impossible Histories: Why the Many Islams Cannot be Simplified", *Harpers*, July 2002.
Warner, M., "Fantasy's Power and Peril", *New York Times Book Review*, 16.12.2001.

Part II
The Islamic Challenge:
Islam and the Secular State

Acknowledgments

Bettina Leysen

Dear Abdullahi An-Na`im,

I must confess that when Prof. Marie-Claire Foblets revealed to me that she had succeeded to have you nominated for the honorary doctor title at the catholic university of Leuven, I had never heard of you before. She told me that your thesis was that the sharia has to be adapted on a voluntary basis by Muslims. Having inherited my father's pragmatic attitude, my spontaneous reaction was: this sounds very interesting, but are his ideas practical and applicable? Marie-Claire Foblets confirmed the latter and as a proof she gave me her copy of your latest book, Islam and the secular state, together with your article 'From Muslims in Europe to European Muslims'. I quote from the article: "As Kurt Lewin rightly said, 'there is nothing so practical as a good theory.' This does not only mean that practice should be guided by good theory, but also that good theory should be practical." End of quote. Her idea of organising a conference in your honour, could therefore count on my family's enthusiasm.

Last month, during a visit to Senegal, I found the time to read your latest book: Islam and the Secular State, Negotiating the Future of Shari'a. You argue that the coercive enforcement of Sharia by the state betrays the Qur'an's insistence on voluntary acceptance of Islam. As it happens, Senegal has a secular constitution since its independence. The Muslim religious brotherhood of the Mourides could not accept the secular character of the newly founded state, and therefore created their own state within the Senegalese state. In the holy city of Touba every aspect of life, such as education, health care and land tenure, is managed by the religious Mouride order independently of the Senegalese state. In the entire country, the Mourides are venerated as saints; one finds depictures of this dynasty in every car rapide and on many mobile phones. The Islam I have come to know during the last years in Senegal first struck me as being totally different from the Qur'anic Islam I have been taught at this very university, by Prof. Emilio Platti. When I confronted Amina Wadud, another distinguished speaker of this Forum, about what I would describe as popular Islam, she replied: "Remember Bettina, this is the only alternative to Wahhabism." As you all know, Wahhabism is the kind of Islam practiced in Saudi-Arabia. What you might not know, is that it is also the legal school under the jurisprudence of which some Belgian Muslims fall. During the month of the Ramadan, Imams of Wahhabite signature are invited with Saudi support to promulgate their fundamentalistic and puritan interpretation of Islam.

In contrast to Amina Wadud, I believe that there is a third alternative to Wahhabism on the one side and popular, devotional Islam, on the other side. I am thinking of Sufism, or more broadly mysticism. Mysticism is the language in which all religions understand each other, as the mystic experience is pre-verbal and pre-conceptional. In Zen the phrase goes: "The greater the mystic experience, the greater the compassion with all sentient beings." Contrary to common prejudice, the mystic way leads into everyday life. I give the example of he great Flemish mystic Hadewijch, who lived in the 13th century in Brabant. One of her followers was indulging in languorous longing for the Lord. Her brief advise was: "Stop it and start working."

However, the mystic way is long and often painful, as described for example by Saint John of The Cross in his famous work 'Dark Night of the Soul'. Mystics of all religious beliefs have been persecuted and sometimes executed by their religious authorities, to mention only the great Muslim mystic Mansur al-Hallaj and Margarete Porete, who lived at the turn of the 14th century in our latitudes.

Dear Abdullahi An-Na`im, I don't know if you are a mystic, and I wouldn't dare to ask. What I know however is that you are striving incessantly to make our society more humane by demanding human rights for every individual, whatever his religion, ethnicity or legal status. (Professor An-Na`im was so kind to tell me later that indeed he is a Sufi).

I am looking forward to your lecture, but first I would like to thank Marie-Claire Foblets for her dedication and expertise in composing the Anne and André Leysen Forum in the past three years. Our gratitude goes also to Isabel Penne, who brought the practical organisation to a good end. Finally I want to congratulate Honorary Rector Roger Dillemans for proposing Marie-Claire Foblets as chair holder for this Forum.

AN-NA'IM AND HIS WORK *TOWARD AN ISLAMIC REFORMATION*: A SHORT INTRODUCTION[*]

Jean-Yves Carlier

The works of Abdullahi Ahmed An-Na'im contributes greatly to intercultural dialogue and discussion of the place of Islamic law, especially in western societies. His first book, *Toward an Islamic Reformation* (1990), defends a modernist interpretation of Islam that combines respect for the foundations of Muslim identity and basic principles of democratic societies. His latest book, *Islam and the Secular State* (2008), lends broad support to the effectiveness of a neutral State from the standpoint of religion. His works as a whole attest to the vitality of innovative thought within Islam. This also represents a major (scholarly) contribution to both intercultural dialogue and integration of Islamic law into international development of law; in particular, international human rights law. Rigorously scientific, a man of dialogue, committed to the defence of fundamental rights, an audacious reformer of Islam, Abdullahi Ahmed An-Na'im deserves to be better known in Europe, since it is in the process of building into an "ethnic society", to use the words of Albert Bastenier.[1] This article will be limited to a general introduction of the author and an analysis of his first work, *Toward an Islamic Reformation*, even though the subsequent articles are more focused on his latest work, *Islam and the Secular State*, which will only be mentioned briefly at the end of this article, to distinguish it from his preceding work.

An-Na'im

Professor An-Na'im was born in Sudan in 1946. He studied law at the universities of Khartoum (1970), Cambridge (1973) and Edinburgh (1976). Since 1995, he has been professor of law at Emory University in Atlanta, Georgia (USA), after having served as Executive Director of the African division of *Human Rights Watch* in Washington D.C.

---

[*] This is a revised edition of a text published in French: "An-Na'im pour une réforme du droit musulman", in *La Revue nouvelle*, Brussels, December 2008, n° 12, p. 75 (www.revuenouvelle.be).

[1] A. Bastenier, *Qu'est-ce qu'une société ethnique?*, Paris, Presses Universitaires de France, 2004.

In 1968, while still a student in Khartoum, he became a member of the Republican Brotherhood, whose leader Mahmoud Mohamed Taha, was executed in 1985 by the regime of Sudanese president Jafar Numayry. Numayry's regime, in turn, fell later that same year. Taha's reform-oriented thinking and these events had a profound influence on An-Na`im, who frequently quotes him as someone he holds, according to Islamic tradition, to be a revered master *(ustadh)*. In 1987, he translated Taha's main work, *The Second Message of Islam,* initially published in 1967.

In the interim, An-Na`im was lecturer at Khartoum University Faculty of Law from 1976 until 1985. He had become a leading spokesman for Taha's ideas, the latter being banned from speaking in the country. President Numayry, who had seized power in 1969 through a coup d'état by young socialist soldiers, succeeded in establishing his power by negotiating an agreement in the 1970s that ended the civil war in Sudan between the Muslim North and the non-Muslim South. However, influenced by the Muslim Brotherhood, the government hardened its stance. It forcefully imposed Islamic law in 1983, thus reopening the conflict between North and South. Taha, moderate Muslim reformer, was openly opposed to the forced Islamisation of Sudanese society. He was arrested along with more than 400 members of the Republican Fraternity, including An-Na`im. With An-Na`im himself serving as their lawyer, all members of the group were released except for Taha, who was tried for sedition and apostasy, sentenced to death and executed.

Later, the Sudanese Supreme Court, to which Taha's daughter had appealed the case after Numayry's fall, quashed the death sentence due to procedural defects but did not rule on the legal basis for the crime of apostasy. Earlier, the movement had been dissolved and An-Na`im had gone into exile. He held temporary teaching positions in various universities in the United States, Canada, Sweden and Egypt while hoping one day to return to his country. An-Na`im eventually reconciled himself to a long-term exile after seeing the evolution of the Sudanese regime towards fundamentalist Islam after the 1989 coup d'état. Thereafter, he accepted more stable positions, joining Emory Law School in 1995.

His Work

The scholarly works of Abdullahi Ahmed An-Na`im focus on two areas. On the one hand, he develops a modern, liberal interpretation of Islam in general and of Islamic law (the *shari'a*) in particular. This is, in fact, the subject of his first fundamental work, published in 1990, *Toward an Islamic Reformation*, as well as more recent studies such as *Islam and the Secular State*. On the other hand, he seeks an "overlapping consensus" on the universality of international human rights law within the different cultural and religious traditions. In the process, without denying either of these, he tries to reconcile universalism and particularism. An Na'im has pursued his work in this area, developed initially in conjunction with his compatriot Francis Deng, the former foreign minister who would later become a Representative of the Secretary-General of the United States to displaced persons, through various publications.

Both themes address the issue of interculturality and the role of Muslims in western societies. Intercultural dialogue is a common thread in all of An-Na'im's work. This dialogue is not only out of kindness – which in itself is already laudable – it is a reasoned dialogue, a structured openness to the other aimed at reconciling the particular interests of persons and groups with the interests of society as a whole. This objective, if it is to be durable, cannot be attained by good will alone; it must come from life-organizing systems in society, of which law is a core component. In this regard, An-Na'im is very close to liberal thinkers such as John Rawls or Will Kymlicka. Like the latter, An-Na'im often uses the images of "walking in the other person's shoes". The writings of An-Na'im are characterized by this capacity to humanize his reflection, to make it come alive by the force of a loving gaze upon humanity, nurtured by hope, in spite of or because of his experiences, without eliminating an indispensable rationalisation.

Toward an Islamic Reformation

Published in 1990, *Toward an Islamic Reformation*[2] ends with a discussion of the Rushdie affair, which erupted after the publication of the *Satanic Verses* in September 1988. If An-Na'im, as a Muslim, can understand the shock and wound that an insult to the prophet can cause, he cannot accept the call for its author to be put to death which was issued both from the masses and from the imam Khomeini. We can see that he is profoundly shocked and worried by these radical manifestations of intolerance. He recalls, in particular, the death sentence for apostasy pronounced on *ustadh* Mahmoud Mohamed Taha. By way of a

---

[2] A.A. An-Na'im, *Towards an Islamic Reformation: Civil Liberties, Human Rights and International Law*, Syracuse, N.Y., Syracuse University Press, 1990.

counterpoint, he believes that "tolerance of unorthodoxy and dissent is vital for the spiritual and intellectual benefit of Islam itself".[3]

And that, indeed, is An-Na`im's project, characterized, by the introduction by John Voll, referring to the republican Fraternity, as "unorthodox reformist".[4]

What he calls for is truly "reform" in the strong sense of the word. No revolution that would reject the entire Islamic message, and no evolution that would be satisfied with adapting a few interpretations. It is a radical reform that transforms the understanding of the very foundations of classic Islamic law. Starting from a common premise, An-Na`im will revisit the major branches of the law, as the subtitle of his work suggests: Civil Liberties, Human Rights and International Law. It therefore follows that, in its current state, classical Islamic law, the *shari'a*, is incompatible with the major trends in these disciplines, notably as regards the principle of non-discrimination. Only a re-examination of its foundations can make it possible to render *shari'a* compatible with these trends and to develop a truly modern Islamic law. It is impossible to go into the details of the arguments that are specific to each branch. We shall examine, in succession, the premise and two examples in two branches before addressing the question of the appropriateness of the process and of its evolution in An-Na`im's subsequent works.

Law is progressively constructed by human societies. It is not handed down definitively by a higher authority. As evident as this affirmation may seem in the secular societies of today, it is not taken for granted in all times and places. In the not so distant past, positive law in the West drew upon natural law, which in turn had its source in the word of God. The drafters of the principal texts protecting human rights largely looked to it for their inspiration.

Today, in Islamic countries or in any society in which religion covers the scope of public life, law remains, to varying degrees, inspired by sacred texts. Thus, classical Muslim law, the *shari'a*, rests upon four foundations. First, the Qur'an, the divine word revealed to the prophet. Second, the Sunna, which records the sayings and practices of the prophet and his first disciples. Third, the *ijma*, or consensus among the doctors in law. And fourth, the *quiyas*, or reasoning by analogy based on precedent. Even if these sources were established long ago, the last two may be considered interpretations subject to revision. This is, however,

---

[3] *Towards an Islamic Reformation, op. cit.*, p. 184.
[4] *Idem*, p. IX.

a complex issue, for *ijtihad*, which is the word for this interpretive effort, is limited in time and object. The gates of *ijtihad* were closed in the ninth century of the common era, so that the interpretation of that time was not further revised or updated with the passage of time. Some modernists advocate reopening the gates of this effort. No matter how admirable that approach, it remains limited by the object of *ijtihad*. Interpretive reasoning is only possible when the Qur'an and the Sunna, the first two sources, are silent.

As a result, there are points such as discrimination against women or non-Muslims, on which the Qur'an expresses a clear position that is therefore impossible to revise. This is where An-Na`im's fundamental premise comes into play. It consists of admitting, as a Muslim, "that Sharia was constructed by the early Muslim jurists out of the fundamental sources of Islam, namely the Qur'an and Sunna", so that "contemporary Muslims may become more willing to accept the possibility of substantial reform" if the fundamental sources are respected.[5]

Hence the first step is the question of the nature of respect due to these fundamental sources and in particular of the Qur'an, the revealed word of God that contains clear prescriptions to be observed by every devout Muslim. This is the locus of the reformist teaching of Taha on the reading of the Qur'an. The revelation of the word of God occurred in two stages: the first, prior to AD 622, in Mecca, and the second after the migration (Hijra) to Medina in 622, which would mark the beginning of the Islamic calendar. During the period in Mecca, Muhammad and his followers were a persecuted minority, hence their decision to leave the city. During the Medina period, they became, together with allied tribes, a strong community. For Taha and An-Na`im, the first message consisted of the ideal to be attained. In the second, the Medina suras, "an adjustment had to be made, and was successfully made, to provide for a specific political community in its concrete historical and geographical context".[6]

On certain points and in certain verses, however, the second message contradicts the first. According to a traditional technique in all legal systems, the interpretation of the doctors of the law consists in regarding the new verses as abrogating the older ones in case of contradiction. This is the so-called *naskh* technique, "the abrogation or repeal of certain texts".[7] "The evolutionary principle of interpretation (by Taha)

---

[5] *Idem*, p. 11.
[6] *Idem*, p. 12.
[7] *Idem*, p. 34 and 56.

is nothing more than reversing the process of *naskh* or abrogation so that those texts which were abrogated in the past can be enacted in the law now, with the consequent abrogation of texts that used to be enacted as Shari'a".[8] The chronological order, according to which the latter prevails over the former, is replaced by a logical and hierarchical order in which the former, more ideal, prevails over the latter. This technique may be applied to two examples of violation of human rights.

Discrimination

The Qur'an contains provisions regarding women and non-Muslims that are clearly contradictory. For example, the prohibition against a Muslim woman marrying a non-Muslim is a discrimination that combines two criteria: religion and sex. A simple interpretation would not make it possible to go against the letter of the Qur'anic text. Thus, it has lead Egypt to ratify the Convention on the Elimination of all Forms of Discrimination Against Women (1979) with a reservation of compatibility with *shari'a*, which allows a prohibition against or the annulment of a marriage such as that of the writer Abû Zayd, which was deemed to be apostate. According to Taha's principle of evolution, the discriminatory verses date from the second, Medina period. Discrimination against women was justified by the principle of protection by man, who is the guardian of woman on account of socio-economic realities. Discrimination against non-Muslims was justified by the need to affirm themselves as a community. Once this context disappeared, in the contemporary context, it is necessary to return to the first egalitarian message dating from the Mecca period.[9]

Slavery

Unanimously condemned today, slavery is forbidden by the principal texts on the protection of human rights. It has not, however, been completely eradicated. Practised in certain regions, it is sometimes even justified in those areas on the basis of Islamic law. It is true that even if Islam wanted to regulate and limit slavery, in line with the custom of the day, it allowed it for prisoners of war. Although the Qur'an advocates the emancipation of slaves, it nonetheless tolerates slavery (sura IX, verse 60; S II, v. 177). Even a modern interpretation would not make

---

[8] *Idem*, p. 35 and 57.
[9] *Idem*, p. 100, 158, 180.

it possible to forbid slavery entirely without going against the letter of the Qur'an. Taha's evolutionist approach allows for the conclusion that "though Shari'a implemented the transitional legislative intent to permit slavery, subject to certain limitations and safegards, modern Islamic law should now implement the fundamental Islamic legislative intent to prohibit slavery forever".[10]

This second example shows that argumentation based on the order of Qur'anic verses between Mecca and Medina is not always equally strong. Regarding slavery, it is not so much the order of the verses that is invoked as justification, but a return to "the fundamental Islamic legislative intent". It is even more true as to criminal law, in which the Qur'an, including its initial message, is clear on certain fundamental crimes, the condemnation and sanction of which elude any form of interpretation. These are known as the *hudud*: *sariqa* (theft), *haraba* (rebellion or highway robbery), *zina* (fornication), *qadhf* (unproven accusation of fornication), *sukkr* (intoxication), and *rida* (apostasy from Islam).[11] Rather than the evolutionary principle in the strict sense, it is, rather, its spirit that leads to a rejection of the application of the *hudud* on account of the uncertainties of *shar'ia* as it stands today in this area and of the risk of abuse.[12] As a result, An-Na`im proposes the development of specific legislation, including procedural guarantees that "must be supported by all segments of the population, including non Muslims and secularist Muslims, and not simply imposed by the Muslim majority".[13] But An-Na`im does recognise that "given current penological and sociological thinking, it may seem extremely unlikely that non Muslims and secularist Muslims would ever accept *hudu* and *qisas* punishment".[14]

Islam and the Secular State: A Step Forward?

The examples above show the limits of the reformist process that would make it possible to establish a Muslim State that is respectful of fundamental rights. This process would, indeed, be criticised both by the fundamentalists and by the advocates of secularity. An-Na`im is undoubtedly aware of this, since, in his second major work, he advocates

---
[10] *Idem*, p. 175.
[11] *Idem*, p. 108.
[12] *Idem*, p. 115.
[13] *Idem*, p. 135.
[14] *Idem*, p. 136.

a "Secular State".[15] This is an important step that distinguishes the two works, and in effect constitutes a clear division. In *Islam and the Secular State*, An-Na'im is more firmly in favour of a separation of religion and State. "This does not mean the exclusion of Islam from the formulation of public policy and legislation"[16] but, as in the influence of all religion or philosophy, "the rationale of all public policy and legislation must always be based on civic reason".[17] It is not a matter of a State imposing secularity on a French or Turkish model, but a neutral political institution that organises the debate within the public sphere (Habermas). This public debate, a permanent negotiation of the values of a society, is not easy, neither for society as a whole in search of the cement that binds it, nor for the various groups that make up that society, for they never obtain complete satisfaction regarding their place in this mosaic. Thus, "allowing Shari'a principles to play a positive role in public life without permitting them to be implemented through state institutions simply because it is the belief of some citizens is a delicate balance that each society must strive to maintain for itself over time. For example matters such as dress style will normally remain of free choice, so that women can never be forced to wear the veil nor be prevented from doing so if they wish to wear it. But style of dress can be an issue for public debate, including constitutional litigation, to balance competing claims when, for instance, it relates to safety concerns in the workplace".[18] To those Muslims who refuse a secular State in the name of respect for Islam, An-Na'im replies, on the contrary, that "in order to be a Muslim by conviction and free choice… I need a Secular State… one that is neutral regarding religious doctrine"[19], for a religion that is imposed and not chosen is nothing but hypocrisy.

If An-Na'im's first book, *Toward an Islamic Reformation*, was attractive to Muslim intellectuals in Islamic countries by providing the keys to an in-depth reform of Muslim States, the second work, proposing an encounter between *Islam and the Secular State*, in turn appealed to intellectuals of the western world keen to integrate a minority Islam harmoniously within their societies. However, even if they take rather different paths, both works make a major contribution through the debate they launch. And in so doing, they allow the western world, in

---

[15] A.A. An-Na'im, *Islam and the Secular State. Negotiating the Future of Shari'a*, Cambridge, Mass., Harvard University Press, 2008.
[16] *Islam and the Secular State, op. cit.*, p. 2.
[17] *Idem*, p. 29.
[18] *Idem*, p. 38-39.
[19] *Idem*, p. 1.

particular, to recognize the diversity and vitality of Islamic thought, which is too often regarded as monolithic. The essence of An-Na`im's writings constitute a form of thought and of relations based on respect. Respect for religious identity, as for any other identity, and respect for the neutrality of the State, together lead to a social organisation in which the autonomy of persons and the self-determination of peoples are core values. Far from a clash of civilisations, it is an encounter among civilisations that An-Na`im invites us to undertake. As a way of thinking based on dialogue, it is also a way of peace.

'European Islam or Islamic Europe': The Secular State for Negotiating Pluralism

Abdullahi Ahmed An-Na`im

Introduction

The first part of my title is a play of words on the title of John Bowen's book, *Can Islam be French? Pluralism and Pragmatism in a Secularist State*[1]. Since the book is not available at the time of this writing, I am not presuming in the least to pre-empt or evaluate Professor Bowen's argument and analysis. Rather, I wish to offer my own personal reflections on the underlying issues and questions, without attempting to respond to Bowen's analysis or to any of the chapters of the present volume, edited by Marie-Claire Foblets and Jean-Yves Carlier. In particular, I propose to reflect on the appropriate role of the state in the constant negotiation of religious identity, citizenship and pluralism.

My point of departure is that it might be instructive to turn the question around to ask, for instance: "Can France, Europe (or any other country or region of the world) be Islamic?" At a basic logical level, this sort of question assumes that there is an agreed or at least identifiable meaning of both sides of the issue, that is, the country or region, on the one hand, and what is Islamic on the other. It is also logically necessary for that meaning of the two sides of the issue to remain at least temporarily stable for the comparison to be applied. That is, we need to have a commonly agreed or accepted understanding of each of the entities we are correlating and the manner of their relationship. This line of inquiry might focus, for instance, on the nature or integrity of the meaning of the two entities being compared, like the quality of being Islamic and the quality of being French or Brazilian, European or Southeast Asian.

Questions that follow from that premise include whether there is a fixed or stable meaning of France, Europe, or other country or region, and of Islam? How are such meanings determined, and by whom? What other actors and factors contribute to those determinations at any point in time? The answer to the initial question, for instance, about Islam

---

[1] J. Bowen, *Can Islam be French? Pluralism and Pragmatism in a Secularist State,* Princeton, NJ, Princeton University Press.

and France or Europe, depends on the answer one accepts for a range of other questions. For example, how can the extreme historical and contemporary diversity of understanding and practice of Islam ever be reduced to a single monolithic definition of what is 'Islamic' in Denmark or the Netherlands. The framing of the question in terms of, for instance, Islam *in* Europe, Islam *of* Europe, or European Islam, has different connotations, and tends to call for different ways of thinking about the issues. In any case, can the question be about Islam, or does it always have to be about particular communities of Muslims, whereby the inquiry would need to be framed in terms of specific location and time-frame?

At another level of analysis, one may question the question itself: why and how can one compare or contrast believing in a world religion to having a national or regional identity? Assuming that the comparison can be made, is it conceivable to ask "can Catholicism be French?" Conversely, is it likely that this question will be raised in relation to Christianity and a Muslim-majority country or region, for instance, "can Catholicism be Indonesian?" Indeed, why does Catholicism or Islam need to be French or Indonesian for a person to identity as both a believer in the religion and a citizen of the country?

I am raising these questions in the hope of clarifying and opening up the issues for different ways of thinking about religious identity and pluralism. When raised in specific European countries or Western Europe in general, I am concerned that these sorts of questions are not really about Islam as a world religion at all. I wonder whether the real issue in the European context is about the capacity and ability of members of certain visible minorities of immigrant origin who happen to be Muslims are now, or can become, accepted as European by those who appropriate the right to define what being European means. My worry is that such inquiries can easily be manipulated to advance exclusionary, sometimes racist, agenda against a racially and religiously pluralistic Europe. Moreover, while such agenda may be advanced by a small and marginal minority of European public opinion, that may create a 'self-fulfilling prophecy'. The exclusionary prophecy can materialize when Muslim Europeans internalize a feeling of exclusion and behave accordingly, thereby re-enforcing popular perceptions of their being permanent, almost genetically, alien who are incapable of ever becoming European.

Despite these concerns about Europe today, it is also clear to me that all human societies are struggling with issues of identity, inclusion and exclusion, religious and racial pluralism, and that is likely to continue into the foreseeable future. I also believe that such debates and contestations are shaped by the particular history, political context, demographic profile, socio-economic conditions and related factors in each society and location. The question is therefore not whether or not struggles over identity, pluralism and so forth should happen anywhere, but how to regulate and facilitate such debates and contestations in order to promote positive outcomes. Moreover, since it is unavoidable for the state to be involved in struggles over identity and pluralism, the question is which sort of state is likely to play a positive role in the process. As I see it, the question is what sort of structures, institutions and process are likely to promote positive outcomes, or at least minimize negative consequences, of continuing negotiations of religious identity and pluralism in various settings. Accordingly, one premise of this brief discussion is that all human societies are struggling with issues of identity, inclusion and exclusion, and pluralism, although the terms and dynamics of this constant process would of course vary with a variety of factors such as history, political context, demographic and socio-economic inter-communal relations.

Another premise is the distinction between the fact of difference and value of pluralism. That is, the need to distinguish between the demographic facts of religious and other forms of diversity or difference, on the one hand, and a normative commitment to pluralism, on the other. As I see it, pluralism refers to the value system, attitudes, institutions and processes that can translate realities of diversity and difference into sustainable social cohesion, political stability and economic development. In other words, diversity is the factual or empirical reality of difference, and pluralism is the ideology or orientation of accepting social, religious or cultural difference as a positive value, and facilitates constant negotiations and adjustments among varieties of difference, without seeking or expecting to eliminate any of them permanently. Religious or racial/ethnic difference is a permanent feature of all large societies, and pluralism is the orientation or normative system of genuine acceptance of this empirical fact in organizing relationships among different religious and belief communities, instead of seeking to fuse them all into one so-called homogenous whole by coercively assimilating minorities into a hegemonic majority.

A third premise of my thinking here is that it is only human beings who can uphold the ideology of pluralism and engage in negotiations and adjustments among different communities, because it is only people who can shape and work with their own differences in order to realize genuine and sustainable pluralism. By the same token, people may fail to accept and negotiate their differences, fail to realize pluralism, but failures or setbacks cannot be final. Since people have to co-exist and find ways of working together, sharing power and resources, all segments will need to continue to negotiate with each other over their differences and conflicts. While painfully aware from my own personal experience that sustainable progression from diversity to pluralism is difficult, often contingent and contested, I am unable to see a better alternative. One way of facilitating this process and improving its chances of sustainable success is to work on creating conducive conditions for the process of negotiating identity and promoting pluralism. It is from this perspective that I will now briefly consider the role of the state.

The Need for a Secular State

In my view, the state must be secular in order to play its critically important role in enabling and facilitating the negotiation of religious identity and promoting religious pluralism. By secular state I mean one that is neutral regarding all religious doctrine. There are many other relevant aspects of the state and politics that are necessary for good constitutional governance, achieving social justice and protection of human rights that are not possible to discuss here. My focus in these brief remarks is on the secular state in the hope of contributing to clarifying its relevance to issues of religious identity and pluralism in Europe in particular. One initial caveat to begin with is that I mean a secular state, and not secularism, secularization and related concepts and terms. Another caveat is that I mean a state that is neutral regarding religion in particular, and not neutral about all issues or matters of public policy. I will briefly elaborate on this proposition and then illustrate its application to mediate and negotiate issues of religious identity and pluralism.

First, let me begin this elaboration with a caution about the risks of misunderstanding or confusion over the use of terms and their implications. Terms and concepts have their own genealogies, histories and associations which are often personal and contextual for each of us. So when I hear a term, I tend to assume that it is being used in the exact meaning that is familiar to me. If I have certain associations with the term, whether positive or negative, I also tend to assume that it is being used with those or similar association. Such preconceived notions and associations of terms and concepts are sometimes powerful enough to override explicit definitions and qualifications a speaker or author is making. I am noting this caution about language here in relation to my use of the term the secular state, as explained below.

A related caution about language is that "naming something does not make it so". I find that we often tend to assume that things are somehow what they are called. In reality of course, calling a state Islamic, for instance, does not mean that it is truly so. Part of my call for a the secular state is the claim that the state cannot be religious, though it may not be secular enough. When I make this point, I often get the response: how about Iran and Saudi Arabia?! Since my argument against the possibility of a religious state is conceptual as well as empirical, regardless of claims to the contrary, neither Iran nor Saudi Arabia today is an Islamic state. Whenever the claim of a religious state is made, it simply means that it is a state controlled by rulers who impose their view of Islam or other religion on the population.[2]

The caution about language and naming also applies to states we assume to be or call secular, in the sense of neutrality regarding all religions, which is the issue in relation to Europe today. As a brief survey of west European states will show, the meaning and implications of being a secular state are deeply historical and contextual, often contested and contingent at any point in time or regarding some issues. For instance, though the close relationship between the Church of England and the state has apparently diminished over time, it still remains intact.[3] Similarly, the history of the adoption of a state religion in Sweden dates back to the sixteenth century, with the mounting drive to unify the country around the Lutheran faith, which was achieved through effective clerical leadership and popular support for the Protestant church. In 1593, the Evangelical Lutheran Church was established as the National Church of Sweden with the declaration that Sweden had become united, with one Lord and one God. As the official church, the Church of Sweden had until the end of the twentieth century been intimately connected to the life of the state and vice versa. While this relationship gave the Lutheran Church enormous influence in Sweden, it also meant that the Church lacked autonomy. The legal separation of the Swedish Church from the state was finally accomplished by 2000 through the Church of

---

[2] I have made this argument in detail in *Islam and The Secular State: Negotiating the Future of Sharia*, Cambridge, MA, Harvard University Press, 2008.

[3] S.V. Monsma and J.C. Soper, "England: Partial Establishment," in *The Challenge of Pluralism: Church and State in Five Democracies* (2nd ed.), Lanham, MD, Rowman & Littlefield Publishers, 2009), 131; D. McClean, "State and Church in the United Kingdom," in G. Robbers (ed.), *State and Church in the European Union*, Baden-Baden, Nomos Verlagsgesellschaft, 1996, 307-322.

Sweden Act.[4] It is interesting to note that England and Sweden followed similar patterns of increasing recognition of religious pluralism through different means. England has sought to moderate the role of the state church while retaining that status for it, in contrast to Sweden which has gone much further in the legal separation of church and state. But the two countries are equally regarded now as secular in the sense of the religious neutrality in substance.

Italy and Spain are another two west European states that also confirm the deeply historical and contextual nature of the secular state. In Italy, the Agreement of 1929 established Roman Catholicism as the sole state religion, a position which was in principle contradicted but not overturned by the terms of the 1948 Constitution, which includes the principles of a secular state, equality of citizens before the law, and freedom of religion and belief.[5] The constitution provided for the free equality of all denominations before the law, yet Article Seven of the constitution makes a special provision for the Catholic Church, whereby the "State and the Catholic Church are, each according to its own order, independent and sovereign. Their relations are ruled by the Lateran Treaties. Amendments to these treaties which are agreed by both sides do not have to follow the procedure prescribed for constitutional amendments."[6]

The Italian system of agreements between the state and various religious denominations has created a three-level system. The top legal position is held by the Catholic Church which is treated like a sovereign state under Italian public law. Other religious communities that have come to an agreement with the state, such as Jewish and certain Protestant denominations, occupy a secondary position. Since these communities have an agreement with the Italian state, they are no longer governed by the 1929 law. Their respective agreement with the state provides for certain privileges regarding such matters as financing, religious education and pastoral care, which are not available to religious communities in the third level. Religious communities in this third and lowest level are those with a shorter history of established communities and institutions, like Muslims and Jehovah's Witnesses. At this lowest

---

[4] R. Schött, "State and Church in Sweden", in *State and Church in the European Union*, 295-306 and L. Friedner, "Church and State in Sweden in 2000," *European Journal of Church State Research* 2001, 255-259.

[5] M. Giovannelli, "The 1984 Covenant between the Republic of Italy and the Vatican: A Retrospective Analysis after Fifteen Years," *Journal of Church and State* 2000, 539-538.

[6] S. Ferrari, "State and Church in Italy," in *State and Church in the European Union*, 171-190, at p. 172.

level, religious communities are regulated by the Law Number 1159 of 1929 and the general law of associations, which means that they are denied some important privileges enjoyed by communities in the two higher levels. Because of this three-level system, there are no provisions under Italian law which are common to all religious communities for issues such as the position of clergy, financing of religious institutions, pastoral care, religious education and marriage law. Moreover, Italian ecclesiastical law allows public authorities great discretion to accept or reject any denominational proposal to enter negotiations to conclude an agreement with the state; there are almost no objective criteria for these decisions.

Spain's relation to the Catholic Church has been governed primarily through treaties or a series of agreements. Following the Reformation and Counter-Reformation, a certain type of fusion between political and religious powers occurred in Spain. Unlike in Protestant European countries, the absolute monarch did not claim religious powers for himself, since that authority rested with the external power of the Pope. Instead, the monarch developed and employed a set of techniques of intervention to exercise influence on the affairs of the Catholic Church in the country. The intimate connection between Church and monarch, and the assumption of the Catholic nature of the country lasted until the brief reign of the 1931 Constitution of the Second Republic which proclaimed that Spain had no official religion. After the Civil War (1936-1939), the church-state fusion was restored under Franco, culminating with the Agreement of 1953. The relative privileges accorded to the Catholic Church are particularly evident in relation to funding and taxation. The Catholic Church is the only denomination to receive direct funding from the state. Like the situation in Italy, while the system by which the Catholic Church receives this money is similar to a church tax system, it is in fact a part of the state tax system. Tax exemptions are only available to the Catholic Church and to those denominations which have treaties with the state. Salaries for Catholic religious education teachers, clergy working in the military and prisons, and financial assistance to Catholic medical and charitable institutions continue to be paid by the state. All these benefits are not available to other religious communities.[7]

As these and other European cases confirm, the secular state is always inherently contextual and historical, and every society has its

---

[7] I.C. Ibán, "State and Church in Spain," in *State and Church in the European Union*, 94.

own experience unique to itself. This conclusion also emerges when we review the relevant experiences of other countries, like Germany,[8] or the Netherlands.[9] Western conceptions and experiences with the secular state are neither identical nor exclusive of religion in the public domain of policy and legislation. The historical contextual development of the secular state as well as persistent controversy about its meaning and implication in practice continue to the present day in all countries of the region. However, this does not imply that there are no unifying principles among these various experiences, or that the meaning and implications of this concept are totally relative to each society. It is indeed possible and necessary to develop a sufficiently specific understanding of the secular state as a product of comparative human experience, provided we do not impose a specific definition or insist on its implications from an abstract theoretical perspective.

I am calling for the institutional separation of religion and the state while recognizing and regulating the unavoidable connectedness of religion and politics. This does not mean that religion and politics should be separated because believers will always seek to advance their religious values to influence public policy and legislation through the democratic process, just as non-believers may seek to advance their philosophical or ideological views. The tension between the need to separate religion from the state despite the connectedness of religion and the state can be mediated through the distinction between the state and politics. The state should be the more settled and deliberate operational side of self-governance, while politics is the dynamic process of making choices among competing policy options. The state and politics may be seen as two sides of the same coin, but they cannot and should not be completely fused into each other. It is necessary to ensure that the state is not simply a complete reflection of daily politics because it must be able to mediate and adjudicate among competing views of policy, which require it to remain relatively independent from different political forces in society. Still, complete independence of state and politics is not possible because those who control the state come to power and keep it through politics, whether in a democratic process or not. In other words, officials of the state will always act politically in implementing their own agenda and maintaining the allegiance of those who support them. This reality of connectedness makes it necessary

---

[8] R. Puza, "The Development of the Relationship between the Church and State in Germany in 2001," *European Journal for Church and State Research* 2002, 9-13.
[9] S. Van Bijsterveld, "State and Church in the Netherlands," in *State and Church in the European Union*, 209-228.

to strive for separating the state from politics, so that those excluded by the political processes of the day can still resort to state organs and institutions for protection against the excesses and abuse of power by state officials.

This paradoxical relationship can be understood with reference to the way in which the state is rooted in the political life of society yet also preserves its autonomy from the latter. The modern state is a centralized, bureaucratic and hierarchical organization which is composed of institutions, organs and offices that are supposed to perform highly specialized and differentiated functions through predetermined rules of general application.[10] Moreover, the state should be distinct from other kinds of social associations and organizations in theory, while remaining deeply connected to them in practice for its own legitimacy and effective operation. For instance, the state must seek out and work with various constituencies and organizations in performing its functions, such as maintaining law and order, providing educational, health and transport services. Therefore, state officials and institutions cannot avoid working relationships with various constituencies and groups who have competing views of public policy and its outcomes in the daily life of societies. These constituencies include non-governmental organizations, businesses, political parties and pressure groups, and any of them can be religious or not in different ways. These working relationships are not only necessary for the ability of the state to fulfill its obligations, but in fact required by the principle of self-determination. The autonomy and distinctive nature of the state are means to the end of enabling all citizens to participate in their own government, and not an end in itself.

The state incorporates the participation of such non-state actors through formal mechanisms of negotiation and representation as well as informal means of communication and mutual influence.[11] These dynamic interactions between state and non-state actors raise risks of conflict and competition among all sides, and can also compromise the autonomy of state actors as each non-state actor seeks to maximize its influence on state policy and administration. These realistic risks should be moderated and checked through the development of stronger state institutions that can keep their relative autonomy in dealing with diverse groups with their competing demands. The question is therefore how can state-actors remain responsive to the wishes of civil

---

[10] G. Gill. *The Nature and Development of the Modern State*, New York, Palgrave Macmillan, 2003, 2-4.
[11] Gill, *The Nature and Development of the Modern State*, 17.

Contextual Mediation of Tensions

Since every society needs to negotiate the relationship between religion and the state in its own specific context, it is not possible, or desirable in my view, to predict policy outcomes according to a preconceived view of that relationship. Instead, we should try to identify relevant factors and actors, and how to regulate their interaction to improve the prospects for genuine and sustainable neutrality of the state. "Neutrality by the state should not be seen in an abstract way, but in a continuous dialogue with individual identity and individual religious freedoms."[12] In the United States, for example, political debates and legal contestations around the role of religion in public policy takes place against a wider political and cultural debate over the meaning of 'traditional' or 'family' values, religious freedom, personal autonomy and freedom of choice. Thus, whether women have a choice about having an abortion is asserted by some as a matter of personal autonomy and objected to by others who believe that the state should protect the life of the unborn foetus. Both sides may claim religious justifications for their position, whether declared or not. The state has to adjudicate by upholding one view or the other in official policy and legislation, but whatever option is adopted, that will probably be contested by those on the other side on the issue.

The basic tension in such negotiations is about the degree and form of autonomy of religious authority from the political and legal authority of the state. On the one hand, the territorial state seeks to control religious institutions in order to fulfil its obligations to keep the peace, maintain political stability, and achieve social and economic development. This is to be expected because the state needs to exercise the necessary degree of control over its territory and population in order to mediate and adjudicate among competing interests and claims. Paradoxically, however, the state cannot maintain its religious neutrality without exercising control over religious activities among its citizens. On the other hand, religious institutions need to maintain their autonomy against the coercive powers of the state in the interest of the legitimacy

---

[12] R. Torfs, "New Liberties and Church-State Relationships: Synthesis," in *'New Liberties' and Church and State Relationships in Europe*, European Consortium for Church-State Research, Milan, Giuffrè Editore, 1998, 10.

of religious doctrine and practice. These matters must be determined in accordance with the internal frame of reference and independent authority of religious institutions, without interference by state officials who will tend to impose their own views.

In practically every society, religious groups are an important policy constituency on fundamental matters of social life, from education to taxation, from issues of public and private morality to charitable social functions. The negotiations between church and state with regard to these issues in each society can be viewed as arrangements whereby religious groups are acknowledged as an important political constituency, which is neither taken over by the state nor allowed to take over the state itself or any of its institutions. The principle of separation of state and religion helps achieve this delicate balance by providing a framework for securing the legitimacy of the state among religious communities while regulating how their concerns are reflected in public policy with due regard to the concerns and interests of all communities and citizens at large. Since citizens who are not religious or do not organize to lobby the state as religious communities are entitled to equal respect for their views and interests, the state and its organs must not fall under the control of one religious community however large its numbers may be. In fact, the neutrality of the state regarding all religious and non-religious perspectives is more important in relation to dominant groups because the risks of state bias in their favor is greater than in the case of minorities. It should also be noted that perception in such matters can be as important as reality because the appearance of bias tends to undermine public confidence in the neutrality of the state even if that is not true in fact. The secular state should seek to ensure that state institutions are neither partial nor perceived to be partial to any one religious or non-religious perspective, while giving due regard to all relevant and legitimate perspectives in the formulation and implementation of public policy.

This balance is achieved through direct as well as indirect negotiations. On the one hand, more or less *direct* negotiations and agreements between state and the dominant religious tradition (and to a lesser extent, other religious traditions), reflect historical precedent, the importance of a particular religious tradition as part of cultural heritage, or the socially beneficial role of religious institutions. It is true that the state may not be entirely impartial in the degree of support it extends to different religions and state policies may contradict the imperative of neutrality towards religion. But in such direct negotiation, the general principle of separation between religion and state is largely reaffirmed while the value and role of a dominant religion in public life is also acknowledged. For instance, while maintaining the formal status of the Anglican Church as the official church, state policies in England are broadly supportive of organized religion in general, and not one specific creed.[13]

The secular state should operate within the framework of constitutionalism and human rights safeguards in order to enables *indirect* negotiations whereby religious as well as non-religious actors can play a role in shaping public policy. This possibility is ensured by the state protection of freedoms of association and expression, the right to organize and protest, right to legal redress, and the use of instruments of commerce, media, and communication, which enable citizens to present their point of view and mobilize resources and public support for their perspective. The freedoms and rights that organize and regulate these processes of indirect or mediated influence on state policy are themselves enshrined as secular principles and protected within secular legal and political frameworks. The political culture of the United States represents a good example of indirect negotiation between religion and state, in the context of crucial policy matters.

While the separation of church and state is a well-established political and social value in American public political culture, conservative as well as liberal Christian groups have undertaken campaigns and moved the courts on issues such as support of prayer in the schools. Liberal churches have lobbied on such issues of race relations, poverty, and on ending the Vietnam War. Both factions as well as other religious and non-religious actors are strongly engaged in debates about judicial appointments, especially at the higher and Supreme Court levels, in order to ensure the strongest possible representation of their perspectives in the application and development of the secular law of the state. The same process and dynamics can be observed in other Western countries, from protests over educational reform in Spain in 1983 reflecting apprehensions on the part of the populace about the Catholic identity of the church schools, to the June 2006 referendum in Italy about specific changes in the country's civil code that were opposed by the Catholic Church as an active powerful political force. In all these cases, the fundamental principle of separation of religion and state was not directly challenged by religious actors who simply exercised their right to attempt to influence state policy while respecting the right of other groups, religious and non-religious alike, to do the same.

---

[13] Monsma and Soper, "England: Partial Establishment", 141-45.

In these direct and indirect negotiations between state and religious actors, all sides clearly accept in practice the distinction between *religion-state* versus *religion-politics*. But as the idea of negotiation itself clearly indicates, there are tensions in these interactions and relations between state and religious actors, as well as the assumptions or implications of their respective positions. The realities of such tensions and the need for maintaining autonomy of both state and religion emphasize the importance of a framework that enables all social actors, whether individuals or groups, to address the state for policy objectives, without compromising the separation of state and religion. This framework must enable the widest range of social actors to compete with each other on a free and fair footing in presenting their views on policy issues. While there are many requirements and aspects of these processes, I will now highlight what I call the 'civic reason' dimension of this process, in which the critical criterion and frame of reference of civic engagement in public policy deliberations is citizenship.[14]

Process of Civic Reason and Reasoning

In my view, civic reason and reasoning, as I will explain below, are the essential framework and medium for mediating the tension of religious identity and pluralism, including the need to separate state and religion, while regulating the interconnectedness of religion and politics. The basic idea of civic reason consists of two elements: First, the rationale and purpose of public policy or legislation must be based on the sort of reasoning that the generality of citizens can accept or reject, and make counter-proposals through public debate. Second, such reasons must be publicly and openly debated, rather than being assumed to follow from personal beliefs and motivation of citizens or officials. It is not possible of course to control inner motivation and intentions of the political behavior of people, but the objective should be to promote and encourage civic reasons and reasoning, while diminishing the exclusive influence of personal religious beliefs, over time. The requirements of civic reasons that are publicly debated are critically important because it cannot be taken for granted that the people who control the state will be neutral. On the contrary, this requirement must be the objective of the operation of the state precisely *because* people are likely to continue

---

[14] On my concept of 'civic reason' and how it relates to 'public reason' according to John Rawls, see my book, *Islam and the Secular State*, 92-101.

to act on personal beliefs or justifications. These requirements are also desirable because they encourage and facilitate the development of broader consensus among the population at large, beyond the narrow religious or other beliefs of various individuals and groups.

I would also emphasize that the operation of civic reason in the negotiation of the relationship of religion and the state should be safeguarded by principles of constitutionalism, human rights and citizenship. The consistent and institutional application of these principles ensures the ability of all citizens to equally and freely participate in the political process, protect them against discrimination on such grounds as religion or belief, and so forth. With the protection provided by such safeguards, citizens will be more likely to contribute to the formulation of public policy and legislation, including objection to proposals made by others, in accordance with the requirements of civic reason. Religious believers, including Muslims, can make proposals emerging from their religious beliefs, provided they are also presented to others on the basis of reasons they can accept or reject.

These theoretical reflections on how civic reason might operate do not mean that the concept is always clear or that it can easily be applied in practice. Theoretical clarity and commitment to the principle are necessary for correcting any problems with its practical operation. The access of citizens to civic reason debates will vary according to the differences in their socioeconomic status, political experience or ability to maximize use of resources and build alliances, and so forth. But such factors are reasons for more fair and inclusive application of the principle, rather than for abandoning it. Marginalized actors can resort to a range of strategies to secure a greater degree of influence over the policy-making process. For example, groups which possess large resources or political influence may adopt moderate positions or be open to compromise in order to have access to civic reason at all. Alternatively, such groups may seek the assistance of the courts or other institutions of the state to ensure access on constitutional or human rights principles that supplement their lack of resources or influence. With regard to abortion policy in the United States, for instance, proponents of the right of women to decide to have an abortion eventually prevailed through the Supreme Court decision in *Roe v. Wade* in 1973. But that did not mean that the opponents of that claim simply conceded and abandoned their position. Instead, these groups adopted different strategies, including seeking to shift policy-making on this issue to the level of state, rather than federal, government because they hope to have more influence at that level. Such exchanges of strategies and counter-strategies will probably continue into the future as long as some people feel strongly about the issues, one way or the other. Contestation in the sphere of civic reason can itself be seen as an indication of social diversity and other forms of difference in any society. Such contestation may also reflect increased access for more individuals and groups to civic reason through processes of democratization, developments in communication, and the like. As access to civic reason becomes more widely available and fair in any society, public policy choices are likely to be more contested and negotiated rather than being imposed by the majority or ruling elites. The wider consensus that can be achieved around public policy choices through this process is likely to promote the legitimacy of the state among its population and thereby enhance political stability in the country. With greater appreciation for the value and credibility of the civic reason process itself, religious believers will have more opportunity for promoting their religious beliefs through the regular political process without threatening those citizens who do not share their religious beliefs. This balance is likely to be achieved precisely because religious views will not be directly enforced through the coercive power of the state without being mediated through fair and transparent political contestations and subject to constitutional and human rights safeguards as noted earlier. In the final analysis, religious beliefs are neither granted special privilege nor suppressed, which make the relationship between religion and the state more dynamic and its outcomes less predictable.

The secular state as the separation of religion and state is a necessary but insufficient condition for the participation in the sphere of civic reason. But the relationship between the secular state and religion can also have a deeper significance, especially in the domain of civic reason. Religion may provide an important framework for many social actors to present their respective claims, as long as these are formulated in the mode of publicly accessible reason. This relationship can also be viewed as mutually sustaining along the following lines. The secular state needs religion to provide a widely accepted source of moral guidance for the political community, as well as to help satisfy and discipline the non-political needs of believers within that community. In turn, religion needs the secular state to mediate relations between different communities (whether religious or antireligious or nonreligious) that share the same political space or space of civic reason.

The secular state as separation of religion and state is characterized by one limitation; it must confine its normative content to a minimum if it is to achieve its purposes - safeguarding political pluralism in heterogeneous societies and ensuring a space of civic reason where such pluralism can flourish. In other words, the secular state is able to unite diverse communities of belief and practice into one political community precisely and only because the moral claims it makes are minimal. It is true that all varieties of the secular states prescribe a civic ethos on the basis of some specific understanding of the individual's relation to the community. Such an ethos may indeed be sufficiently complex and deeply entrenched as to address some major moral issues facing the society in question. But the ability of the secular state to achieve the necessary degree of consensus that enables and sustains political stability in religiously diverse societies means that it cannot tackle fundamental ethical and moral questions on which there is serious disagreement among different communities.

A related concern is that the secular state is unable to address the objections or reservations that religious believers may have about specific principles of secular governance. A purely secular discourse can be respectful of religion in general, but its ability to rebut religious justifications of certain policies is unlikely to convince believers. An assertion of equal citizenship for non-Muslims is unlikely to persuade Muslims without an Islamic justification of that principle. In other words, the minimal normative content that makes the secular state conducive to inter-religious coexistence, pluralism, and supportive of a space of civic reason diminishes its capacity to legitimize itself as a universal principle without reference to some other moral source.

The Contingent Role of Religion in Influencing Public Policy

Religion (whether taken to indicate organized groups, communities of faith and practice, or the domain of personal views and beliefs) is an important force that competes in the sphere of civic reason to influence policy. In social and cultural developments and changes in Western countries nations in the last few decades, personal concerns regarding quality of life issues, education policy, abortion and other aspects of family policy, religious freedom, and immigration and naturalization policies, have all gained importance as matters of public policy.[15] In other words, civic reason as rationale and process is increasingly

---

[15] M. Minkenberg, "The Policy Impact of Church–State Relations: Family Policy and Abortion in Britain, France and Germany," *West European Politics* 2003, 205.

diminishing the dichotomy between the public and private realms of social existence, thereby making it more difficult to separate religion and politics. But the role of religion in the contested space of civic reason should not be viewed as predetermined or given because such policy outcomes are contingent on various factors.

The ability of religious actors to influence public policy is shaped by historical relations of religion to the state, and current conditions like urbanization, demographic changes, level of religiosity in the society and relations among religious communities. Moreover, since such factors themselves tend to shift and change over time, the impact and outcome of religion on public policy tends to adjust to such changes. For example, in the second half of the twentieth century, the French Catholic Church did not intervene against moderately innovative reform in family policy even though it takes a more traditional view on social values and gender roles than the populace at large among which the level of religiosity is very low. The country's strong cultural emphasis on *laicite* tended to constrain the ability of the Church to maneuver as an interest group. The involvement of the Church in family-related matters was also limited in Germany and England due to a combination of partial establishment of state religion and a moderate level of religiosity among the population. Consequently, the Church tended to act as an institution rather than an interest group in family-related matters. Paradoxically, where the Church is not established as a state religion at all, religious actors may have more room to maneuver in politics, which may enhance its ability to influence public policy, as can be seen in the case of the United States.[16] Recent events in the United States also indicate the role of the ideological orientation of the government of the day in shifting or even transforming the terms and dynamics of the role of religion in civic reason.

For example, the policies of the administration of President George W. Bush in the United States regarding faith-based initiatives may be viewed as a reconfiguration of the space of civic reason, allowing religion, or more precisely specific religious groups, a greater influence in public life through increased funding opportunities from the state. Shortly after taking office for his first term, President Bush issued several executive orders to establish a White House Office of Faith-Based and Community Initiatives in addition to removing obstacles to faith-based funding. But these initiatives have raised serious concerns among Native American communities who have questioned whether

---

[16] Minkenberg, "The Policy Impact of Church-State Relations," 209-210.

they would qualify for, or be able to significantly benefit from, the new policies.[17] This clearly indicates that the category of 'religion' itself was defined in limited terms in these faith-based initiatives, reflecting the President's own understanding of religion and his personal beliefs. The list of religions drawn up by the administration was restricted to monotheistic religions that are most familiar to the dominant secular culture and to Christians. Certain groups, like the Nation of Islam, were also excluded.[18] While such factors tend to define the domain of civic reason and participation of some groups in it, the process would correct itself if applied within the appropriate safeguards noted earlier.

While religion has the potential to operate as a hegemonic discourse in civic reason, non-religious forces or ideologies can also play a similar role. The separation between religion and state is compromised when the dictates of a particular religion, as interpreted by religious authorities or ruling elite, are made a prerequisite condition of participation in civic reason. But this can also happen from a nationalist or so-called secular perspective. This is seen, for example, in the controversy over recent French legislation that prohibits Muslim girls from wearing a headscarf in schools. The decision to ban the use of the Islamic headscarf in the name of French secularism reflects the higher priority given to the assimilation of immigrants into French cultural citizenship as a policy goal over possibilities of ethnic or cultural identity within a national framework of multiculturalism that prevails in North European countries and Canada. The French republican conception of secularism that was invoked here functioned as an instrument of enforcing cultural uniformity among French citizens, especially among immigrant populations.

The debate over the headscarf and French secularism must also be located in a wider context of post-colonial relations, including the ambivalent relationship of France to its former colonies, as well as in the context of stereotypical perceptions and anxieties about Islam and Muslims.[19] Often the victims of racism and discrimination, Muslims are uniformly perceived and treated as outsiders to French society, although significant numbers of them have French citizenship.[20] This raises

---

[17] M.C. Churchill, "In Bad Faith? Possibilities and Perils in the Age of Faith-Based Initiatives," *Journal of the American Academy of Religion* 2002, 844, 845.

[18] R.N. Brock, "The Fiction of Church and State Separation: A Proposal for Greater Freedom of Religion", *Journal of the American Academy of Religion* December 2002, 856.

[19] J. Freedman, "Secularism as a Barrier to Integration? The French Dilemma," *International Migration*, 2004, 6.

[20] Freedman, "Secularism as a Barrier to Integration", 8.

important questions about the extent to which Muslims in France have representation in, and access, to civic reason through French state and non-state institutions. The French case also illustrates how secularism can be invoked as a hegemonic idea of national culture to the exclusion of other identities, thereby violating the requirements of civic reason indicated earlier. The exclusion of persons and groups from the scope of civic reason is always objectionable, whether done in the name of nationalism, secular ideology or religion. In other words, the French case therefore illustrates how the principles of secularism itself can be violated in the name of protecting it. This conclusion can of course be disputed, but competing views on the issue cannot be fairly evaluated without safeguarding the requirements of civic reason for all points of view in the first place.

The secular state precludes any specific understanding of religious doctrine from being directly enforced as state policy, but that is not sufficient for addressing the need of religious believers to express the moral implications of their faith in the public domain. That is why I have emphasized that the secular state as separation of religion and the state is necessary but insufficient without acknowledging and regulating the political role of religion. Both elements of this broader definition of the secular state can be enhanced by insisting on a contextual understanding of the rationale and functioning of secular government in each location. And it is here that religion can play a vitally important role. The condition of the secular state is likely to be seen as merely expedient and temporary by religious adherents unless they are also able to find the secular state to be at least consistent with, if not mandated by, their religious doctrine.

This requirement is not difficult to achieve because the dichotomy of demanding a choice between religion and the secular state has already failed because the "concept of the secular cannot do without the idea of religion."[21] Politics and religion do not operate in distinct realms; the one continually informs and is informed by the other. The concept of the secular lacks independent motivating power for believers and lives off that of the religions it checks and balances. As Harold Berman said, "people will not give their allegiance to a political and economic system, and even less to a philosophy, unless it represents for them a higher, sacred truth. People will desert institutions that do not seem to them to correspond to some transcendent reality in which

---

[21] T. Asad, "Religion, Nation-State, Secularism," in P. van der Veer and H. Lehmann (ed.), *Nation and Religion*, Princeton, NJ, Princeton University Press, 1999, 192.

they believe - believe in with their whole beings, and not just believe about with their minds."[22] In the final analysis, the secular state cannot motivate believers to uphold its own principles without engaging religion, but religion also needs the secular state to secure the space for free and valid religious belief and practice. As I have attempted to explain elsewhere, the relationship between religion and the secular state should therefore be one of synergy and mutual support, instead of hostility and confrontation.[23]

Concluding Remarks

Recalling my opening remarks about Islam and Muslims in Europe today, the main conclusion of my analysis in this paper is that it would be much more productive and helpful if European policy makers, scholars, media and public opinion deal with Islam as a European religion, like any other religion. It would also be most conducive to positive negotiations of religious pluralism and identity in Europe if all concerned take various communities of citizens (or immigrants) who happen to be Muslims on their own terms as a community of human beings, not of 'Muslims'. As a Muslim myself, I know that Islam is important to Muslims in general, but people who are Muslims are influenced by all sorts of motivations, aspirations and needs, like all other human beings. However important to a person his or her Islamic identity might be, it cannot exhaust who that person is, or in any way diminish or change her or his humanity. In short, I am calling on European scholars, policy makers, media and public opinion to reflect on what appears to be an irrational fixation and obsession with Islam and Muslims, and think of just people who happen to be religious believers, just like being Christian or Jewish. Once that happens, I believe, most of the issues and concerns that appear to be major obstacles for social cohesion, political stability, and other concerns will all become as amenable to political, social and legal mediation and negotiation as any other issue of public policy for the population at large.

Shared concerns facing all human societies which must necessarily struggle with the relationship between religion and the state include the question of the constitutional and legal status of religion. As current

---

[22] H. Berman, *The Interaction of Law and Religion*, Nashville, TN, Abingdon, 1974, 73.
[23] A.A. An-Na`im, "The Interdependence of Religion, Secularism, and Human Rights," *Common Knowledge*, Winter 2005, 56-80.

experience of European and other countries show, the secular state allows for a variety of options for the constitutional status of religion. One possibility is that religious leaders participate in state institutions and legislative bodies and attempt to promote their religious values as any other democratically elected representative. Another possibility suggested by the European experience is the system of special bilateral agreements between the state and religious entities, as is the case in Spain and Italy today. This view can be a third alternative between theocracy and strict state neutrality that permits flexibility in reconciling competing claims and reassuring minority religions.

Other examples of the relevance of the secular state to the mediation and negotiation of issues of public policy and practice, like issues of religious education, can offer helpful models for dealing with similar issues in relation to European Muslims. For instance, both the similarities and differences between the Catholic and Islamic traditions, and within and across Western and Islamic societies can be instructive in this regard. For instance, the United States and France have taken different approaches to how the doctrine of separation between religion and state applies in the field of education. State funding of religious education or religious educational institutions remains a controversial issue in both countries. The content and control of education is also contested between secular, liberal governments and the Catholic Church. If religious education is permitted in public schools, should the state pay the salaries of teachers from different religious communities and, correspondingly, have a say in the content or methods of education? What might be the principles that would regulate the role of the state in private education? Regardless of whether the state subsidizes religious education in private schools or the community bears the entire cost, should the state have the power to ensure the promotion of broader civic values of equality and non-discrimination in the curriculum? Can state officials ever be neutral and independent enough to implement such a supervisory role without imposing their own beliefs or those of dominant communities? For example, traditional Islamic schools (*madrasas*) have played an important educational and social role, often in places where other educational possibilities have been limited, or to students who would otherwise have little access to education. But the autonomy of such schools can also raise serious questions, especially when the curriculum tends to promote values that undermine the requirements of constitutionalism, human rights and equal citizenship.

Similar concerns apply to the broader question of financial and organizational issues in the relationship between religion and the state.

If religious precepts and principles are not to be limited to purely private affairs, then what financial obligations should the state have regarding the salaries of religious scholars and functionaries, the maintenance of churches, mosques and other religious buildings, and taxation? Such questions should also be considered in the context of the powerful role of religious leaders and institutions on the political stage, and their ability to challenge state policy on a wide range of social and moral issues. Every state must therefore find ways of negotiating potential conflicts that are bound to arise between freedom of religious association and expression, and the maintenance and promotion of values associated, for instance, with the human rights of women and minority religious communities.

In the final analysis, there is a permanent paradox in the competing roles of religious autonomy and authority, on the one hand, and the political authority, legal powers and material powers of the state, on the other. This paradox derives from the inherent nature of the two types of institutions. On the one hand, religious communities need the cooperation of the state in order to fulfill their own mission. However rich and well-organized a religious community may be, it cannot avoid conflict with the state because both sides seek to influence, if not control, the behavior of the same population living within the same territory. On the other hand, the state has to seek some measure of control over religious institutions in order to limit ways in which they can influence or shape the public behavior of believers in their communities. In other words, even when the state is not required or allowed to provide material and administrative support for rich and well-organized religious communities, it cannot afford to grant them complete freedom to propagate whatever values or engage in whatever activities they wish to independently pursue in the name of freedom of religion and belief.

The approach I have attempted to clarify and advance in this essay would first acknowledge this permanent paradox and then seek to mediate its consequences through a range of mechanisms, rather than claim to impose a categorical and final solution. To begin with, this paradox must be acknowledged through a categorical and consistent commitment to the combination of religious neutrality of the state and acceptance of the role of religion in public life of the society. However, this difficult combination cannot be sustained in the context of the modern state without a clear legal and political framework for mediating inevitable tensions and conflicts. For this, I propose the principles of constitutionalism, human rights and equal citizenship which can work only when they enjoy sufficient cultural and religious legitimacy to inspire and motivate people to participate in organized and sustained political and legal action. That is how, I believe, the secular state will succeed everywhere in mediating and negotiating the most complex and protracted issues of public policy, whether Muslims are a majority or small minority.

The 'Secularization' of Shari'a in Iran

Ziba Mir-Hosseini

I would like to begin by thanking the organizers of the conference and in particular Professor Foblets for inviting me to be here. It is a great privilege to participate in a conference in honour of Professor An-Na`im, whose scholarship and advocacy for justice and human rights have been the source of great inspiration for many, including myself. He has stated that his latest book – *Islam and the Secular State*, which has brought us here – is 'the culmination of' his life's work and his 'final statement on the issues' he has been struggling with for nearly a half century.[1] It is indeed an intellectual tour de force, but I hope it is not his final word, and that he will continue reflecting on the struggle for justice and human rights within an Islamic framework, a struggle that has now entered a critical phase.

In his new book, An-Na`im offers an elegant theory of the tripartite relationship between religion, state and society in the development of Islamic societies. He calls his theory 'secularism from an Islamic perspective', and opens the discussion with a faith-based statement:

> In order to be a Muslim by conviction and free choice, which is the only way one can be a Muslim, I need a secular sate. By a secular state I mean one that is neutral regarding religious doctrine, one that does not claim or pretend to enforce 'Shari'a' – the religious law of Islam – simply because compliance with Shari'a cannot be coerced by fear of state institutions or faked to appease their officials.[2]

One important aim of the book is to lay the theoretical grounds for a 'creative Islamic reform that balances the competing demands of religious legitimacy and principled political and social practice.' He calls for the notion of 'Islamic state' to be abandoned, and sees even retaining it as an ideal to be counterproductive, because 'it precludes debates about more viable and appropriate political theories, legal systems, and development policies.'[3] He reminds us that, once Shari'a is adopted as the law of land, it paradoxically ceases to be religious law.

---

[1] Abdullahi Ahmed An-Na`im, *Islam and the Secular Sate: Negotiating the Future of Shari'a*, Cambridge, Mass., Harvard University Press, 2008, p. vii.
[2] An-Na`im, *Islam and the Secular State*, p. 1.
[3] An-Na`im, *Islam and the Secular State* pp 34-35.

While concurring with these contentions, here I want to examine the other side of the paradox, and to shift the focus from theory to ethnography. I shall refer to the experience of political Islam in Iran, and to the emergence of feminist voices in Islam: the so-called 'Islamic feminism'.

There are two elements to my argument. First, the rise of political Islam, and the Islamist project of a ' return to the Shari'a', have had certain unintended yet neglected, and in my view positive, consequences; notably, the opening of a dialogue between Islamic law, on the one hand, and feminism and secularism, on the other. This dialogue, in turn, led to the emergence, by the 1990s, of democratic and feminist interpretations of Islam's sacred texts that are slowly but surely changing the terms of reference of Islamic discourses from within. And it is in the context of this dialogue that An-Na`im's latest book should be placed.

The second strand of my argument is that the transformation of Shari'a from an ideal into an ideology makes it a site of political contestation, and opens its legal mandates to scrutiny and public debate, which is the prerequisite for any meaningful rethinking of relations between state, law and society. In other words, the application of Shari'a mandates through the machinery of a modern nation state sets in motion a process of desanctification and secularization of the notion of law, which can bring about a much-needed paradigm shift in Islamic discourses. In the end, the very slogan of 'return to Shari'a', from which Islamists draw their legitimacy when in opposition, becomes their Achilles heel when they are in power.

I examine these propositions with reference to Iran, where one version of the Islamist vision was realized in 1979 after a popular revolution ended '2500 years of monarchy'.[4] The resultant Islamic Republic merged religious and political authority, and the new rulers embarked on a fierce process of Islamization of law and society according to their understanding of Shari'a.

Yet, three decades later, Iranian society is more 'secular', and in some respects more democratic and 'modern' than it was before the revolution; and – by contrast with other countries in the Muslim world – Islamist ideology has lost its popular support and political lustre. There is a popular reformist movement that advocates an egalitarian and democratic interpretation of the Shari'a and is seeking a gradual but definite separation of the institution of religion from the state –

---

[4] The following account draws on Z. Mir-Hosseini and R. Tapper, *Islam and Democracy in Iran: Eshkevari and the Quest for Reform*, London, I.B. Tauris, 2006.

The 'Secularization' of Shari'a in Iran

if not of politics from religion. There is a vibrant and daring grass-roots women's movement that is striving for equal rights in law and society.

To understand the paradox that is Iran today, we need to remember the two core challenges that the Islamic Republic has had to confront since its birth: the demands for democracy and for women's rights. These two challenges encapsulate the essence of a tension that is inherent in the very quest for an Islamic state in modern times – a tension that by the early 1990s became a powerful catalyst for transforming the Islamic Republic from within.

The Islamic Republic of Iran combines not just religion and the state, but also theocracy and democracy. The founders made two broad assumptions: first, that, given free choice, people will choose 'Islam' and will thus vote for clerics as the interpreters and custodians of the Islam; secondly, that what makes a state 'Islamic' is adherence to and implementation of the Shari'a. The new constitution included both democratic and 'Islamic' principles and institutions. Some institutions, including parliament and the presidency, are elected by direct popular vote, but they are subordinated to clerical oversight and veto, exercised through the concept and institution of the Ruling Jurist (*Vali-ye Faqih*), which gave Ayatollah Khomeini the mandate to rule, as well as the Guardian Council (*Shura-ye Negahban*) of Islamic jurists, who are charged with ensuring that the legislation of parliament does not contradict the constitution and the Shari'a.[5]

In practice, as the revolutionary fervour subsided, neither of the initial assumptions proved as valid or clear-cut as the framers of the constitution hoped, and cracks in the system soon appeared. Either the notion of 'Islamic', as defined by the ruling clerics, must adapt to the political exigencies of a modern democracy, or the people's choice must be restricted or bypassed, which meant betraying the revolution's ideals and losing the popular support from which the new regime drew legitimacy. The story of the Islamic Republic is told by how the rulers have managed this basic problem of legitimacy, and their success or failure has been measured in regular general elections.

An important development in this story is popular disillusionment with the policy of 'return to Shari'a'. In Iran as elsewhere, this policy in practice has amounted to little more than legislating and enforcing rules devised by pre-modern Muslim jurists, *i.e.* classical *fiqh*, most notably a

---

[5] See Asghar Schirazi, *The Constitution of the Islamic Republic: Politics and the State in the Islamic Republic*, London, I.B. Tauris, 1998.

dress code for women, and an outdated, patriarchal and tribal model of social relations enforced in courts dealing with penal cases and familial disputes. The results have been so out of touch with social realities, with the current sense of justice and with women's aspirations, that ordinary people and religious intellectuals alike have come to rethink and redefine their notions of sacred and mundane in the Shari'a.

By the early 1990s, a number of dissident thinkers, both lay and clerical, were developing a critique of the Islamic state from within an Islamic framework. Displaying a refreshingly pragmatic vigour and a willingness to engage with non-religious perspectives, they sought a rights-based political order that could open Muslim polities to dissent, tolerance, pluralism and women's rights and civil liberties. Their ideas and writings, which came to be known as the 'New Religious Thinking', were the mainstay of the popular reformist movement that emerged in the aftermath of the unexpected victory of Mohammad Khatami in the 1997 presidential elections.

The novelty in the 'New Religious Thinking' is not the argument that Islamic jurisprudence or *fiqh* is temporal and changeable, which al-Ghazali argued as early as the 11th century. Nor is it the attempt to consolidate conceptions of Islam and modernity as compatible, which has been the aim of all Muslim reformers since late 19th century. What is new is the political context within which these ideas were shaped and operated, that is, the experience of living in a theocracy at the end of the 20th century. It is not that the Shari'a is losing its sanctity, nor that people are turning away from Islam. Rather, the state's ideological use of the Shari'a and its penetration into the private lives of individuals have brought home the urgent need for legal reform and for the separation of religion from the state.

Khatami's election, and the theological and ideological challenges posed by the New Religious Thinking, unleashed a power struggle in the very heart of the Islamic Republic. For about eight years, that is, Khatami's two terms in office, there was in effect a dual state, where the unelected bodies – now identified with the 'Islamic' side of the state – saw their hold on power as dependent on preventing the elected bodies – now identified with the 'republican' side of the state – from carrying out their election promises. Between 1997 and 2003, all elections were victories for the reformists, but their opponents successfully used the power of the theocratic institutions to frustrate government reformist initiatives and the legislative moves of the reformist Sixth parliament (2000-2004). They also silenced key reformist personalities, first by assassinating, then by prosecuting and jailing them, and closed down the vibrant free press that was one of the main early achievements and platforms of the reformists.

Unable to deliver on their electoral promises and bring change in the structures of power, the reformists lost popular support. In February 2003 and 2004, the theocratic forces won back the city councils and the parliament, and in June 2005 they brought the 'dual state' to an end, when one of their candidates, the hardliner Mahmoud Ahmadinejad, won the presidential election – a victory that astounded both insiders and outsiders. The means by which the theocratic forces regained their monopoly of state power – disqualifying reformist candidates from running for elected office, rigging ballot boxes and interfering with electoral processes through organizing mass votes for their candidate – undermined the popular legitimacy and mandate on which the Islamic Republic has so far rested.

The 2005 presidential election introduced a new round in a power struggle that is far from settled, and the outcome of the next round, the presidential election of June 2009, is unpredictable at the time of writing. But two things are clear. First, Ahmadinejad's election, and the current dominance of the theocratic forces, are not an indication of their popularity or of the end of the reformist movement – as was concluded early on by Western media. Iran's current leaders owe their dominance largely to the blunders of US policy in the Middle East. President Bush's inclusion of Iran in the Axis of Evil in 2002 and the subsequent rhetoric of regime change and refusal to talk to Iran about nuclear and other issues, all tipped the balance in favour of the theocratic forces, and blind-sided the reformists. Then the invasion and occupation of Iraq in 2003 gave the rulers of Iran an opportunity to aim for regional influence and popularity in the Muslim world.

Secondly, the original assumptions underlying the formation of the Islamic Republic – that given free choice people will vote for Islam, and that what makes a state Islamic is application of the Shari'a – have proved unwarranted and unworkable. In all elections since 2004, the clerical leadership not only had to show its hand by disqualifying reformist candidates from running, but also had to mobilize the revolutionary guards under its control to ensure the outcome it wanted. Clearly, the people could no longer be trusted at the ballot box.

Let me now turn, very briefly, to the second unintended consequence of the rise of political Islam, that is the emergence of a new gender consciousness and of feminist scholarship in Islam.

Political Islam, and the slogan of 'return to Shari'a', brought the classical jurisprudential texts (*fiqh*) out of the closet and – unintentionally – exposed their patriarchal ethos to critical scrutiny and public debate. The Islamists defended classical *fiqh* rulings as God's will and the authentic Islamic way of life, but attempts to translate them into policy have provoked many women to increasing criticism and greater activism. Paradoxically, this has opened a space, an arena, which has allowed the articulation of a vigorous internal critique of patriarchal readings of the Shari'a that is unprecedented in Muslim history. A new gender discourse, which has come to be known as Islamic Feminism, has been arguing for equal rights for women on all fronts but within an Islamic framework. This discourse is nurtured by a feminist scholarship that is both discovering a hidden history in Islam and rereading the textual sources to unveil an egalitarian interpretation of the Shari'a.

Among others, I have written and spoken at some length about this emerging feminism, which is quite diverse and speaks with many voices.[6] Here I want to stress that a brand of feminism that takes Islam as the source of its legitimacy has the potential to challenge both the hegemony of patriarchal interpretations of the Shari'a and the authority of those who speak in the name of Islam. This places so-called Islamic feminism in a unique position to expose the inequalities embedded in current interpretations of the Shari'a as constructions by male jurists rather than manifestations of divine will. This exposure can have important epistemological and political consequences. Epistemological, because if it is taken to its logical conclusion, then it can be argued that some rules that until now have been claimed as 'Islamic', and part of the Shari'a, are in fact only the views and perceptions of some Muslims, and are social practices and norms that are neither sacred nor immutable but human and changing. Political, because it can both free Muslims from taking a defensive position and enable them to go beyond old jurisprudential dogmas in search of new questions and new answers.[7]

Both Islamic feminism and the reformist movement in Islam are still in their formative phases, and their fortunes are tied to political developments all over the Muslim world – and to global politics. I will conclude with two comments. First, during their two terms in government (1997-2005), the Iranian reformists failed to bring tangible changes in the structure of power; they lost many battles, and they faced,

---

[6] There is a growing literature of feminist scholarship in Islam, too large to list here; for a review of the literature, see Z. Mir-Hosseini, "Muslim Women's Quest for Equality: Between Islamic Law and Feminism", *Critical Inquiry* 2006, 32 (1), 629-645.

[7] See for instance, 'Musawah Framework for Action', which brings Islamic and human rights framework together to argue for equality and justice in Muslim family law, available at www.musawah.org.

and continue to face, many political setbacks. But they had one major and lasting success: They demystified the power games, which until then had been conducted in a religious language, and the instrumental use of Shari'a to justify autocratic rule. In the end that is what the reform movement in Islam is about.

Secondly, the notion of Shari'a as an ideal has enabled the reformists in Iran to argue for democracy, and Muslim feminists to challenge patriarchal laws enacted in the name of Islam. They have done so by appealing to its higher values and principles, and by invoking concepts from within Islamic legal theory, notably the distinction between Shari'a as the divine law and *fiqh* as human understanding of the terms of the divine law.

Now, an important premise of An-Na`im's theory is negation of this distinction between Shari'a and *fiqh*. He argues that it is difficult to maintain the distinction in practice, that 'any attempt to do so will itself necessarily be the expression of human opinion that is subject to the same risks and limitations.' In his words, both Shari'a and *fiqh* are 'the products of human interpretation of the Qur'an and the Sunna of the Prophet in a particular historical context.'[8] However, both epistemologically and historically, it is this distinction that underlies the emergence of various schools of Islamic law and within it a multiplicity of positions.[9] In other words, the very possibility of changing and reforming the mandates of the Shari'a depends on the contestedness of the concept and disputes over its correct interpretation through *fiqh*. Absent a distinction between Shari'a and *fiqh*, those who are struggling for democratic and feminist interpretations of the Shari'a have little to work with. Given the deep connection between religion and law in Muslim societies, I suggest that denial of the distinction not only impedes the reception of An-Na`im's great theory where it needs most to be received, but makes it unusable in contexts where Islamists have the loudest voices in defining the terms of political and gender discourses among Muslims.

---

[8] An-Na`im, *Islam and the Secular State* p. 35.
[9] For an exchange of views on this with An-Na`im see the transcript of a discussion that took place in Yogyakarta, Indonesia during a workshop organized in 2004 as part of the New Directions in Islamic Thought and Practice project, in K. Vogt, L. Larsen and C. Moe (ed.), *New Directions in Islamic Thought: Exploring Reform and Muslim Tradition*, London, I.B. Tauris, 2008, 200-219.

RESURRECTING *SIYAR* THROUGH *FATWAS*? (RE)CONSTRUCTING 'ISLAMIC INTERNATIONAL LAW' IN A POST–(IRAQ) INVASION WORLD[*]

Shaheen Sardar Ali[1]

Abstract

This article seeks to explore the impact of the Iraq war on *siyar* or 'Islamic international law' from a range of Muslim perspectives by raising some critical questions and addressing these through the lens of a selection of *fatwas* solicited by Muslims from a range of countries and continents, on the Iraq war and its implications for popular understandings of *siyar* and *jihad*. This article suggests that the Iraq war presents an opportunity to revisit and potentially revive historical *siyar* pronouncements of a dichotomous world, *i.e., dar-al-harb* and *dar-al-Islam*. I argue that in so doing, this discourse has invigorated the notions of a universal *Ummah* within the normative framework of *siyar* hitherto marginalized by ascendancy of the nation state, international organizations and contemporary Muslim state practice. Finally, I argue that a wider Internet access to Muslim communities in the global

---

[*] This article was first published in: *Journal of Conflict and Security Law*, 2009, 1-30. We wish to express our gratefulness to the editorial board for giving us permission to publish the text in the present volume.

[1] Professor of Law, University of Warwick; Professor II, University of Oslo, Norway; and Vice-Chair of the United Nations Working Group on Arbitrary Detention. Formerly, Professor of Law, University of Peshawar, Pakistan. This article draws upon some of my earlier research on the subject including: S. Ali, "Religious Pluralism, Human Rights and Muslim Citizenship in Europe: Some Preliminary Reflections on an Evolving Methodology for Consensus", in T. Leonon and J. Goldschmidt (ed.), *Religious Pluralism and Human Rights in Europe*, 2007, 57-79; S. Ali, "The Twain Doth Meet! A Preliminary Exploration of the Theory and Practice of *as-Siyar* and International Law in the Contemporary World", in J. Rehman and S. Breau (ed.), *Religion, Human Rights and International Law: A Critical Examination of Islamic State Practices*, 2007, 95-136; S. Ali and J. Rehman, "The Concept of *Jihad* in Islamic International Law", *Journal of Peace and Security Law* 2005, 10, p. 321, p. 343. I am grateful to Mamman Lawan, Ayesha Shahid, Amila Jayamaha and Shahbaz Cheema for their research assistance in writing this article and my colleagues Prof. Javaid Rehman, Dr. Andrew Williams and Dr. Barbara Roberson for their incisive comments on earlier drafts of this article. I would also like to record my appreciation for constructive feedback provided by Prof. An-Na`im and participants of the conference on 'Islam and the Secular State' in honour of Professor Abdullahi Ahmed An-Na`im held in Leuven, Belgium, 30-31 January 2009, where this paper was presented.

South has facilitated a modified institution of *ifta* to reflect popular understandings of *siyar* and *jihad* and influence its reformulation in the backdrop of the Iraq war.

Introduction

This article seeks to explore the impact of the Iraq war on *siyar* or 'Islamic international law'[2] from a range of Muslim perspectives. There is little doubt that the war has caught the attention of people and governments worldwide, finding expression at multiple levels and in diverse forums and disciplines. Within Muslim communities,[3] the challenge and the resulting discourse is two-fold: to reiterate to themselves and the world at large the belief that Islam is the only basis for authority for any action, individual or collective in local, national and international affairs. The second, and following on from the first point, is a renewed focus on conceptions of *siyar* and *jihad,* and whether under its principles, the Iraq war imposes a religious duty on Muslims, individually and collectively, Iraqi and non-Iraqi, to engage in armed struggle against the occupying forces. Which particular constituency of Muslims poses this question and to whom? What textual definitions of *siyar* and *jihad* inform their understandings of the resistance/insurgency in Iraq? Why is the duty under *siyar* and *jihad* understood by most Muslims in religious terms rather than in a political or ideological framework? Is there a unified 'popular' position amongst Muslims regarding legitimacy or otherwise of this resistance or, do understandings and approaches differ from 'official' positions of governments in Muslim jurisdictions? Under popular Muslim understandings of *siyar,* do governments in some Muslim countries as allies of the West, comprise 'Islamically' legitimate targets of armed struggle? Has this discourse revived a historical *siyar* categorization of the world as *dar-al-Islam* (territory of peace) and *dar-al-harb* (territory of war)? And finally, in the absence of a single religious authority and the existence of multiple sects *(Sunni, Shia)* and schools of juristic thought *(madhab;* plural *madahab)* within Islam,

---

[2] I use this term in inverted commas to indicate that this is a contested term and has generated an on-going debate among scholars whether it is indeed an accurate and acceptable translation of *siyar*. For further discussion, see the section on *siyar* below.
[3] At the grassroots, at governmental and intergovernmental level including the Organisation of Islamic Conference (OIC), the Arab League and the United Nations, within the Muslim diaspora of Europe and North America and, at the level of a transnational Muslim *Ummah*.

what are the implications of a 'global' articulation of *siyar* by Muslims today.

For an increasing number of Muslims, the above questions resonate in a transnational 'Muslim' discourse generated by a proliferation of *fatwa*-giving websites and 'Internet *Muftis*' on the legitimacy of the Iraq war and the resistance to it by Iraqis and other Muslims.[4] The present article attempts to address some of the questions posed above through the lens of a selection of *fatwas*[5] solicited by Muslims from a range of countries and continents, on the Iraq war and its implications for popular understandings of *siyar* and *jihad*. This article suggests that the Iraq war presents an opportunity to revisit and potentially revive historical *siyar* pronouncements of a dichotomous world, *i.e., dar-al-harb* and *dar-al-Islam*.[6] I argue that in so doing, this discourse has invigorated notions of a universal *Ummah* within the normative framework of *siyar* hitherto marginalized by ascendancy of the nation state, international organizations and contemporary Muslim state practice. Finally, I argue that a wider Internet access to Muslim communities in the global South has facilitated a modified institution of *ifta* to reflect popular understandings of *siyar* and *jihad* and influence its reformulation in the backdrop of the Iraq war.

Contextualizing *Siyar, Jihad* and *Fatwas* in the Islamic Legal Tradition and the Contemporary World: An Analytical Overview

This section presents a brief analytical overview of what constitutes the Islamic legal tradition, highlighting its diversity, plurality and inherent dynamism insofar as these have a bearing on our exploration of the

---

[4] This article does not claim to establish a direct connection between the proliferation of *fatwa* websites established since 11 September 2001 and the insurgency and resistance to the Afghanistan and Iraq wars. It simply uses the questions posed to 'Internet *Muftis*' regarding legitimacy of the resistance, duty of Muslims in these circumstances and clarifications regarding *as-siyar* and *jihad* as indicative of a parallel discourse competing with 'official' views of governments in Muslim jurisdictions on the subject. It also draws attention to Gary R. Bunt describing an increasing usage of the Internet as an 'Islamic tool'. See G.R. Bunt, "Islam Interactive: Mediterranean Islamic Expression on the World Wide Web", in B.A. Roberson (ed.), *Shaping the Current Islamic Reformation*, London and Portland, Oregon, Frank Cass, 2003, 165.

[5] The present paper is confined to a discussion of *fatwas* as experienced within the Sunni jurisprudence and practice.

[6] This is encouraged in some respects by the 'Bushian' worldview of 'you are either with us or against us.'

impact of the Iraq war on *siyar*. The core concept of the Islamic legal tradition is the *Shari'a*, forming an overarching umbrella of rules, regulations, values and normative framework covering all aspects and spheres of life for Muslims. It is composed of the Divine injunctions of God *(Qur'an)*, Divinely inspired *Sunna* (words and deeds of the Prophet Muhammad recorded as *hadith)* as well as the human articulation and understanding of these sources.[7] *Shari'a*, is therefore more than the black-letter law and legal principles and encompasses social, moral and ethical normativities affecting human lives.[8] I define the legal component of *Shari'a* as the 'Islamic legal tradition' rather than 'Islamic law', to avoid creating a restrictive fence around an evolving tradition. This description is especially important in a discussion within Western scholarship that imagines law largely as formal, black-letter, written law.[9] By the same token, and following An-Na`im, Kamali, Hallaq and others, I distance myself from those writers on the subject who believe that ('Islamic law')

> was the result of a speculative attempt by pious scholars working during the first three centuries of Islam, to define the will of Allah. In self imposed isolation from practical needs and circumstances they produced a comprehensive system of rules, largely in opposition to existing legal practice which expressed the religious ideal.[10]

Coulson's notion of the 'isolationist development' of what he defines as Islamic law, does not reflect the entire landscape of legal development in Islam. As a later section of this article will describe, throughout Muslim

---

[7] See A. Rahim, *Muhammadan Jurisprudence*, Lahore, Mansoor Book House, 1995; M. H. Kamali, *Principles of Islamic Jurisprudence* (3rd ed.), Cambridge, Islamic Texts Society, 2003; A.A.A. Fyzee, *Outlines of Muhammadan Law* (4th ed.), Delhi, Oxford University Press, 1974; A.A. An-Na`im (ed.), *Islamic Family Law in a Changing World: A Global Resource Book*, London, Zed Press, 2002, 1-2.

[8] For this particular viewpoint, see, generally, F. Rehman, *Islam* (2nd ed.), Chicago, University of Chicago Press, 1979, 68; A. Allot, *Limits of Law*, 1980; A.A.A. Fyzee, *Outlines of Muhammadan Law* (4th ed.), Dehli, Oxford University Press, 1974; D. Pearl and W. Menski, *Muslim Family* Law (3rd ed.), London, Sweet & Maxwell, 1998.

[9] I am conscious of the fact that some scholars and students believe that the term 'Islamic law' is more appropriate and by defining it as the 'Islamic legal tradition', we are somehow taking away its authoritative status. My reason for choosing this manner of description is to widen the remit and reach of the concept.

[10] J. Coulson, "The State and the Individual in Islamic Law", *International and Comparative Law Quarterly* 1857, 6, p. 57, as cited by W.B. Hallaq in "From *Fatwas* to *Furu*: Growth and Change in Islamic Substantive Law", *Islamic Law and Society* 1994, 1, p. 29 and accompanying footnotes.

history, *muftis* and other scholars at the grassroots level have influenced and have been influenced by the existing practices of Muslims and feeding these into the transformative and evolutionary processes of the Islamic legal tradition.

Sources of the Islamic legal tradition have been categorized as primary, *i.e.,* the *Qur'an*[11] and *Sunna,*[12] and secondary, including *Ijma* (consensus of opinion)[13] and *Qiyas* (analogical deduction).[14] Juristic techniques include *ijtihad* (many established jurists place it in the category of a source of law),[15] *Taqlid,*[16] *Iikhtilaf*[17],

---

[11] The *Qur'an* is believed by Muslims to be the word of God and was revealed to the Prophet Muhammad through the Angel Gibrael over a period of 22 years, 2 months and 22 days. It is divided into 114 chapters and has a total of 6666 verses and 30 sections.

[12] *Sunna* means the words and deeds of the Prophet Muhammad also known as traditions, which are compiled as *hadith* (singular) and *ahadith* (plural). A tradition or *hadith* is composed of the *matn* (text) of the tradition and the *isnad* (chain of transmitters). For an excellent exposition, see M. Z. Siddiqi, *Hadith Literature Its Origin, Development and Special Features*, 2006.

[13] It is defined by A. Rahim as 'agreement among the Muslim jurists in a particular age on a question of law'; see A. Rahim, *Muhammadan Jurisprudence*, Lahore, Mansoor Book House, 1995, 97. '*Ijma* is defined as the unanimous agreement of the *mujtahidun* of the Muslim community of any period following the demise of the Prophet Muhammad on any matter': see M.H. Kamali, *Principles of Islamic Jurisprudence* (3rd ed.), Cambridge, Islamic Texts Society, 2003; N.J. Coulson, *A History of Islamic Law*, Edinburgh, Edinburgh University Press, 1994, 230.

[14] As a source of law, *Qiyas* comes into operation in matters not covered by an express text of the *Qur'an* and *Sunna* nor dealt with by *Ijma*. The law deduced by application of what has already been laid down by the three sources is *Qiyas*. See Rahim, *op. cit.*, fn. 12, p. 117.

[15] The literal meaning of which is striving hard and strenuousness denotes exercising independent juristic reasoning to provide answers when the *Qur'an* and *Sunna* are silent on a particular issue. A person qualified to undertake *ijtihad* is known as a *Mujtahid* and there are specific qualifications for a person to be so acknowledged.

[16] *Taqlid* is translated as the duty to follow and is considered by most students of Islamic law as mere 'imitation' or to emulate or copy. As a term of jurisprudence, *taqlid* may be used in the context of accepting someone's intellectual authority. The reality of the Islamic legal tradition, however, shows that *taqlid* was used by Muslim jurists to engage in juristic methods and processes that were anything but blind emulation. Whilst inhibiting independent legal formulations, *taqlid* allowed later day jurists a choice from among variant views recorded in authoritative texts. See A. Rahim, *Muhammadan Jurisprudence*, Lahore, Mansoor Book House, 1995, fn. 12, 44-145; N.J. Coulson, *A History of Islamic Law*, Edinburgh, Edinburgh University Press, 1994, 80-81.

[17] It means the 'unity in diversity' doctrine, *i.e.* jurists of the various schools of thought as well as practitioners, arrived at positions that were as varied as the colours of the rainbow. See Coulson, *A History of Islamic Law*, 86.

Takhayyur[18], *Talfiq*[19], *Maslaha*[20], *Darura*[21], *Istishab*[22], *Istihsan*[23], *Sadd al-Dharai*[24], *Ijtihad*, also translated as personal reasoning, has been described as

> ... the most important source of Islamic law next to the Qur'an and the *Sunnah*. The main difference between *ijtihad* and the revealed sources of the *Shari'ah* lies in the fact that *ijtihad* is a continuous process of development whereas divine revelation and prophetic legislation discontinued after the demise of the Prophet. In this sense, *ijtihad* continues to be the main instrument of interpreting the divine message and relating it to the changing conditions of the Muslim community in its aspirations to attain justice, salvation and truth.[25]

---

[18] A process of selection. As a term of jurisprudence, it is used to consider possible alternatives from a range of juristic opinions on a particular point of law, with the intention of seeking less restrictive legal principles in application to issues arising. *Takhayyur* has been of enormous significance in developing a number of women-friendly codes of family laws in Muslim jurisdictions. For example, regarding circumstances where a married Muslim woman may seek dissolution of her marriage, the Hanafi school is restrictive whereas the Maliki is flexible and allows a wife to seek dissolution on the grounds of cruelty of her husband. This was incorporated in a number of Personal Status laws in the Muslim world. Likewise, the Hanbali doctrine of abiding by stipulations (based on the *hadith* of the Prophet Muhammad) led this school of thought to declare that the marriage contract could stipulate monogamy of the husband, the wife could choose the place of residence and so on. Examples of *Takhayyur* include the *Dissolution of Muslim Marriages Act* 1939, the *Moroccan Code of Personal Status* 1858, *Jordanian Law of Family Rights* 1951, *Syrian Law of Personal Rights* 1953 and the *Ottoman Law of Family Rights* 1917 and the latest, *Moroccan Family Code* (*Moudawana*) 2004 and others.

[19] Translated literally as a 'patchwork', this term implies the process whereby Muslim jurists constructed legal rules by the combination and fusion of opinions derived from different schools of thought on a particular issue.

[20] The public good or in the public interest or *masalihu'l-mursala wa'listislah* is a doctrine propounded by Imam Malik who allowed 'a deduction of law to be based on general considerations of the public good.' See Rahim, *op. cit.*, fn. 12, p. 140 and Coulson, *A History of Islamic Law*, *op. cit.*, fn. 15, p.144.

[21] Necessity/duress is a technique applied where it becomes imperative to make prohibited things and situations, permissible.

[22] Literally meaning 'escorting' or 'companionship'. Technically it has been defined by Shafis and Hanbalis as 'continuation of that which is proven and negation of that which had not existed'. Kamali, *op. cit.*, fn. 6, p. 297.

[23] Literally means 'to approve or to deem something preferable'. It was applied by Malikis, Hanafis and Hanbalis. Kamali, *op. cit.*, fn. 6, p. 246.

[24] Literally means 'blocking the means'. It is based on the idea of preventing an evil before it actually materializes. Kamali, *op. cit.*, fn. 6, p. 285.

[25] Kamali, *op. cit.*, fn. 6, p. 468.

Resurrecting Siyar *Through* Fatwas?

Last but not the least, is custom or *'urf,* also termed *ta'amul* or *'adah.* At times controversial,[26] this source of law plays an important role in the growth of the Islamic legal tradition as it engages with commonly held beliefs and convictions of communities.[27] Whilst emerging as a pivotal point in the evolution of *siyar,* the contested position of *'urf* within the various schools of juristic thought in Islam is also evident from how this source of law is perceived historically and in contemporary Muslim communities. Kamali also makes the fine distinction between *'urf* and *'adah* stating that scholars have used *'adah* as denoting repetition or recurrent practice of individuals and groups whereas *'urf* is the collective practice of significant numbers of people in a community.[28] *'urf* (meaning, 'which is known') and its derivative, *Ma'ruf* (also meaning 'known', appears in the Qur'an but its usage is equated with 'good') thus inform norm-making, potentially to influence the course of *siyar* except where the collective practice violates an established basic rule of the Islamic legal tradition.[29] This analysis is useful in querying the nature of *fatwas* responding to the question whether armed resistance to the invading army by some, can constitute *'urf* and an emerging norm under contemporary *siyar.* Despite wide acceptance of *'urf* as one of the manifestations of the living law, susceptible to evolution, Imam Malik[30] created a hierarchy of *'urf* going so far as to equate the customs and practice of the people of Medina, *'amal ahl al-madinah* with *ijma,* thus elevating the customs and practice of Medina to a source of law rather than as one of the several evidential factors of what constitutes

---

[26] For example, where some Muslim communities uphold customs in violation of Islamic law including that of widow re-marriage to the late husband's brother against the wishes of the widow; custom of '*swara*' or giving a woman in marriage to the 'enemy' in return for pardoning a murder; killing men and women in the name of honour; excommunicating men and women who choose to marry outside the community to name a few.

[27] *Ta'amul/amal* has been applied by Malikis restrictively to the practices of people of Medina. Some communities of South Asia relied upon 'urf to interpret Muslim laws of inheritance. For example, in the Pakistan province of Punjab, among the Khojas of Bombay and some Pukhtun tribes of the North West Frontier Province of Pakistan. For application of customary norms intertwined with Islamic concepts of inheritance and other family law matters, the Indonesian *adat* is a fascinating example. See J. Bowen's excellent work in this area entitled, *Islam, Law, and Equality in Indonesia: An Anthropology of Public Reasoning* (American title: *Entangled Commands*), Cambridge, Cambridge University Press, 2003.

[28] Kamali, *op. cit.*, fn. 6, p. 369. 28 *Ibid.*

[29] *Ibid.*

[30] Founder of the Maliki school of juristic thought in Islam.

'*urf*[31]. By extension, and as An-Na'im notes, it also arguably, leaves *'urf* of later day Muslim communities as of lesser normative value.[32]

A major objective of the present paper is to explore the normative status of *fatwas* in the evolution of *siyar*. It is therefore important to note the connection and interface, both juristic and historical, between *ijtihad, 'urf* and *fatwa*.[33] To this end, it is useful to present an insight into the place and role of *fatwas* within the Islamic legal tradition generally and as an interpretative vehicle and process in particular.

The *fatwa* has been defined in a variety of ways, ranging from being compared to 'proof' or evidence of *Shari'a* (when handed down by a *sahabi*, or Companion of the Prophet Muhammad), a considered opinion of a *mujtahid*[34] or a nonbinding advisory opinion to an individual questioner.[35] Hallaq defines a *fatwa* as, ' ... consisting of a question *(sua-al, istifta)*, addressed to a juriconsult *(mufti)*, and an answer *(jawab)* provided by that jurisconsult'.[36] It is a non-binding opinion of a *mufti* given in response to a question (posed by a *qadi*, a private person or an institution). The *fatwa* is perceived by many as the 'meeting point between legal theory and social practice'[37] serving a number of functions. These include employing *fatwa* as a legal tool,[38] a social instrument,[39] as inputs to the political discourse[40] or as a device for reform.[41] It has historically 'formed the vital link between academic theories of pure scholarship and the influences of practical life, and

---

[31] Kamali, *op. cit.*, fn. 6, p. 372; Rahim, *Muhammadan Jurisprudence*, 137; Mahmassani, *Falsafah*, 123; A.A. An-Na'im, "Competing Visions of History in Internal Islamic Discourse and Islamic-Western Dialogue", in J. Rusen (ed.), *Time and History: The Variety of Cultures*, 2007, 135-150,142-145.

[32] A.A. An-Na'im, "Competing Visions of History in Internal Islamic Discourse and Islamic-Western Discourse", in J. Rusen (ed.) *Time and History: The Variety of Cultures*, Oxford, Berghahn Books, 2007, 135-150, 142-145.

[33] The institution of *fatwas*.

[34] Kamali, *op. cit.*, fn. 6, p. 315.

[35] M.H. Masud, B. Messick, and D.S. Powers, "Muftis, Fatwas, and Islamic Legal Interpretation", in M.H. Masud, B. Messick and D.S. Powers (ed.), *Islamic Legal Interpretation. Muftis and Their Fatwas*, 2005, 3-32, 34.

[36] W. B. Hallaq, "From Fatwa to Furu: Growth and Change in Islamic Substantive Law", *Islamic Law and Society* 1994, 1, p. 29, p. 31.

[37] A. Caeiro, "The Shifting Moral Universes of the Islamic Tradition of Ifta: A Diachronic Study of Four Adab al-Fatwa Manuals", *The Muslim World* 2006, 96, p. 661.

[38] In assisting the adjudication process at the behest of a *qadi*.

[39] In the form of questions by private persons in the community.

[40] Seeking a *fatwa* in relation to an act of state or government either within the state or to another state or states.

[41] Where a *mufti*, in response to a question, presents his viewpoint for reform in existing practice.

through them the dictates of the doctrine were gradually adapted to the changing needs of Muslim society'.[42]

Hallaq states that there exists strong evidence to indicate that *fatwas* went beyond responses to individual questions and played a considerable role in the growth and evolution of Islamic substantive law.[43] This is likely to have been the case as compilations of *fatwas* issued by leading jurists, were often published and used as authoritative precedents.[44] The history of *fatwas* is therefore uniquely placed within the Islamic legal tradition standing at the crossroads between theory and practice of Islam, the formal and non-formal structures of authority and their relational location within Muslim communities. It provides both 'text' (the *fatwa)* and context (the space within which questions are posed and responses applied) for application of plural understandings of the Islamic legal tradition. Records indicate that whilst *fatwas* contributed to legal discourse within the Islamic legal tradition, they were also an important social instrument and helped in shaping societal views on issues from the mundane to the sublime. In particular, it is important to bear in mind that in view of the high rates of illiteracy among Muslim populations and their dependency on the mass media (public meetings, lectures, radio and television), reliance on 'verbal' *fatwas* delivered to an audience has increasingly become a popular offering of radio and television channels today. More recently, internet *fatwa* sites have emerged to add to the offerings.

It would be fair to state that the *fatwa* as a socio-legal advisory process has undergone transformation due to its wider reach to the ordinary Muslim. From its departure point as a response by an individual *mufti* to an individual questioner, it appears to have acquired a collective and public nature and a deeper normative influence.[45] Questions (as a later section of this paper attempts to demonstrate) of a transnational nature, personal and political, individual and collective, place *fatwas* at the intersection of *'urf* and *ijtihad* throwing up a range of questions regarding its nature within the Islamic legal tradition. For instance, in the present context, were it to be established that a significant body of

---

[42] Coulson, *loc. cit.*, fn. 15, p. 142.
[43] Hallaq, *op. cit.*, fn. 35, p. 34.
[44] The list of such *fatwa* collections is too numerous to be included here. For some of the most prominent *fatwa* collections, see *ibid.*
[45] This view is advanced bearing in mind increased media access of the ordinary Muslim and the input of non-governmental organizations, regional and international organizations into the norm-making and law-making processes of Muslim states and governments.

Muslims across the world believe as *'urf* that it is both *fard ayni* and *fard kafaya* to engage in *jihad* against the invading/occupying armies in Iraq, and that this belief was confirmed by multiple *fatwas* of *muftis* who qualified as *mujtahids*,[46] would such *fatwas* qualify as inputs to the nature of *siyar*?

What is the status of contemporary Muslim state practice regarding interstate/intergovernment relations and actions, *i.e., siyar,* especially where there are no express dissenting voices? From an *usul-ul-fiqh* perspective, where do these actions fall as well as edicts and *fatwas* of state-employed *muftis*?

The Nature of *Siyar* and *Jihad* Within the Islamic Legal Tradition

Siyar, translated variously as the 'Islamic law of nations',[47] 'Muslim law of nations', or 'Islamic international law', forms an integral component of the Islamic legal tradition and unlike its Western counterpart, its status within the legal system is never in doubt.[48] The above terminology used in translation into some western European languages including English, French and German by various scholars has generated a robust on-going debate on the subject. An-Na'im and Baderin are of the view that *siyar*

---

[46] One qualified to make *ijtihad*. Details of qualifications of *mujtahids* are the subject of numerous scholarly works including, Rahim, Kamali, Fyzee and a range of earlier Muslim jurists cited in these works.

[47] M.A. Baderin, "The Evolution of Islamic Law of Nations and the Modern International Order: Universal Peace through Mutuality and Cooperation", *American Journal of Islamic Social Sciences* 2000, 17, p. 57-80; K. Bennoune, abstract of presentation at the 2004 Annual Meeting of the American Association of Law Schools Workshop on Islamic Law, <http://www.aals.orglam2004/islamiclaw/international.htm> accessed on 31 December 2008 and others.

[48] See K. Bennoune, "As-Salamu Alaykum? Humanitarian Law in Islamic Jurisprudence", *Michigan Journal of International Law* 1994, 15, p.605, p.611. For sources of *siyar*, see H. Kruse, *The Foundations of Islamic International Law,* Karachi, Pakistan Historical Society, 1956, cited in Bennoune (n. 42); S.G. Vasey-Fitzgerald, "Nature and Sources of the Sharia", in M. Khadduri and H.J. Liebesny (ed.), *Law in the Middle East*, Washington, D.C., The Middle East Institute, 1955); A. Rahim, *Muhammadan Jurisprudence*, Lahore, Mansoor Book House, 1995; J. Schacht, *Origins of Muhammadan Jurisprudence*, Oxford, Oxford University Press, 1959; J. Schacht, *An Introduction to Islamic Law*, Oxford, Clarendon Press, 1964; N.J. Coulson, *A History of Islamic Law*, Edinburgh, Edinburgh University Press, 1994; A.A.A. Fyzee, *Outlines of Muhammadan Law* (4th ed.), Delhi, Oxford University Press, 1974.

to mean 'Islamic international law' is a misnomer and one that does not present an accurate representation of this section of the Islamic legal tradition.[49] In An-Na`im's view, there can only be one international law, but it has to be truly international by incorporating relevant principles from different legal traditions, instead of the exclusive euro-centric concept, principles and institutions of international law commonly known today. When the essential nature and purpose of international law are clarified in the present global context, I will argue, one will find that Islamic law can be fully supportive of the *possibility* of international law.[50]

Bouzenita's expose on the subject highlights the difficulty of designating *siyar* as 'Islamic law of nations' on a number of counts. Due to different historical developments, *siyar* is not presented within the framework of a territorial state and its relations with other states that form a basic element of 'modern international law'.[51]

The rules of *siyar* are, contrary to the modern law of nations, not 'international' in the sense that they came into existence on the ground of a legal order *inter* nations. They are due to the monistic character of Islamic law, rather deduced from the same sources like any other Islamic legal rule. Due to the respective historical developments, *siyar* lacks the concept and definition of a territorial state which constitutes one of the basic elements of modern international law.[52]

While accepting that there exist issues of terminology, theoretically and conceptually divergent understandings and approaches towards *siyar* and international law, it is submitted that a comparatively useful methodology might be evolved where substantive content and contours of *siyar* may be compared with what we term international law. Whether the point of departure is a legal order based on a post-Westphalian

---

[49] Remarks by Prof. Abdullahi Ahmed An-Na`im and Prof. Mashood Baderin at the 2nd Islamic Law Curriculum Development Workshop, University of Warwick, 2 July 2008.

[50] A.A. An-Na`im, "Islamic Law and International Law", abstract of presentation at the 2004 Annual meeting of the American Association of Law Schools Workshop on Islamic Law, <http://www.aals.org/am2004/islamiclaw/international.htm> accessed on 31 December 2008 and others.

[51] Ibid.

[52] A. Bouzenita, "The Siyar – An Islamic Law of Nations?", *Asian Journal of Social Sciences* 2007, 35, p. 19-46, p. 44.

premise of territorially based nation state or a universal Islamic world order based on *Shari'a* and intended to apply universally to all people in every time and place, the fact is that both legal orders propose to regulate beyond national boundaries, religious denominations and (interstate, intergroup, intercommunity, interfaith) alliances. That is not a failure to acknowledge the differences in remit and reach between the two legal orders but to note that the overlaps between the two offer a common discursive space and engagement with a view to some mutually useful transformative processes.

As part of the Islamic legal tradition, *siyar* grew into a fully functional body of the *Shari'a* several centuries in advance of any similar developments in the Western world.[53] Hamidullah defines it as '[t]hat part of the law and custom of the land and treaty obligations which a Muslim *de facto* or *de jure* State observes in its dealings with other *de facto* or *de jure* States.[54] Majid Khadduri is of the view that *siyar*, if taken to mean the Islamic law of nations, is but a chapter in the Islamic *corpus juris,* binding upon all who believed in Islam as well as upon those who sought to protect their interests in accordance with Islamic justice.[55] Gamal Badr makes the important point that in trying to understand *siyar,* we must neither lose sight of the historical framework of Islam nor of the living and developing Islamic view of international

---

[53] One of the reasons for the early development of *siyar* since the eighth century AD may well have been the conviction in Muslim theology that the Islamic nation was one entity, the *Ummah*, and so laws to cover various nationalities in this *communitas islamica*, were necessary. The various schools of Islamic juristic thought thus set out to deduce rules of international law from the sources of Islamic law. The Hanafi school of juristic thought was particularly active and two of Abu Hanifa's (founder of the Hanafi school of thought) followers came to be known as 'fathers' of the Islamic law of nations. Abu Yusuf authored the *Kitab al Kharaj* and *al-Radd Ala Siyar al-Awai*, and al-Shaybani wrote his famous *al-Siyar al-Kabir* (translated by M. Khadduri, *The Islamic Law of Nations*, Baltimore, Johns Hopkins Press, 1966. These works date back to the second and third centuries of hijra, the Islamic calendar (eighth and ninth centuries of the Christian calendar). For a discussion of the history of the codification of Islamic international law, see M. Hamidullah, *Muslim Conduct of State: Being a Treatise on Siyar, that is Islamic Notion of Public International Law, Consisting of the Laws of Peace, War and Neutrality, Together with precedents from Orthodox Practices and Precedent by a Historical and General Introduction*, Lahore, Sh. Muhammad Ashraf, 1977, 61-72.

[54] Hamidullah, *op.cit.*, fn. 52, p. 3.

[55] M. Khadduri, *The Islamic Law of Nations*, Baltimore, Johns Hopkins Press, 1966, 6, 55.

law and relations.[56] Within this historicity of *siyar* lies its most important element: the 'Islamic' conceptualization of a dichotomous world, *i.e.*, *dar-al-Islam* and *dar-al-harb* and the legitimacy of armed *jihad* to bring *dar-al-harb* into the fold of *dar-al-Islam*.[57]

Equally on record in world history, are extended periods of peaceful coexistence of Muslim and non-Muslim communities described as *dar-al-sulh* (territory of peace), *dar-al-ahd* (territory of peace as a result of an agreement) or *dar-al-darura* (territory where Muslims reside under necessity), and hence a component of *siyar*. The practice of Muslim governments, communities and the Muslim diaspora, or *'urf*, also forms an important indicator of the current norms of *siyar*, a point that the present article attempts to signify in the context of Muslim responses to the Iraq war. Membership of Muslim states of the United Nations Organization, active participation in the formulation of various human rights and other treaties, accession to these treaties (albeit with reservations in the name of Islam) as well as the formation of the Organization of the Islamic Conference (OIC) by Muslim states in 1969 is evidence of this norm. The Charter of the OIC, among other statements, contains pronouncements implying agreement to conduct their relations with other states on the basis of equality and

---

[56] G.M. Badr, "A Survey of Islamic International Law", *Proceedings of the American Society of International Law* 1982, 76, p. 56.

[57] M.A. Baderin, "The Evolution of Islamic Law of Nations and the Modern International Order: Universal Peace through Mutuality and Cooperation", *American Journal of Islamic Social Sciences* 2000, 17, p. 57-80 drawing upon classical Muslim scholars, e.g., Ibn Khaldun, *The Muquaddimah*, trans. F. Rosenthal, vol. 1, 1958, p. 473. The concept of *Dar Al-Harb* was first introduced in the Fiqh Hanafi. According to Abu Hanifah, a territory becomes a Dar Al-Islam if: (a) Muslims are able to enjoy peace and security; and (b) it has common frontiers with some Muslim countries (other Dar Al-Islam). (Assarkhasi, (b) 101114; Azuhaili, 1962: p. 192-196; al-Qardawi, 2005) cited by M. Abo-Kazleh, "Rethinking International Relations Theory in Islam: Toward a More Adequate Approach", *Alternatives: Turkish Journal of International Relations* 2006, 5, p. 41-56 at 42 (also available in pdf at: <http://alternativesjournal.net/volume5/number4/kazleh.pdf>). A Muslim majority nation not ruled by Islamic law is still, traditionalists believe, bode of war, while a Muslim-minority nation ruled by Islamic law could qualify as being a part of bode of Islam (al-Kasani, 7/131;) (cited in *ibid.*, p. 43). A place is not a Domain of Islam where Muslims' lives, property and faith are not safe although its ruler may be a Muslim (as-Sarkhasi, 5/2197; Ibn al-Qayim, 1/366) (cited in *ibid.*, p. 43).

reciprocity and recognizing core universal human rights norms and may be considered as an example of contemporary *siyar*.[58]

The inclusive view of *siyar* described above has not gone uncontested and a number of writers have challenged both the intent of Muslim governments as well as the extent to which the non-statist premise of *siyar* has been dislodged by post-United Nations developments. Tibi appears unconvinced of Muslim states purporting to subordinate themselves to international law through membership of the United Nations. He argues that without 'cultural accommodation' whereby Muslims and Muslim governments recognize the reality of territorial nation states and the illegality of war, United Nations membership by itself will not modify historical understandings of *siyar* and *jihad*.[59]

The doctrine of *jihad* is one of the most prominent concepts in *siyar* and is frequently equated with the Islamic notion of 'Just War'[60]. In response, others argue that Islam is a religion of peace and *jihad* in the form of armed conflict is mainly defensive in nature, particularly in the persistent state of war in seventh century Arabian society.[61] Further, it is argued that much confusion stems from the fact that *siyar* and laws of

---

[58] H. Moinuddin, *The Charter of the Islamic Conference and Legal Framework of Economic Cooperation Among Its Member States*, 1987, 14. The preamble of the OIC affirms this position by stating the following: "REAFFIRMING their commitment to the United Nations Charter and Fundamental Human Rights, the purposes and principles of which provide the basis for fruitful cooperation among all people" <http://www.oicoci.org/english/main/charter.htm> accessed 12 September 2007. Likewise, the *Arab Charter on Human Rights* adopted by Muslim member states of the Arab League in 1994 (with a revised version adopted in 2004), also invokes international human rights instruments in its preamble: "Reaffirming the principles of the Charter of the United Nations and the Universal Declaration of Human Rights, as well as the provisions of the United Nations International Covenants on Civil and Political Rights and Economic, Social and Cultural Rights and the Cairo Declaration on Human Rights in Islam."

[59] B. Tibi, "War and Peace", in S.H. Hashmi (ed.), *Islamic Political Ethics, Civil Society, Pluralism and Conflict*, 2002, 187. In response, it may be said that similar arguments may be applied to some non-Muslim United Nations member states to question their commitment to the United Nations Charter, particularly in the context of the Iraq war that breached and indeed defied the United Nations Charter.

[60] See H.M. Zawati, *Is Jihad a Just War? War, Peace, and Human Rights Under Islamic and Public International Law*, Lewiston, NY, Edwin Mellen Press, 2001, 55-58.

[61] For an incisive article on this line of argument, see S.A. Jackson, "Jihad and the Modern World", *Journal of Islamic Law and Culture* 2002, 7, p. 1-26; F. Donner, "The Sources of Islamic Conceptions of War", in J. Kelsey and J. T. Johnson (ed.), *Just War and Jihad: Historical and Theoretical Perspectives on War and Peace in Western and Islamic Traditions*, 1991, 31-70.

armed conflict within the Islamic legal tradition has, until recently, not received due attention in Western legal scholarship.[62] when speaking of *Islamic* perceptions of the use of force, particularly in the current phase of international relations, we should remember that there is no unified perception among Islamic law experts or politicians in Islamic countries. It is not unusual that Islamic schools of jurisprudence have different interpretations of the provisions of primary sources of Islamic law, particularly verses of the Koran.[63]

According to a popular interpretation, the totality of *jihad* ideology represents a religiously sanctioned aggressive war to propagate or defend the faith.[64] In fact, so strong is the ordinance to use aggressive war, that *siyar* values are regarded as synonymous to those of the *jihad*.[65] This notion of *jihad* and *siyar* as being synonymous also draws strength from the normative framework of historical *siyar* that perceived the

---

[62] See M.A. Boisard, "On the Probable Influence of Islam on Western Public and International Law", *International Journal of Middle East Studies*, 1980, 11, p. 429; T. Landscheidt, "Der Einfluss des Islam auf die Entwicklung der Temperamenta Belli im Europäischen Volkerrecht", Unpublished Dissertation, 1955; M.C. Bassiouni, "Protection of Diplomats under Islamic Law", *American Journal of International Law* 1980, 74, p. 609; for a rare, though useful, contemporary European perspective on Islam, see S. Ferrari and A. Bradney (ed.), *Islam and European Legal Systems*, Aldershot, Ashgate Publishing.

[63] S. Mahmoudi, "The Islamic Perception of the Use of Force in the Contemporary World", *Journal of the History of International Law* 2005, 7, p. 55-68.

[64] Professor Abdullahi Ahmed An-Na`im makes the observation that 'the term can also refer to religiously sanctioned aggressive war to propagate or 'defend' the faith. What is problematic about this latter sense of jihad is that it involves direct and unregulated violent action in pursuit of political objectives, or self-help in redressing perceived injustice, at the risk of harm to innocent bystanders ...'. See A.A. An-Na`im "Upholding International Legality against Islamic and American Jihad", in K. Booth and T. Dunne (ed.), *Worlds in Collision: Terror and the Future of Global Order,* London, Palgrave, 2002, 162-172.

[65] J. Busuttil, "Humanitarian Law in Islam", *Military Law and Law of War Review*, 1991, 30, p. 113; M. Khadduri, *War and Peace in the Law of Islam*, Baltimore, Johns Hopkins Press, 1955, 51-54; M. Khadduri, "Islam and the Modem Law of Nations", *American Journal of International Law* 1956, 50, p. 358, p. 358-359.

world as *dar-al-Islam* and *dar-al-harb*[66] and a religious obligation to transform it into one *dar-al-Islam* by armed struggle, if need be.

In contrast to the above interpretation, another view states that *jihad* ideology is exclusively one of self-exertion and peaceful coexistence. Proponents of this viewpoint place reliance upon the literal interpretation of the meaning of *jihad* as well as the primary sources of *siyar* -the *Qur'an* and *hadith* of Prophet Muhammad. The term *jihad* comes from the Arab verb *'jahada'*, meaning to struggle or exert.[67] The Prophet Muhammad is believed to have stated that exertion of force in battle is a minor *jihad*, while 'self-exertion in peaceful and personal compliance with the dictates of Islam (constitutes) the major or superior *jihad*'.[68] The Prophet Muhammad is also reported to have said that the 'best form of *jihad* is to speak the truth in the face of an oppressive ruler'.[69] In Islamic jurisprudence, *jihad* has been defined as 'exertion of one's power to the utmost of one's capacity.[70]

It is evident from the foregoing discussion that opposing interpretations of the religious text in Islam as well as the historical process impacted on the meaning, scope and application of *jihad* and Muslim perspectives on international law. Since the *Qur'anic* verses lend themselves to multiple readings and extrapolations, the controversy over the concept and what it means for Muslims today continues. In

---

[66] Virtually every writer on Islamic law has considered these divisions. *Dar-al-Islam* corresponds to territory under Islamic sovereignty. Its inhabitants were Muslims by birth or conversion, and the people of the tolerated religions (Jews, Christians and Zoroastrians) who preferred to remain non-Muslims at the cost of paying a special tax. The *dar-al-harb* consisted of all the states and communities outside the territory of Islam. Its inhabitants were called *harbis* or people of the territory of war. See Khadduri, *op. cit.*, fn. 64, p. 359. Also see, S. Mahmassani, "International Law in the Light of Islamic doctrine", *Recueil des Cours*, 1966, 117, p. 201, p. 250-252.

[67] Bennoune, *loc. cit.*, fn. 47, p. 615.

[68] *Ibid.* See also A.A. An-Na`im, *loc. cit.*, in. 31, p. 145 (citing Al-Kaya Al-Harasiy, Akhan Al-Ouran 1:89 1983).

[69] *Ibid.*

[70] Bennoune, *loc. cit.,* in. 47, p. 615. Some *Quranic* verses supporting this view include the following: 'And if they incline to peace, incline thou also to it, and trust in God', Verse VIII: 61. 'So do not falter, and invite to peace when ye are the uppermost. And God is with you, and He will not grudge (the reward of) your actions'. Verse XLVII: 35. That peace is the preferred state of affairs is borne out by the following *Quranic* verse: 'And make ready for them all ye can of armed force and of horses tethered, that ye may dismay the enemy of God and your enemy and others besides them whom ye know not: God knoweth them. And whatsoever ye spend in the path of God, it will be repaid to you in full, and ye will not be wronged. And if they incline to peace, incline thou also to it and trust in God. Lo! He is the Hearer, the Knower'. VIII: 60-61.

the context of the on-going Iraq war as well as the first Iraq war in 1991, the Iran-Iraq war, the Soviet invasion of Afghanistan and the so-called *'jihadi'* resistance to it, the question of what constitutes *jihad* and whether Muslims are obligated individually and collectively, to participate in it, remains a central issue for Muslims worldwide. There is no doubt that these conflicts have created deep fissures in the Muslim body politic and deepened rifts within Muslim nations, various Islamic movements and Muslim communities.[71] Governments of Muslim states found themselves torn between popular opinion demanding solidarity with their Muslim brethren in Iraq and pressure of the United States and her allies to facilitate their occupation and 'war on terror'. This strain inevitably led to a war of *fatwas* where pro-government *fatwas* matched anti-government pronouncements in favour of Muslims under attack from the Western powers. Within Sunni Islam, the Sheikhs of al-Azhar University, Cairo, have an authoritative voice in advising an Islamic position. In recent years, they have been called upon to provide guidance to Muslims regarding *jihad* mainly in the form of issuing *fatwas* on the subject. Their scholarship has contributed towards a narrow reinterpretation of *jihad* and hence *siyar,* discouraging armed conflict. This approach has widened the rift between what may be described as 'establishment' Islam and its more radical counterparts including Hasan al-Banna, Syed Qutb and others, who emphasize the warlike characteristic of *jihad* and the dichotomy of the world into *dar-al-Islam* and *dar-al-harb*.[72] In fact, *fatwas* became an intellectual battleground where muftis presented opposing viewpoints regarding *siyar*, *jihad* and Muslim responses to American and Allied troops in Iraq and Saudi Arabia. Titles of academic articles included: 'Operation Desert Storm and the War of *Fatwas*'; 'The War of *Fatwas* and the *Fatwas* of War'[73] with scholars challenging the role of Muslim governments to pronounce the 'Islamic' position on war and peace. This state of confrontation and uncertainty continues and indeed appears to have escalated in the on-going Iraq war where 'Islamic' positions including those of al-Qaeda lay claims to authoritative declarations of the content of *siyar* and *jihad*.

---

[71] Haddad expressed similar thoughts in her study on *fatwas* following the first Iraq war in 1990-91.
[72] Tibi, *loc. cit.*, fn. 58, p. 183.
[73] Y.Y. Haddad, "Operation Desert Storm and the War of Fatwas", in M. K. Masud, B. Messick, and D.S. Powers (ed.), *Islamic Legal Interpretation Muftis and their Fatwas*, Oxford, Oxford University Press, 297-309; M. Khalifa, "The War of Fatwas and the Fatwas of War", cited in Haddad.

Fatwas as an Interpretative Vehicle of *Siyar* and *Jihad*: An Exploratory Overview in Light of 'Internet *Fatwas*' on the Iraq War and Muslim Responses to the Invasion[74]

As indicated above, one of the most powerful interpretative processes within the Islamic legal tradition lies in the role played by the institution of *ifta*, embracing all aspects of a Muslim's life. Despite this importance, compared to some other aspects of the Islamic legal tradition, muftis and their *fatwas* are an underexplored area in Western scholarly writing. It has acquired prominence in recent years as a result of (initially) the *fatwa* of Imam Khomeini issued against Salman Rushdie, author of The Satanic Verses; the Palestinian resistance to Israeli occupation and the invasion of Kuwait by Iraq in 1990. More recently, post-9/11 and its aftermath in the form of invasions of Afghanistan and Iraq, there appears to be a proliferation of *fatwas* seeking clarification and guidance on 'Islamically valid' responses of Muslims to these wars. Less publicized globally (until recently) are *fatwas* issued by what may be termed '*fatwa* institutions' or '*fatwa* committees', both 'official' and 'unofficial', responding to political, economic or other situations within Muslim jurisdictions.[75] The recent surge of *fatwas* has opened up discursive space for an ideological basis to the resistance in Iraq (as well as its precursors in the form of events of 9/11 and 7/7), inviting serious Western attention to this genre of the Islamic legal tradition placing it on the agenda of Western legal scholarship. Easily accessible English language translations of *fatwas*, originally issued in Arabic (less so in other languages), available on Internet sites, have led to an increasing number of 'fatwa-sighters'.

The increasing number of *fatwa* websites and the presence of Internet muftis led to the present exploratory study. Muqtedar Khan, an 'Internet alternative Mufti', in an interview with Emily Wax, a reporter with *The Washington Post*, made an interesting comment regarding this emerging 'generation' of Internet *muftis*: 'In the past there was only

---

[74] The present study confines itself to the discourse generated by internet *fatwas* in the backdrop of the Iraq war and the potential impact on *siyar*, *jihad* and international law. It recognizes the limitations of adopting such an approach and acknowledges that inferences arrived at and analysis based on the Internet *fatwas* accessed, is only exploratory in nature and may form the basis of a more detailed and comprehensive study on the subject.

[75] Such as the Al-Azhar House of *Fatwa*, the *Fiqh* Council of North America, the European Council for *Fatwas* and Research, the Islamic Fiqh Council, the Palestinian Scholars League, the Islamic Fiqh Academy India, the Permanent Committee for Research and *Ifta* (Saudi Arabia) and the Islamic Research Academy.

the local *mufti*. The Internet has opened up a variety of opinion. It's the globalization of the *mufti*.'[76] Bunt terms such online contexts 'Cyber Islamic Environments'.[77]

In order to address the questions set out in this article, I undertook a study of some Internet sites dedicated to *fatwas* on *jihad* in general and obligations of Muslims to support the resistance against the Allied invasion, in particular. The study is essentially exploratory and does not qualify either as comprehensive or exhaustive, nor does it purport to be representative in its sample.[78] The *fatwas* analyzed provide a preliminary insight into the range and variation of questions posed to muftis on the subject and reflective of the fluidity of the discourse amongst Muslim scholars as well as the laity.

The first website studied was www.islamonline.net. It has a well-organized homepage with a section dedicated to *fatwas*. The user has the option of reading the contents in Arabic or English and to identify the theme she/he wishes to seek guidance on. Between 14 August 2000 and 4 November 2007, a total of 287 *fatwas* were recorded under the theme of international relations and *jihad* covering a comprehensive range of international law issues.[79]

The titles of the questions posed reflect an amazing sense of awareness of norms of *siyar* as well as general international law and human rights, citizenship, private international law, issues of multiple identities of Muslims and so on. The questioners appear to be persons of all conceivable nationalities, male and female and of all ages and professions. Access to the Internet and being computer literate as well as being able to communicate in Arabic or English are serious limiting factors that rule out a large percentage of Muslims that are unable to read and write these two languages and/or unable to access the Internet.

After collecting *fatwas*, delivered on this website falling broadly within the *siyar* category of the Islamic legal tradition, I set about

---

[76] E. Wax, "The Mufti in the Chat Room: Islamic Legal Advisers Are Just a Click Away from Ancient Customs", *Washington Post* 31 July 1999, C01, <http://www.ijtihad.org/Mufti.htm> accessed 02 August 2008.

[77] Bunt, *loc. cit.*, fn. 3, p. 165.

[78] The Google search engine was employed in the first instance, to search for the theme: '*Fatwas* issued on *jihad* and the Iraq war'. This was further refined by a keyword search of 'fatwa', 'jihad', 'Imam Sistani', 'Al-zawahiri', 'Osama bin Laden' and 'Fatwas on Iraq war'. Only English translations of *fatwas* on the subject were included in the analysis and *fatwas* in Arabic and or other languages were not included in this preliminary study. After searching a range of Internet sites, the following *fatwas* were selected for analysis through a process of random sampling.

[79] It is interesting to note that the format and presentation of the *fatwa* remains the same as used in the classical period of Islamic jurisprudence.

to shortlist a few that appeared representative of the major issues highlighted in the present paper, *i.e.*, the main concerns and questions of Muslims globally, the invasion of Iraq; how are these questions being addressed through *fatwas* invoking the *shari'a* and *Siyar*; does this discussion and evolving discourse embedded within these *fatwas* have the potential of moving beyond websites impacting on the broader stage of globalized Muslim communities and Muslim state practice, or is it likely to remain within the confines of a cyber Islamic environment, to recall Bunt's phrase above.

The first *fatwa* is by Sheikh Ahmed Kutty issued on www.islamonline.net when the invasion on Iraq was imminent. It addresses a number of issues in the field of international law and relations from the viewpoint of a Muslim. This *fatwa* invokes solidarity with the Iraqis against the United States in the name of Islam and offers a range of options through which to express this solidarity and support. The *fatwa* is reproduced below:

> Question: In case the war on Iraq breaks out, what can Muslims do in order to help their brothers and sisters there? Is it allowed to fight Americans outside the Iraqi soil. Like in Kuwait and Saudi Arabia and other places?
>
> Answer: In the Name of Allah, Most Gracious, Most Merciful. All Praise and thanks are due to Allah, and peace and blessings be upon His Messenger.
>
> In case the American invasion on Iraq happens, then it is obligatory upon Muslims all over the world to help their fellow Iraqis in fending off this invasion and aggression with all possible means.
>
> As for fighting against the aggressive American troops, this is a basic and a required duty from all Muslim countries each according to its capabilities.
>
> In addition, Muslim peoples are required to declare their full sympathy with the Iraqi people. They are also required to totally deny and condemn the American invasion and aggression against Iraq. Part of the required steps they should apply is to boycott the American products and to earnestly implore Allah to grant victory to their Muslim brethren and to help them financially by all possible means.

The peoples in the Arab and Muslim world are required to do all what they can do to defy the existence of the American forces in their countries. They can do so through arranging peaceful demonstrations to declare their total rejection to the mere existence of the American troops on their soil and the use of their lands as a launching point of such troops against Iraq.

Not only that but those people should seriously ask their governments to end existence of such troops in their countries or at least not to give them facilities they need in their aggression against Iraq.

Allah Almighty knows best.

The above *fatwa* presents the prototype of the *fatwas* researched for the present study. It is important to note that the mufti recites the name of Allah and His Prophet, indicating that this opinion is delivered from an Islamic perspective, drawing upon Islamic sources and to the best of his knowledge and competence. The *fatwa* closes with the acknowledgement that this opinion is in no way a claim to the only truth/ opinion as only Allah knows best. This apparently religious invocation may also be construed as the *mufti's* disclaimer (to use a legal term) that he has done his best within the realm of human reason and that there may be other truths that he has not been able to extract from his knowledge of the Islamic legal sources.

As to the substance of the *fatwa*, if one were to remove 'religious' overtones from the opinion, it has a number of ingredients of international law norms of expressing concern, displeasure and protest at an illegal action or imminent action on the part of a member of the international community. Also noteworthy is the suggestion of the economic boycott, diplomatic disengagement, and disallowing troops of the aggressor to use neighbouring or neutral territory. The democratic right to peaceful protest is also stated to be one of several peaceful mechanisms to register protest against the imminent US invasion. A question that comes to mind regarding this *fatwa* is the following: while it imposes an obligation on Muslim countries to fight against the aggressive American troops, individual Muslims are told to defy the invasion through peaceful means. Why the distinction? Is *jihad* no longer a *fard ayn* (individual duty) as the *fatwa* decreed by the Azhar Academy below?

The second *fatwa* raising international law issues is in response to a questioner from Canada on 20 November 2006. The question is directed at Shaikh Ahmed Kutty:

    Question: Dear scholars, As-Salamu 'alaykum. In light of the current crisis in Iraq, what should be the attitude of all Muslims living there, in particular that of the Sunnis and Shiites towards one another and towards the occupying forces? Should these Muslims fight one another or try to come closer to one another in order to join forces against the invaders?

    Also, is it obligatory upon the Iraqi people to resist the American occupation and its authority? Jazakum Allah khayran.

    Answer: Wa 'alaykum As-Salamu wa Rahmatullahi wa Barakatuh.

    In the Name of Allah, Most Gracious, Most Merciful. All praise and thanks are due to Allah, and peace and blessings be upon His Messenger.

    Dear questioner, we are greatly pleased to receive your question which shows the confidence you place in us. May Allah reward you abundantly for your interest in knowing the teachings of Islam.

    In the first place, we would like to stress that it is a religious duty of Muslims to demonstrate remarkable solidarity among themselves regardless of their different inclinations. The Iraqis should mobilize themselves and constitute a united front so as to force the occupiers to leave their lands. In this regard, Muslims must stay away from committing any act that may weaken their strength.

    Responding to your question, Sheikh Ahmad Kutty a Senior Lecturer and Islamic Scholar at the Islamic Institute of Toronto, Ontario, Canada, states the following:

    To answer the first part of your question concerning the attitude of Iraqi Muslims with their different inclinations and sects, I would like to highlight the following:

1. I consider it a religious duty of every Muslim to establish solidarity among all Muslims regardless of sectarian differences.

2. We, as Muslims, must establish law and order, because anarchy and lawlessness cannot be tolerated in Islam at any time.

3. All Muslims should mobilize themselves and show a united front and force the occupiers to leave their lands.

4. We must open our hearts to Allah and seek His Mercy and Grace by earnestly establishing the laws of Allah within ourselves and by dealing with each other on terms of justice and compassion. Allah says: ("O ye who believe! If ye help Allah, He will help you and will make your foothold firm.") (Muhammad 47: 7)

By doing so, we merit and earn the support of Allah Almighty, for ultimately all victory belongs to those who are conscious of Allah. Allah Almighty says, ("And Moses said unto his people: Seek help in Allah and endure. Lo! the earth is Allah's. He giveth it for an inheritance to whom He will. And lo! the sequel is for those who keep their duty (unto Him).") (Al-'Araf 7: 128)

As to the second part of the question, concerning resisting the American invasion, I say that Muslims should never tolerate occupation of their lands, so they should present a united front of solidarity and impress upon the occupiers that they must vacate their territories.

However, Muslims must do this through using *hikmah* (wisdom) and strategic methods that are effective rather than simply resorting to rash methods that would only empower the invaders.

Islam does not allow us to commit collective suicide. He Almighty says, ("Spend your wealth for the cause of Allah, and be not cast by your own hands to ruin; and do good. Lo! Allah loveth the beneficent.") (Al-Baqarah 2: 195)

He Almighty also says, ("O ye who believe I Squander not your wealth among yourselves in vanity, except it be a trade by mutual consent, and kill not one another. Lo! Allah is ever Merciful unto you.") (An-Nisa' 4: 29)

> Thus, the methods we use must be appropriate to the circumstances so that the enemy will eventually be forced to leave.
>
> An extremely crucial point to remember here is that Muslims must stop bickering among themselves and abstain from all activities that would promote disunity and dissension among themselves. It is high time for Muslims to heed the call of Allah Almighty Who says, ("Lo! Allah loveth those who battle for His cause in ranks, as if they were a solid structure.") (As-Saff 61: 4)
>
> May Allah guide you, dear brother, to the straight path, and guide you to that which pleases Him, Amen.
>
> Allah Almighty knows best.

The above-cited *fatwa* reiterates the illegality of the Iraq invasion and the obligation of Muslims to defend the country and the faith. Simultaneously, it calls for restraint, caution and strategic wisdom in offering resistance to the invading army in Iraq. This *fatwa* does not expressly enjoin use of force against the occupying forces. It merely says Muslims should unite 'and force the occupiers to leave their lands'; 'should present a united front of solidarity and impress upon the occupiers that they must vacate their territories'. 'However, Muslims must do this through using hikmah (wisdom) and strategic methods that are effective rather than simply resorting to rash methods that would only empower the invaders.' Yet it invokes a verse (As-Saff 61: 4) that expressly talks about physical *jihad*. Meaning and implication of 'caution', 'strategic wisdom', are not explicitly set out in the context of the question raised.

A third *fatwa* chosen for analysis, was solicited by a questioner from Riyadh on 11 March 2003 in relation to a ruling of the al-Azhar scholars:

> Question: Dear scholars, As-Salamu 'alaykum. We heard about Al-Azhar's statement regarding the attack on Iraq and the Middle East, describing it as an unjust aggression, a new Crusade that has no international legitimacy, and that Al-Azhar called for *jihad*. Is this true? Jazakum Allah khayran

Answer: Wa 'alaykum As-Salamu wa Rahmatullahi wa Barakatuh. In the Name of Allah, Most Gracious, Most Merciful.

All praise and thanks are due to Allah, and peace and blessings be upon His Messenger.

Dear brother Riyadh, we would like to thank you for the great confidence you place in us, and we implore Allah Almighty to help us serve His cause and render our work for His Sake.

Let us stress that Islam does not call for violence; rather it abhors all forms of violence and terrorism, whether against Muslims or non-Muslims. Islam, moreover, calls for peace, cooperation, and maintaining justice, and provides for the happiness and welfare of humanity as a whole. This fact is declared in the Qur'an when Allah says: "Allah commands justice, the doing of good, and liberality to kith and kin, and He forbids all shameful deeds, and injustice and rebellion: He instructs you, that ye may receive admonition." (An-Nahl: 90)

Islam makes it obligatory upon Muslims to stand by the oppressed regardless of their race, color, religion or affiliation and say NO to the oppressor and ask him to respond to the voice of reason and justice.

Bearing all this in mind, the Islamic Research Academy at Al-Azhar has issued a statement explaining its view of the prospective war on Iraq and calling upon Muslims to unify their efforts and join forces in facing this illegitimate and aggressive war. In its statement Al-Azhar declares:

The Islamic Research Academy has studied the serious events occurring in our Arab and Islamic World and the signs of evil and destruction in our present world. They are a result of power's mania that disregards all values, norms and international laws for which humanity has striven, sacrificed lives and wealth, and withstood pain in order to declare and guarantee them due respect.

The Academy has discussed these events, considering the signs of destruction and evils surrounding the Arab and Islamic World, which are represented by the military troops armed with the most powerful and dangerous weapons of destruction.

Al-Azhar's Academy has realized that our Arab and Islamic *Ummah* (nation) and even our religious belief (Islam) are undoubtedly the main goal of these military troops, whose targets will be millions of the members of our *Ummah* as well as our belief, sacred places and all sources of power and wealth that Arabs and Muslims possess. The first stage to achieve these goals is to attack Iraq and occupy its land and seize its abundant reserve of oil wealth.

The Academy has also realized that the persistence to attack Iraq is, no doubt, just a beginning to be followed by other attacks targeting the rest of the Arab countries. The anti-Arab and anti-Islam powers have declared that after grabbing hold of Iraq, they will divide and arrange positions in the Arab region in a way that achieves American and Israeli interests and put an end to the Palestinian resistance.

In light of all the above-mentioned circumstances, Al-Azhar's Academy issues to all the powers in the civilized world and the peace-loving forces as well as our Arab and Islamic *Ummah* the following declaration:

First, the Academy appreciates and hails the countries that condemned attacking Iraq and rejected the prospective war for their stances and diplomatic striving in the United Nations and UN Security Council to stop war.

Second, the Academy welcomes and stresses the importance of the stands of people all over the world and in America, particularly those who declared their rejection of war and called for resorting to peaceful means to solve the crisis under the umbrella of International Law and the Security Council.

Third, the Academy hails and backs the resolution of the Islamic Summit, which refused attacking Iraq and stressed the necessity of resorting to peaceful means in solving the crisis, considering this as a permanent declaration of all Arabs and Muslims, stressing their unanimous refusal of attacking Iraq.

In light of all the current events, most people think that attacking Iraq is inevitable. According to Islamic Shari'ah, *jihad* becomes an individual duty *(fard 'ayn)* upon all Muslims if the enemy occupies a Muslim land. Our Arab and Muslim *Ummah* will face a new inhumane campaign that aims to deprive us of our land, belief, honor, and dignity.

Accordingly, the Islamic Research Academy at Al-Azhar calls upon all Arabs and Muslims all over the world to be on high alert to defend themselves, their belief and lands. They should all hold fast to their religion, not separate, and forget all their internal differences. The Academy calls upon all Arabs and Muslims not to surrender to prospective attacks, as Allah has guaranteed to render His religion victorious. Finally, the Academy reminds (Muslims) of Allah's saying: "Allah will certainly aid those who aid His (Cause). Lo! Allah is Strong, Almighty." (Al-Hajj: 40)

Allah Almighty knows best.

This *fatwa* echoes the contents of the first two on the subject. The tone in a number of paragraphs appears to be more in line with contemporary international law. There is an acknowledgement of the United Nations, the Security Council and norms of international law generally[80]. At the same time, it draws upon *Qur'anic* sources to invoke justification for armed *jihad*, but using it as defensive rather than offensive/aggressive

---

[80] Note the mention of phrases such as 'illegal war' and 'inhumane campaign to deprive us of our land'. This *fatwa* from al-Azhar, considered the base of 'establishment' Sunni Islam, however, is different from the position adopted by al-Azhar during the first Gulf War when it justified the American invasion of Iraq.

jihad.⁸¹ The *fatwa* is also an example of the ordinary Muslim's concern regarding 'Islamicness' of actions and issues around her/him (legal and non-legal).⁸² The third *fatwa* above merely reproduces the *fatwa* given by the Islamic Research Academy in Al-Azhar (which expressly calls for physical *jihad*). It neither endorses it nor rejects it, thus raising a question in jurisprudential terms of *taqlid*, imitation or following another.

A second website, http://english.bayynat.org.lblFatawa/index.htm owned by one Sayyid Fadlullah, described as a 'religious authority', also issued *fatwas* on national defence and self-defence in his (online) collection *Al-Fatawa Al Wadeha*.⁸³ He states that according to the present-day international codes of conduct, any aggression directed through occupation or any other form against any Muslim state, or a country where Muslims form the majority must be regarded as aggression against the population. In any such invasion by a foreign power among the 'infidels', it is the duty of the people by way of *wajibun kifa'ie*, to use (all means at their disposal) to liberate their land and push back the aggressor. If they fail, it becomes obligatory on those closest, then the closer to them and so on, to come to their rescue.⁸⁴

As noted in an earlier section of this paper, *fatwas* are opinions of individual muftis or groups of muftis that vary in the position and approach adopted regarding questions posed to them. The range of opinions offered on the same subject is potentially infinite and one that in the context of our present study gives cause for concern and confusion.

---

⁸¹ Sheikh Hamed Al-Ali, a prominent Kuwaiti Sheikh, issued a *fatwa* posted at <http://memri.org/bin/articles.cgi?Page=archives&Area=sd&ID=SP156307 > that describes the resistance in Iraq as defensive *jihad* stating: "The banner [of jihad in Iraq] is a banner of defensive jihad. Generally speaking, the [members of] the known jihad groups [in Iraq] are righteous men who have spared no effort in jihad and have all brought the [Muslim] nation a tremendous victory ... Nevertheless, [Iraq] is still under occupation. They must continue their jihad until the final victory is achieved, and nothing must distract or hinder them from [achieving] this goal. Only after [they achieve it] should they, along with everybody else, begin to lay down the foundations for the revival of Islam and [for the establishment of] an inclusive Islamic rule that will incorporate all the forces of *da'wa* and *jihad*, [as well as] the rest of the nation."

⁸² Whilst the *qadi* pronounces binding judgments in response to questions arising from the litigant public and at times with assistance of *muftis*, *fatwas* have a wider and more informal remit in responding to questions that were not necessarily litigational (in the legal sense). They could be clarifications of existing circumstances and/or legal rules, moral or social, ethical, political and economic questions.

⁸³ <http://english.bayynat.org.lb/Fatawa/index.htm>.

⁸⁴ This website and its *fatwa* collection are not restricted to pronouncements on *jihad* but also contain opinions affecting all spheres of life, from the personal to the political, moral and economic.

Hence, *fatwa* 'proliferation' presents examples of *'jihad*ists' including Al Zarqawi who validate the use of force and killings by claiming that: it is permissible to commit this evil- indeed, it is even required in order to ward off a greater evil, namely the evil of suspending *jihad*. To claim that (such means of war) are not permissible here, especially in light of present form of fighting, means inevitable suspending *jihad* and stopping it-indeed, burying it alive and completely shutting the gate of *jihad* ... This inevitable means surrendering the land and the believers to the hands of infidels who bitterly hate Islam and its people, allowing them to impose at will humiliation and inferior status on Islam and its people, ... [85]

How do the various *fatwas* discussed above as well as ones available on the many websites, differ from one another? For instance, a *fatwa* handed down by the Islamic Research Academy declares *jihad* as an individual obligation (*fard ayn*) that every Muslim must discharge. But the *fatwa* pronounced by Sayyid Fadlullah states that: 'it is the duty of the people by way of *wajibun kifa'ie*, (*fard kifaya*) to use (all means at their disposal) to liberate their land and push back the aggressor', *i.e.*, it is a collective obligation dischargeable by some people in the *Ummah* on behalf of all.

The foregoing selection of *fatwas* are drawn from a range of '*fatwa-giving*' websites that have emerged over the past decade. They are but a very small sample of the available *fatwas* studied and by no means representative of the questions and responses of the global Muslim communities. Despite the limitation of the present study, it is submitted that the *fatwas* do provide some useful insights into the use of this interpretative tool within the Islamic legal tradition. Muslims globally appear to refer to it to raise questions and address issues affecting their lives, communities, countries and the world they live in. In particular, we have focused on *fatwas* that have generated a discourse on the impact of the Iraq war on the Islamic legal tradition, institutions of *siyar* and *jihad* and more broadly, contemporary international law. The sample analyzed raise a number of important points in informing our understandings of views of Muslims on norms and principles of *siyar*

---

[85] <http://www.islamtoday.net>. Likewise Saudi clerics Al-'Odeh and Al-Hawaii have issued several *fatwas* pronouncing the legitimacy of *jihad* in Iraq. A communiqué of 26 Saudi clerics was published on the Al-'Odeh official website (published in November 2004) sanctioning *jihad* against the United States in Iraq. Despite Al-'Odeh's claim that the communiqué calls upon Iraqis only to resist the occupation in Iraq, it was widely regarded as a call upon all Muslims, Iraqis and non-Iraqis alike, to support jihad on US forces in Iraq. See <http://www.islamtoday.net>. a website supervised by one of the signatories, Sheikh Salman Al-'Odeh.

and the role and obligations of Muslims, individually and at a collective level. The concluding part of this article presents some observations and reflections in this regard.

Siyar, Jihad, Fatwas and International Law: Past, Present and Futures in a Globalized World

One of the most publicized events today is the invasion of Iraq and the resultant resistance against occupation of that country. All parties to the conflict, caught in the grip of competing interests, invoke a range of legalities to provide legitimacy for their actions and appropriate the moral high ground. Materially and politically advantaged, the alliance of predominantly Western governments aided by a few non-Western allies, are waging the 'war on terror'. For the alliance, this war is being waged in the name of human rights and democracy, the aspiration being for Iraqis, indeed, the whole world, to embrace it as a global ideology. 'Others', equally robust in advocating their position of resistance to this alliance, describe it as a 'war of terror' (recalling Upendra Baxi's expression[86]) on the sovereign states of Iraq and Afghanistan in particular and Muslims in general. The ideology stimulating and propelling this counter-war (of resistance) ranges from contemporary international law principles demanding respect for Iraqi sovereignty, notions of Iraqi nationalism, as well as a global appeal to *jihad* and solidarity from a universal Muslim *Ummah* (nation) derived from the principles of *siyar* and the Islamic legal tradition. This article therefore set out to explore the extent to which the Iraq war and resistance to the occupation of the country has generated a discourse both within the Islamic legal tradition and in international law in general. It problematized the concepts of *siyar*, *jihad* and *fatwas* as discursive sites in Muslim legal and political history. It initiated the discussion by outlining traditional contours of the Islamic legal tradition highlighting the plurality of its sources and juristic techniques. It also noted two parallel trends in its evolution: the formal, scholarly and juristic endeavour to understand the intention of the Qur'an and its interpretation by the prophet Muhammad (recorded as *hadith*). Simultaneously and equally important is the urge and autonomy of the common Muslim to explore, understand and implement

---

[86] See U. Baxi, "The 'War *on* Terror' and the 'War *of* Terror': Nomadic Multitudes, Aggressive Incumbents, and the 'New' International Law – Prefatory Remarks on Two 'Wars'", *Osgoode Hall Law Journal* 2005, 43, p. 7-43.

'Islamic law' to the best of their knowledge and ability. *Fatwas* may be seen as a critical response to this urge of accessing and understanding 'Islamic' law from below. In the context of the present study, there is evidence that *fatwas* as an interpretative vehicle, has grown in stature, profile and use mainly through the mass media (Internet, audio and visual recordings and dissemination thereof). Akil N Awan notes, " ... the traditional *ulama* (religious scholars) are no longer considered to be the ultimate repositories for moral authority and guidance they once were"[87]. Rather than remaining a purely academic and jurists' activity, the discourse on what is 'Islamically valid' has widened its remit to include the concerns and understandings of common Muslims.[88]

But the present exploration in the field of Internet *fatwas* also alerts us to the danger of Internet muftis and *fatwas*, "With the advent of globalization and an age of virtual *fatwas*, it can prove increasingly more difficult for the uninitiated to discern the authentic and eminently trustworthy from those who are not."[89]

The question that the present study therefore raises is the following: whilst the Internet is a facilitatory tool for Muslim communities in accessing responses to questions they perceive as critical to their lives and faith, what is the danger of this proliferation of Internet muftis and *fatwas*? What are the potential dangers of anyone being able to claim or be accepted as an authority on the subject simply by expressing one's opinion online? A faceless person on the Internet handing down factually incorrect or ill-informed advice? And finally, in the absence of a uniform, agreed, global, authoritative voice across the Muslim world, regarding the accuracy or otherwise of a *fatwa*, what/how might *fatwa* pronouncements be regulated, if at all?[90] This point is evident in the disparate views reflected in the sample of *fatwas* presented in the present study. In Bunt's words:

---

[87] A.N. Awan, "Antecedents of Islamic Political Radicalism Among Muslim Communities in Europe", *Political Science & Politics* 2008, 41, 13-17.

[88] The identity of hundreds of questioners seeking *fatwas* supports this view. They included students, researchers, members of political parties, public servants, members of the armed forces and so on. *Fatwas* also potentially pose a challenge to the (Muslim) state's legislative prerogative of *siyasa Shari'a* and *qanun* as it provides alternative opinions on issues of public importance such as supporting the resistance in Iraq, not paying taxes to a government that fails to provide social justice and an Islamic form of government. This is in keeping with its historical antecedents. See Coulson, Rahim, Fyzee, Hallaq, Masud and others, and Jackson.

[89] Awan, *loc. cit.*, fn. 86, p. 16.

[90] Websites purporting to be the public face of al-Qaeda are an example of this concern raised.

The Internet is unique as a media form, in that it offers individual or minority views an opportunity to present themselves to a wide readership internationally. It can be difficult to determine the difference between an 'official' site and one generated by an individual. What makes a website 'authoritative' and 'Islamic' is a key question to consider when reading Cyber Islamic Environments, particularly for readers who may not be overly familiar with the nuances and various shades of meaning that exist between diverse Muslim interests.[91]

A further observation of the present study is that the Iraq war has thrown up existing as well as new issues within the framework of *siyar* as the Muslim worldview of international relations. This includes *jihad*, the modern nation state and multiple identities of Muslims residing within its borders, as well as the global Muslim *Ummah*. The range of *fatwas* reviewed reveal a consistently similar view regarding armed struggle as only one of several aspects of *jihad*. Muftis emphasize, in line with norms of public international law, that armed struggle is the last and NOT the first response to aggression. Peaceful avenues of resolution must be exhausted before undertaking armed *jihad*. Muftis in the sample surveyed, appear unanimous in their opinion that the situation in Iraq calls for armed *jihad* and that this struggle is defensive in nature. As Mahmoudi notes, 'when [*jihad*] is used by religious, resistance or other groups and individuals, the purpose is however to carry out "radical resistance to Western 'aggression' against Muslim peoples"'[92]

The *fatwas* reviewed in the present study conceptualize the territorial nation state vis-à-vis a global Muslim *Ummah*. They not only place their discussion of the Iraq invasion and resistance to it in the framework of *jihad*, and a universal Muslim *Ummah* tradition but also forcefully reinforce this approach. Viewed in this light, it would seem that global questioners and their global respondent muftis place a significant premium on the belief that all Muslims are bound together in a common fraternity based on their commonly held faith. The evolutionary element in the *fatwa* discussion of the *Ummah* is acknowledgement of the territorial state, Muslim and non-Muslim as well as the United Nations and other regional organizations including the OIC. Similarly Mahmoudi remarks, 'even if in normal political

---

[91] Bunt, *loc. cit.*, fn. 3, p. 175.
[92] A. Sachedina, "From defensive to Offensive Warfare: The Use and Abuse of Jihad in the Muslim World", in J.I. Coffey and C.T. Mathews (ed.), *Religion, Law and the Role of Force: A Study of Their Influence on Conflict and on Resolution*, Ardsley, NY, Transnational Publishers Inc., quoted in Mahmoudi, *loc. cit.*, fn. 62, p. 108.

rhetoric politicians may refer to "just war" or *jihad*, they still try to defend their positions legally by referring to the [United Nations] Charter and the norms of international law.'[93] It is suggested that in light of the above observations, *siyar* has, albeit marginally, brought within its fold a modified *Ummah* whose members are global as well as members of territorial states. As I have stated elsewhere,

> The contours of contemporary *siyar* as well as its sources have undergone an enormous modification both structural as well as ideological. It no longer draws inspiration from a pristine *Shari'a* based on the primary and secondary sources of Islamic law but is subject increasingly to *siyasa* (state power) *Shari'a*.[94]

In other words, Muslim states have acquired unto themselves the power to make laws (*qanun*) based on their understanding of the norms of *Shari'a*. Muslim state practice in the domestic and international arena has thus undergone major reconstruction.[95] The presumption of unqualified universality of historical *siyar* encompassing the Muslim *Ummah* becomes questionable in the face of *siyasa Shari'a* and individual Muslim states promulgate overriding laws of entry and exit for persons within their jurisdiction. State practice of Muslim jurisdictions has moulded *siyar* to become more open to contemporary realities of coexistence in an increasingly globalized world.[96]

Historically, *siyar* was rarely called upon to address and develop comprehensive norms and guidance regarding plural identities, *e.g.*, a Muslim also being a Pakistani and a British citizen, an American of Iraqi origin and a Muslim and so on. The Islamic legal tradition, in particular *siyar,* is thus under pressure to respond to the anxieties of Muslims in Muslim majority countries as well as in the 'Western' predominantly non-Muslim jurisdictions and having to make decisions impacting on their lives and those of their families and communities. A number of *fatwas* seek to resolve the question of whether as a British or American Muslim it is 'Islamically' valid to go to war against a fellow Muslim

---

[93] Mahmoudi, *loc. cit.*, fn. 62, p. 109.
[94] S.S. Ali, "The Twain Doth Meet! A Preliminary Exploration of the Theory and Practice of As-*Siyar* and International Law in the Contemporary World", in J. Rehman and S. Breau (ed.), *Religion, Human Rights and International Law: A Critical Examination of Islamic State Practices*, Leiden, Martinus Nijhoff Publishers, 2007, 93.
[95] O. Arabi, *Studies in Modern Islamic Law and Jurisprudence*, The Hague, Kluwer Law International, 2001, 18.
[96] Ali, *loc. cit.*, fn. 93, p. 93.

in Iraq or elsewhere.[97] From the sample studied for the present project, responses are not categoric and there does appear a certain degree of ambivalence in the responses provided. The dilemma of divided loyalties is not confined to the Muslim diaspora and has affected millions of Muslim citizens residing in Muslim countries[98] as well. A significant result of the Iraq (and Afghanistan) invasion was alignment of some Muslim governments with the United States and her allies in the so-called 'war on terror'. This brought into serious question the 'Muslimness' of these governments vis-à-vis their Muslim population, creating a vacuum of credibility and legitimacy. Disappointed with establishment Islam (represented by, *e.g.*, governments of Pakistan, Jordan, Egypt, Saudi Arabia and others) as well as the US-backed Iraqi government, they rallied around traditional modes of validating their feelings and actions against the aggressors including acquiring *fatwas*. Ought Muslims of these countries to defy their governments and rise to the defence of the Iraqis and in so doing, undermine their governments through acts of violence? Who could the Muslim population of these countries trust to respond to these and similar questions from the perspective of *siyar*? The institution of *ifta* verbally available through the Friday sermon, audio, through private radio channels, and visually through private television channels as well as websites; became a popular and sought-after method of seeking guidance about how Muslims should react to the crisis from an Islamic perspective. But, despite minor differences in opinion as to when a Muslim is obliged to defend her/his faith and territory against aggressors, a broad consensus on some crucial issues falling within the broad remit of *siyar,* is evident.

This study also reveals some *fatwas* canvassing a revival of the historical *siyar* divisions of the world as either falling into *dar-ul-harb* or *dar-ul-Islam*. Theoretical perceptions of the world as *dar-ul-harb* and *dar-ul-Islam* are now being translated into popular perceptions of the

---

[97] For instance, a question posted on the website www.islamonline.net on 14 October 2003 by a questioner called Haneef from the United States: "As Salaamu 'alaykum. Are Muslims allowed to join an un-Islamic military such as that of the United States, where they may be put in a position to kill a fellow Muslim brother or sister? Also what is Allah's Punishment for this if such thing happens? Because I hear some Muslim leaders say it is okay to join the US Military. Jazakallah Khayran?" Another questioner, Salah, asked www.islamonline.net *muftis* on 20 March 2003: "Dear scholars, As-Salamu 'alaykum. Are Muslim American soldiers allowed to participate in the war on Iraq? Jazakum Allah khayran".

[98] By Muslim country I mean those countries where the predominant population espouses the Muslim faith.

United States and her allies as constituting *dar-ul-harb* against which defensive (and in some cases, offensive) *jihad* is considered legitimate. The neutral space of *dar-u-sulh, dar-ul-ahd* or *dar-ul-aman* consisting of friendly non-Muslim jurisdictions is shrinking since the invasions of Afghanistan and Iraq. This mirrors the rigidity of approach and action of "you are either with us or against us" policy of international relations espoused by the United States during the Bush era. Thus, the *dar-ul-harb* (abode of war) of historical *siyar* (meaning the non-Muslim world) now translates into the *dar-ul-harb* of the secular West (meaning the 'rogue' Muslim world). Both sets of regimes are thus building their own adversarial versions of *dar-ul-harb*.

For at least two centuries, the international law scene has witnessed the hegemony of Western legal doctrine. Scant attention is paid to exploring and including concepts of non-Western legal systems including *siyar* in discussions on the modern law of nations, including humanitarian law and laws of armed conflict.[99] International law, including international human rights law, are termed 'international' and 'universal' but this internationalization and universalization fails to recognize and engage with other legal systems including the Islamic legal tradition. Framing this debate in terms of compatibility/incompatibility in An-Na`im's view, is to present an either/or situation to Muslim communities and an inappropriate frame of reference to generate a positive discourse. He believes that transformative processes through serious and sincere engagement between various legal and knowledge systems is the way forward to evolve a truly 'international' law.[100] Drawing upon these views, the present study submits that it is no longer possible to ignore rules developed in the Islamic legal system as regards the conduct of inter-state relations including laws of war, which even today form a coherent body of rules comparable to any legal system of the world. By generating an international law discourse on the Iraq war through the lens of *siyar, fatwas* and other Muslim discursive sites have attracted the attention of the world community inviting engagement with the Islamic legal tradition and its concepts and normative framework. It has been argued that *siyar* generates a legal and moral doctrine, including rules of humanitarian law, treatment of prisoners etc. conceptually similar

---

[99] A few exceptions include the drafting process of the United Nations Convention on Rights of the Child and some comparative academic discourse on water policy. See T. Naff and J. Dellapenna, "Can There Be Confluence? A Comparative Consideration of Western and Islamic Fresh Water Law", *Water Policy* 2002, 4, p. 465-489.

[100] A.A. An-Na`im, "Why Should Muslims Abandon *Jihad*? Human Rights and the Future of International Law" *Third World Quarterly* 2006, 27, p. 785-797.

to later Western constructs.[101] This discourse has found a variety of contemporary manifestations, of which the use of Internet discussions, chat rooms, email and *fatwas* is one. In Bunt's words:

> The Internet's application, in conjunction with related computer applications such as 'chat rooms' and e-mail, makes a significant impact in creating a cohesive electronic identity in cyberspace for Islamic political agendas and concerns. Whether this means that it also contributes to a global electronic *umma* could be open to question: many political platforms are interlinked, but the concept of a free-flowing dialogue and shared agendas between all shades of opinion remains an aspiration rather than a reality. Whilst issues regarding accessibility still remain, increasingly for participants as well as observers with access to the Internet, Cyber Islamic Environments are a primary medium for religious, political and ideological guidance.[102]

A final observation on the impact of the Iraq war on *siyar* and international law: norms of international law espousing and cherishing state sovereignty and inter-state relations stand fragmented, diminished and challenged in a post-Iraq invasion world. State practice is no longer the primary source of international law and non-state actors, in the form of institutions, organizations and communities, make robust and challenging inputs into the normative discourse in this field. Despite the rhetoric of many Muslims that international law and the language of globalization is an alien and oppressive construct, almost all the *fatwas* reviewed in this study employ contemporary language of international law and international relations. Communication systems and technology invented and employed by the West, including the Internet, are increasingly being appropriated by the most traditional, conservative mufti to disseminate responses to questions covering all aspects of life. A 'popular', accessible version of contemporary Muslim jurisprudence, responsive to questions of (Islamic) international law in a post(Iraq) invasion world is emerging, demanding global engagement.

---

[101] T.S. Thomas, "Jihad's Captives: Prisoners of Wars in Islam", *Journal of Legal Studies* 2002, p. 12; *US A. F. Acad.*, 87-101; Bennoune and others.

[102] G.R. Bunt, *Virtually Islamic: Computer-mediated Communication and Cyber Islamic Environments*, Cardiff, University of Wales Press, 2000, 102-103.

The Indian Dimension of An-Na`im's *Islam and the Secular State*

Prakash Shah

The Global Relevance of *Islam and the Secular State*

As a London LLM student in the early 1990s I recall An-Na`im's writing (An-Na`im 1990a) as one of the few then available discussions of human rights not only within the Islamic world, but also more widely in non-Western contexts. At the time, the voice of non-Western jurisprudence, particularly in light of the universal claims of essentially Western concepts of human rights, was hardly heard and, even in the post-cold war period, this field is still not exactly replete with deeper reflections about the significance and relevance of human rights concepts and ideas for non-Western peoples. An-Na`im's contributions therefore stand out as the foremost in that field.

An-Na`im's writings also went beyond, on the one hand, the glib and complacent assertions of some apologist Muslims who tended to say that Islam was naturally compatible with human rights and, on the other hand, the strategy of those Islamists who insisted that everything must be based on Islam. Instead, An-Na`im was so securely grounded in the Islamic tradition that he was not afraid to argue that, in times past and in the contemporary era, Islamic societies face major problems in terms of the treatment of women and of minorities, problems about which human rights ideals were at least a partial answer, as long as they could be adequately domesticated (An-Na`im 1990b). Some of this earlier thinking is continued and built upon in *Islam and Secular State*, where An-Na`im also confronts other problems such as the role of the state and the need to carve out and recognise a secular space which is the domain of civic reason, not empty of religious concerns but, at the same time, a space of compromise where a *modus vivendi* among *all* citizens, and groups of citizens, can be worked out.

The book *Islam and the Secular State* naturally deserves deeper reflection by the ongoing collaboration of multiple minds and perspectives of the kind assembled in the workshop out of which this book emerges. However, much will naturally depend on the reception of the book within the Muslim *ummah* (global community of Muslims) for it is they who must test their ideas against its challenges, and this should guard us against academic elitism. If the book's message does not 'speak to' academicians, this may partly be because it has not necessarily been addressed to us. But while the addressees of the book are primarily meant to be Muslims (9), I think a wider readership would gain much from the intensive *ijtihad* (juristic effort) which must have been exerted in its writing.

In discussing, in a few words, the Indian dimension of *Islam and the Secular State* I must first declare my interest as a non-Muslim and see no reason, even being mindful that I may not be part of the primary intended addressees of the book, why I should not find something within it of value. I found it particularly interesting and important that An-Na'im confronts the Indian dimension in his book. This may partly have to do with my own biography and the parallels An-Na'im's work introduces and the mirror images which it produces. An-Na'im is an African Muslim, taking a deep interest *inter alia* in India. I myself was born in Kenya of parents who were themselves born in Gujarat, India. We, I think, share the sense of an Indo-Islamic-African nexus in our lives and studies. Not that such globality and transnationalism is unique to us. However, An-Nai'im speaks as a Muslim from within the Islamic fold, whereas I comment as an outsider with an interest in global legal pluralism.

Our lives have also brought us into deep contact with the West and we have been privileged to gain access to the Western academic world through which we can develop our ideas and critiques not only about the problems of our societies of origin but also of the West and its troubled historical encounter with the rest of the world. To overcome modernity and colonialism is also to come to terms with the Western impact on our mother cultures and countries so that we can chart our way into a post-modernity and post-coloniality, efforts which of necessity have had to last longer than the formal process of decolonisation. The 'decolonisation of the social sciences', an academic reflection of personal struggles which are taking place daily, is a critical agenda and unfinished process today. Discussing the Indian case, An-Na'im explicitly asks us to think along those lines when he says (179-180):

> One aspect of the difficulty is that recollections of ideas and the meaning of institutions and relationships of the precolonial past are filtered through the lenses of European notions of what counts as history and how to interpret it. Another aspect is that possibilities of implementing policies emerging from such recollections are inhibited by ways in which the world today is organized and operated on the basis of European knowledge and

understanding. To achieve continuity of historical experiences in the process of building constitutionalism over time ... Indians need to reconnect to their precolonial past as if colonialism and its aftermath never happened. But since colonialism and its aftermath did happen, the challenge here is to the imagination of Indians to see and act on what might have happened, and to seek ways to read their own history in the most positive light possible.

While directed to Indians, this sentiment is extended throughout the book, first and foremost, to the worldwide community of Muslims. An-Na`im is therefore concerned to challenge the claim of an Islamic state as a postcolonial discourse that relies on European notions of the state and positive law. More strongly he says (7):

The notion of an Islamic state is in fact a postcolonial innovation based on a European model of the state and a totalitarian view of law and public policy as instruments of social engineering by the ruling elites.

In expressing such forthright but incisive criticism An-Na`im identifies a much wider problem for law and legal theory and, while set within the context of Muslim societies, his critique should be regarded as a serious contribution to a post-modern vision of law which is of relevance globally. It is possible to extend his critique, I believe, to all parts of the world where the belief now strongly persists, particularly among legal professionals of all kinds, that law is the law made by the state; otherwise it is either not proper law at all or is at best a deficient form of extra-legal regulation. This positivist and modernist 'colonial consciousness' (Balagangadhara 2006) appears to apply as much to the generality Indian lawyers (Menski 2003: 3-11).

This ideology has done much damage to the state-society-religion balance. Indulging in counterfactual thinking for a moment, it might be considered that, were it not for the intervention of colonialism and modernity, these elements would have interacted in much more harmonious forms. In fact, this job of recalibrating among various constitutive legal elements – in his case those of Muslim law – seems to be the massive task that An-Na`im argues for and elaborates in *Islam and the Secular State*. An-Na`im goes through a fairly detailed explanation of Muslim history to explain how such balance has been achieved in times past and how the lessons of that history, which require much modesty among state officials and religious spokespersons, continue to be of relevance in the contemporary period. Each aspect of law – be it state law (*kanoon*), the religious law (*shari'a*) or social laws (*urf, adat, riwaj*) – must be recognised to have its own role, although each might also influence the other in complex conglomerations of legal pluralism or 'inter-legality' (Santos 1995). In this sense, An-Na`im's work echoes writings by others who discuss the non-singularity, indeed, the inherently plural essence of law in non-Western contexts (Menski 2006) as well as in Western contexts (Berman 1983), no matter how much that legal reality has been denied particularly in the West. The non-recognition of aspects of Muslim and other minority laws in Europe today is, at least in part, a direct consequence of the strangulation of legal pluralism in the Western legal consciousness.

I hope in what I have said so far that it is evident that An-Na`im's book should provide the locus for many a fruitful discussion and debate about the nature of law and regulation in Muslim societies, but also of law globally. For reasons of space, and not wishing for this discussion to descend into some sort of hagiography of *alim* An-Na`im, I turn to introducing some of the ways in which the debate could be moved further into the interesting terrain which *Islam and Secular State* pushes us.

India and Secularism

The choice of India is a fascinating one for *Islam and the Secular State*. Unlike the other countries, Turkey and Indonesia, which are also discussed in the book in some detail, Muslims are seen as being in a minority position in India. This characterisation is predicated on the assumption of a 'majority' of Hindus which really comes about as an 'artefact of census categorisation' which casts Hindus as a *residual* class (Poddar 2009). However, one must, as An-Na`im does, have some regard for the pre-partition history of India where Muslim civilisation, culture and religion have had a profound influence to arguably lead to the emergence of an Indo-Islamic civilisation, the boundaries of which stretch beyond the political borders of modern, post-colonial India. Nevertheless, and despite this history, Muslims today find themselves as a vulnerable set of minority communities within the Indian state. They are often proxy hate objects for the existence of an unneighbourly and virtually ungovernable Pakistan next door, and depleted in numbers and talent because of the huge emigration that occurred in the months preceding and following the partition of 1947.[1] All South Asian countries continually experience a people drain due to the global market for skill and talent and the emigrants' own desire to do better or to escape problems at home, in the process transnationalising their cultures and laws to the diasporic sphere. In December 2008 I was informed by a Nepali restaurateur that, just in Leuven, there are some 700 Nepalis. Still, unlike other minorities in India, Muslims are not so few in number that they can easily be neglected, like the less vocal Christians[2], Parsis and the virtually disappeared Jews.

The analysis of the Indian dimension in *Islam and the Secular State*, and its account of the vulnerability of Muslims in contemporary India, is based largely on a taken-for-granted vocabulary of 'religion' and 'faith'. This creates problems for Indians most of whose traditions are not based on religion. This sounds like an odd thing to argue since it is conventional wisdom that Indians are very religious and spiritual people, despite the fact that they unleash vicious fury against fellow citizens from time to time, and perhaps increasingly so. Many Indians would indeed be aghast at the charge that they have no religion. To analyse this problem one needs to go back to the time of the British encounter with India. As De Roover and Balagangadhara (2007) show, the British assumed that they were tolerant and secular, but in so doing brought in Protestant concepts to interpret their experiences of India. On the assumption that 'religion' was a cultural universal and that all peoples had one, Indians too were assumed to have religion, 'Hinduism'[3], and that their customs and rituals could be seen as the expression of the beliefs of their religion.

Not unlike earlier Islamic understandings of Indians, it was thought that their religious beliefs were false beliefs leading to worship of false gods. However, the British also thought that whatever the correctness of the Indians' beliefs, those beliefs motivated their actions. This was a misrepresentation of the pre-existing Indian conception that it was not necessary to hold any particular belief; what mattered was ancestral

---

[1] See the recent issue of the International Institute for Asian Studies *Newsletter* on Pakistan at http://www.iias.nl/.
[2] It is not that there are no tensions with respect to Christians; there are, particularly around the subject of conversion to Christianity, which have led several Indian states to pass anti-conversion laws. In the north-eastern Indian state of Tripura, allegations have been made that the Baptist Church has been supporting separatist militancy in the area.
[3] In fact, early British legislation in India referred to Hindus as Gentoos and I am informed that it derives from the term Gentiles.

tradition and 'best practice'. Still, as De Roover and Balagangadhara (2007) demonstrate, it followed that if the Indians could not demonstrate a religious basis to act in the way they did, then British colonial laws could legitimately rule against objectionable practices, like *sati*, etc. With the branding of their religion as false, and the assumption that textual sources were the key to establishing the source, and therefore the legality, of Hindu religious practices, there became entrenched a clash of visions. The new system of thinking which the British inspired was a contradiction of the previous understanding that traditional practices have value because they are practiced as customs or performed as rituals, not because they are sourced in foundational texts. This should be familiar to Africans as ancestral practices, consistently under attack from one side by Christianity and on the other by Islam. Indeed, African official legal systems appear to have largely ignored such traditions in what is argued to be a massive conspiracy of silence (Mutua 2002).

The process of rethinking along the lines presupposed by Western Christianity – specifically Protestantism – led to reactions by Indians, particularly those who styled themselves the spokespersons of the Hindus, and led to a conversion of Hindu thought into a Protestant version of *religion*. This led to the contemporary phenomenon of *Hindutva* (Hinduness) which has, meanwhile, made its rhetoric more sophisticated by an appeal to the 'Hindu nation' and its 'religious rights', particularly when it seemed that looking for answers in so-assumed foundational sources would only produce contradictory results, as the British had themselves eventually discovered. The advocates of *Hindutva* are therefore concerned to elaborate the contours of a modernist Hindu nation in which, as with all nationalisms, non-belongers would be tolerated citizens as long as they conformed to the (however unreasonable) demands of what was assumed to be the majority's cultural order.

Let us note in passing that by contrast, and contemporaneously, Indians living and trading along the East African coast were referred to in Kiswahili as *wahindi*, a term which shares the etymology of 'Hindus' but does not appear to have the *religious* connotations of the latter term.[4] Thus, from an African perspective which was not predicated on Protestant assumptions, it seemed irrelevant to interpret the ethnicity of Indians in religious terms, a difference of detail that speaks volumes about how interactions between differently premised

---

[4] I am grateful to Prof. Abdulaziz Lodhi of Uppsala University for confirming this point (e-mail exchange 30 January 2009).

cultural understandings give rise to a quite different series of reaction and counter-reaction.

My point is that the contemporary discourse of secularism, including the Indian constitutional commitment to it, depends heavily on this colonial experience, as An-Na`im also appears to acknowledge, albeit on the basis of a slightly different reading of the colonial encounter. He also refers inter alia to Ashis Nandy who now diagnoses that there is a problem with secularism because it is not matched in the vernacular traditions of Indian people (167-168). Balagangadhara (2006: 175) develops this analysis by pointing out the problems associated with the transplantation of the epistemology of the Semitic religions' claims to truth and their acceptance by the secularist post-colonial Indian state:

> By forcing the framework of the Semitic religions on the Indian traditions, the "liberal" state in India is also coercing the communities to solve their internal conflict in a religious manner. That is to say, it is forcing the pagan traditions in India to mould themselves along the lines of the Semitic religions. The growth of so-called Hindu fundamentalism is a direct result of this coercive straightjacket. Traditions, which never systematically persecuted the other on the grounds of religious truth, are forced into a systematic persecution of religions precisely on this basis. When secularists fight "Hindu fundamentalism" by appealing to liberal theory, they merely feed and strengthen what they intend fighting. It is precisely a liberal conception that generates the phenomenon of "Hindu fundamentalism" in the pagan culture.

This diagnosis should lead to a much deeper reconsideration of the colonial impact and a working out of a specifically Indian brand of *modus vivendi*. However, this mode of living together in respect, I believe, should not be referred to as secularism since that imports a specifically *religious* understanding of the world. Furthermore, it is not simply a problem associated with the vocabulary of religion and secularism, but also the uses to which the European concept of nationalism is put. To that extent, this is not a uniquely Indian problem but arises elsewhere in cases of ethnic conflict the roots of which lie in colonialism and missionary activity, but which are ostensibly not underpinned by religion as in Rwanda (Longman 1997). How should one characterise such conflicts, among which I would include the Indian problem? We basically need a more sophisticated vocabulary and conceptualisation of inter-ethnic relations or of relations of otherness which do not depend on a *secular* space for civic reason.

The *Shari'a* and Judges

The basis of the argument in *Islam and the Secular State* that the state cannot be Islamic, because religion and politics are fundamentally different activities is underpinned by An-Na`im's conviction that the relationship between the individual Muslim and *Allah* does not countenance any delegation or interference by another person:

> The fact that knowing and upholding Shari'a is the permanent and inescapable responsibility of every Muslim means that no human being or institution should control this process. (14)

This guardedness about trusting others for deciding what is effectively right and wrong under *shari'a* seems to come from the principle that, ultimately, one is answerable to *Allah* directly and cannot blame another for one's mistakes in ascertaining his will. However, it is interesting to ask how far one can go with this claim of 'detached idealism' (Coulson 1964: 82) without running into problems. Although we cannot delve into the issue in depth here, it is instructive first of all to note that, much as the Western concept of secularism depends on the theological assumptions of Christianity, so does An-Na`im's advocacy of a secular state relies on his essentially Islamic theological claim for non-interference by the state in matters of religion.

Another question which An-Na`im's arguably purist, but not unorthodox, position raises is about judging activity from the point of view of Islam. Does his stance mean that Muslims should not have any recourse to *qadis* (among other legal experts) for help in finding Islamically acceptable solutions to their problems? Surely, however possibly tainted a particular judicial authority or opinion might be, Muslim societies have, through the centuries, relied on such personnel for guidance on *shari'a*? There are many historical and contemporary examples of this phenomenon. In fact, I don't think that An-Na`im's position is so cut and dried. After all, he accepts that the 'practical need for administration and adjudication will continue, as will the need to seek benefit from the knowledge and views of scholars' (16). However, one might disagree with the view put forward in *Islam and the Secular State* that history does *not* support the view that the 'Shari'a was enforced by the state' (146). The largely ignored book on Mughal India by Hasan (2004) presents contrary and fascinating evidence of the adjudicative and other functions of *qazi* courts which are said to have been established in almost all towns in the Mughal Empire (99).

The Indian Dimension of An-Na`im's 'Islam and the Secular State'

Drawing on a rich resource of archives he manages to recreate a picture of how, not just Muslims, but also local Hindu Brahmins and Banias invoked *shari'a* principles and rules, in the process also re-shaping them because of the pervasiveness of non-*shari'a*, local normative structures.

A trickier question relates to the position of, for example, European or Indian judges deciding on matters about which Muslims are litigating. Are these judges any different to Muslim *qadis* who assist parties in finding adequate solutions to their problems? This is not a hypothetical issue being posed for heuristic purposes, since European or Indian judges daily rule on matters that concern Muslims in areas which have, at least historically, been regarded as core concerns of *shari'a*, especially to do with family life. Should Muslims living in these states accept the decisions of such judges too? Are they, or should they be, regarded as capable of ruling on questions of Muslim law at all if one falls back on the argument that ultimately it is between a Muslim and his God? Is there room for the intervention of a multiplicity of different actors, including non-Muslims, to come in as intermediaries to help the devout (and those not so devout) along the way? These concerns underlie the problems in the development of a *fiqh* in situations where Muslims are a non-ruling minority, in Europe today, but this also remains an issue in India. The principle of *ikhtilaf* (tolerated diversity) points to the probability that there is no one answer and, naturally, there will be a multiplicity of responses depending on how the individual evaluates the legal dilemma that she is caught up in. This also means that not all Muslims will ever agree to be subject to state law in *shari'a* matters either and may inevitably prefer to stay as far as possible away from state rule and resort to 'private ordering' (Galanter 1981). As is central to An-Na`im's argument, the state is after all the secular, possibly even irreligious, realm of power politics.

Yet, and acknowledging all this, it is still tempting to pose the questions above which are evoked by the basis of An-Na`im's argument. This is because it niggles somewhere if we accept the full extent of the argument that only the individual conscience is the relevant legal actor in *shari'a* terms. The aetiology of dispute processing, in the Islamic world as elsewhere, after all shows that there is a variety of intercessors including familial and other local interveners, official judges, and so on. From a socio-legal and legal pluralist perspective judging activity must be considered as one component of Islamic law, notwithstanding internal Muslim reluctance to accept human interpretation of God's will. However, the inexorable logic of An-Na`im's starting point therefore requires him to pursue a definition of Islamic legality that is ill at ease with a more socio-legally embedded and pluralistic conceptualisation of law.

The theme of judging activity in plural contexts is a very important one particularly at present. In the UK we are having debates about the extent of power and regulation that may be legitimately and realistically applied to control the activities of unofficial *shari'a* tribunals. In Canada there was a controversy a few years ago regarding the same issue. Individual questions concerning Muslims are coming up all over Europe (Rohe 2007), although in Euro-American settings we are far from developing any depth in Muslim jurisprudence given the self-declared secularity of official legal systems. This flip-side of secularity means that many judges, certainly in Britain, do not feel able to use Islamic sources of authority to settle matters out of a concern not to impose one particular interpretation in matters of faith. Besides, Muslims are still largely 'the other', certainly from a legal perspective. The underlying issue of 'on our terms, not theirs' continues to be a ground of contestation, but also the basis of sometimes dishonest posturing and sometimes confusion on all sides.

But India presents a different case from European jurisdictions with their Christian backdrop. This is where An-Na`im's call to re-examine the Indian past to draw out lessons for the present comes to be of critical relevance. Here it can be suggested that Indian norms of plurality-consciousness must be re-examined and re-enacted for contemporary, post-modern circumstances. It could be asked, in light of current inter-ethnic tensions in Indian society and the state's ambivalent approach to protecting minority people which An-Na`im also identifies, what the jurisprudential basis for this claim to plurality-conscious thinking is. One does not have to go much further than invoking *Manusmriti*, a pre-modern document of Indian jurisprudence and sometime favourite of the Hindutva fundamentalists who tend to interpret it as a code, which is of course not what it is. *Manusmriti* says (at 8.41-42):

> A ruler who knows (his duties according to) *dharma* must inquire into the customary laws of castes, of districts, of guilds, and of families, and thus settle the law peculiar to each. For men who follow their respective occupations and who abide by their respective duties become dear to the people, even though they may live at a distance.

This legal-pluralistic approach (and this is not the only such example) shows that the law professors of old were working along the lines of principles completely different from modern positivist and natural law based absolutisms. This plurality-conscious thinking is reflected frequently in contemporary examples from Indian law. The lessons from the pre-modern past have not escaped those who are facilitating justice-conscious approaches for post-modernity, but to establish this one must go into the details of law and judging activity in India, not something frequently achieved by non-Indians (and I include myself in that category).

In *Islam and the Secular State* An-Na`im discusses the aftermath of the *Shah Bano* case (A.I.R 1985 S.C. 945) in which the issue of principle was whether a Muslim ex-husband was liable to maintain his wife beyond the *idda* period (of three menstrual cycles). The ruling of the Supreme Court in that case, which confirmed the findings of earlier cases that there is indeed such a requirement according to principles of Muslim law, provoked outrage among some Muslim leaders. The fact the five Hindu judges had ruled on this matter of Muslim law added fuel to the fire. As a result the *Muslim Women (Protection of Rights on Divorce) Act, 1986* was enacted by the Indian Parliament. As my *guruji* Prof. Werner Menski (e.g. 2006) has untiringly been pointing out, the provisions of this legislation have been widely misinterpreted as reinstating the understanding of traditionalist Muslims that no maintenance was liable to be paid beyond the *idda* period. Unfortunately, An-Na`im follows this line of interpretation also, probably being misled by widespread misreporting by Indians writers who should have known better, and whose unfortunate reading has been quite influential among non-Indian scholars also.[5] Perhaps An-Na`im is justified in interpreting this legislation as instantiating another case of Muslim-bashing, but the Muslim-bashers and others could not have got it more wrong. In subsequent cases the judges, clearly basing their decisions on terms of the 1986 Act, confirmed that there was now a potentially time-unlimited obligation on a Muslim ex-husband to provide, under Muslim law, 'a reasonable and fair provision and maintenance' for his ex-wife. And this was dramatically reiterated by the Supreme Court just after 11 September 2001 in the case of *Danial Latifi v Union of India* (2001 (7) SCC 740), upholding the constitutional validity of the 1986 Act.

The question then is what senior Indian judges are doing when ruling on matters of Muslim law as exemplified by the *Shah Bano* and *Danial Latifi* cases. In her study of women under Muslim personal

---

[5] For an example of continuing overlooking of the post-*Shah Bano* scenario among non-Indian writers see Vatuk (2008), while an example of more alert scholarship on the same issue can be found in MacKinnon (2006).

law in India Ephroz (2003: 335) says the following of the response of Muslim politicians and *ulema* to the *Shah Bano* judgment:
> It may be reiterated that the reason of the condemnation of the said judgment is the desire of the concerned community to maintain its separate political identity. It is noted that there is no solid or legal objection to the legality of the said judgment, except the popular objection that a non-Muslim judge is not competent to cite the *Quranic* verse because of his lack of faith in the same. If it is done, it amounts to an 'interference' to the Muslim personal law.

This recalls the earlier-mentioned potential objections to non-Muslims pronouncing on matters of Muslim law. Alternatively, one could hypothesise that, in fact, the deeper identity postulate (Chiba 1989) of Indian judicial decision making is *dharma* as pluralistically enunciated long ago by the law professors. It may be possible to argue that even when the laws of non-Hindus are being debated by judges, ultimately, they are concerned to enunciate what they view as 'best practice' according to the *dharmic* ideals. Furthermore, it is precisely because Indian judges are super-conscious of the demands of *dharma* that they continue to develop Muslim law using its emic principles, while *simultaneously* being informed by the etic perspective of *dharma*. While this leads to fundamental questions for Muslims about the fate of their law within an overarching *dharmic* domain, the matter of Muslim law in India is probably not reducible to the division (and tension) between religious and secular law.

It is not entirely clear from *Islam and the Secular State* what An-Na'im's position is on the existence of multiple personal law systems for India's citizens, plus the 'secular' options built into the official law, but there is an impression that he sees too much of the British inheritance there. However, in the discussions during the workshop out of which this book emerges, it became clear that An-Na'im favours the enactment of a uniform civil code, one assumes along the lines of those adopted by European jurisdictions. The idea of a uniform civil code remains a long-standing constitutional promise in India too, but one which remains unfulfilled in legislation. While occasionally making utterances to the effect that Parliament should enact a uniform civil code, arguably an example of judicial lesson-teaching through the invocation of ultimate options, Menski (2009) shows that judges have slowly created a harmonisation of personal laws for India's different communities. Of course, any uniform civil code, if one were ever to be enacted, would not prevent it from referring to local customary and religious norms of the parties (as already happens for example in the *Hindu Marriage Act, 1955*) since, in light of India's huge diversity, one cannot see the prospect of a total effort at uniformisation ever being seriously countenanced. Even if that were to be the case, one cannot see how Indian judges could remain totally blind to religious and cultural factors in cases which they have to deal with – this is a reality frequently faced by European judges too.

A deeper reading of post-colonial developments, and particularly of the activism engaged in by the senior Indian judges in the area of personal laws, shows a remarkable level of pluralist creativity. This practice of *harmonisation* should not be unfamiliar to Europeans who have also developed legal ways to achieve a unity of their national states, but through diversity, not despite it. The Indians are trying to build this unity among their constituent communities, and not nations. Nationalism is a European inheritance that Indians would do better to forego.

References

An-Na`im, A., "Human rights in the Muslim world: Socio-political conditions and scriptural imperatives", *Harvard Human Rights Journal* 1990a, Vol. 3.

An-Na`im, A., "Problems of universal cultural legitimacy for Human Rights", in An-Na`im, A. and Deng, F.M. (ed.), *Human Rights in Africa: Cross-Cultural Perspectives*, Washington, DC, The Brookings Institution, 1990b.

An-Na`im, A., *Islam and the Secular State: Negotiating the Future of Shari`a*, Cambridge, Harvard University Press, 2008.

Balagandhara, S.N., "Secularism as the harbinger of religious violence in India: Hybridisation, Hindutva and post-coloniality", in Schirmer, D., Saalmann, G. and Kessler, C. (ed.), *Hybridising East and West: Tales Beyond Westernisation*, Berlin, LIT Verlag, 2006.

Berman, H.J., *Law and Revolution: The Formation of the Western Legal Tradition*, Cambridge, Mass., and London, England, Harvard University Press, 1983.

Chiba, M., *Legal Pluralism: Toward a General Theory Through Japanese Legal Culture*, Tokyo, Tokai University Press, 1989.

Coulson, N., *A History of Islamic Law*, Edinburgh, Edinburgh University Press, 1964.

De Roover, J. and Balagandhara, S.N., *The dark hour of secularism: Hindu fundamentalism and colonial liberalism in India*, Lecture given at the Mahatma Gandhi Center for Global Nonviolence, James Madison University, Harrisonburg, Virginia, 15 November 2007.

Ephroz, K. N., *Women and Law: Muslim Personal Law Perspective*, Jaipur, Rawat Publications, 2003.

Galanter, M., "Justice in many rooms: Courts, private ordering and indigenous law", *Journal of Legal Pluralism and Unofficial Law* 1981, Vol. 19.

Hasan, F., *State and Locality in Mughal India: Power Relations in Western India, c. 1572-1730*, Cambridge, Cambridge University Press, 2004.

Longman, T., "Christian Churches and genocide in Rwanda", in O. Bartov, and P. Mack, (ed.), *In God's Name: Genocide and Religion in the Twentieth Century*, New York and Oxford, Berghahn Books, 2001.

MacKinnon, C.A., "Sex equality under the Constitution of India: Problems, prospects and 'personal laws'", *International Journal of Constitutional Law* 2006, Vol. 4 No. 2.

Menski, W.F., *Hindu Law: Beyond Tradition and Modernity*, Oxford, Oxford University Press, 2003.

Menski, W.F., *Comparative Law in a Global Context: The Legal Systems of Asia and Africa* (2nd ed.), Cambridge, Cambridge University Press, 2006.

Menski, W.F., "Indian secular pluralism and its relevance for Europe", in R. Grillo et al. (ed.), *Legal Practice and Cultural Diversity*, Farnham, Ashgate, 2009.

Mutua, M., *Human Rights: A Political and Cultural Critique*. Philadelphia, University of Pennsylvania Press, 2002.

Poddar, P., *Vernacular Articulations: Indianness and Nineteenth-Century Hindi Writers* (unpublished paper, on file with author), 2009.

Rohe, M., *Muslim Minorities and the Law in Europe: Chances and Challenges*, New Delhi, Global Media, 2007.

Santos, B. de Sousa, *Toward a New Common Sense: Law, Science and Politics in the Paradigmatic Transition*, London, Routledge, 1995.

Vatuk, S., "Islamic feminism in India: Indian Muslim women activists and the reform of personal law", *Modern Asian Studies* 2008, Vol. 42 No. 2/3.

EUROPEAN FOREIGN POLICY AND THE UNIVERSALITY OF HUMAN RIGHTS

Cedric Ryngaert*

Abstract

In some Muslim quarters, there is a lingering, and even increasing skepticism over the universal validity of human rights. Those quarters may consider human rights as vehicles of Western arrogance and supremacy that run roughshod over deeply held cultural and religious convictions. Such skepticism demonstrates that human rights are still in what An Na'im has termed 'a process of universalization'. Their full realization is an aim to which all States have committed themselves, and which is dependent on (1) domestic political willingness and strong institutions, (2) grassroots support, (3) international assistance, and (4) evenhandedness. In order to further universalize the discourse of human rights, it is proposed that the European Union and European governments (1) support (at times fledgling) State institutions in partner countries, (2) shore up support for local civil society organizations, (3) assist in the realization of economic and social rights in the global South, and (4) ensure that all receive their fair share of deserved criticism.

The debate over the universality of human rights is very much perceived as a debate over the compatibility of international/universal human rights standards, supposedly derived from Western values, with traditional values typically held in the global South (Asia, Africa, the Muslim world).[1] The discussion may seem to have somewhat subsided as we write, as many states have become parties to international human rights conventions and have incorporated human rights standards into

---

* This article is based on the advisory opinion which the author wrote for the Dutch Advisory Council on International Affairs (AIV). The Council's final advisory opinion to the Dutch Government, opinion nr. 63, 'Universality of Human Rights: Principles, Practice and Prospects', of November 2008, is available at http://www.aiv-advies.nl (accessed 24 February 2009).

[1] In the 1990s, this debate was very much a debate over supposedly 'Asian' values, which were seen as incompatible with international human rights standards. *E.g.*, R. Bauer and D.A. Bell (ed.), *The East Asian Challenge for Human Rights*, Cambridge University Press, 1999; J. Donnelly, *Universal Human Rights in Theory and Practice* (2nd ed.), Cornell University Press, 2003, 107-126.

their domestic legal systems (Section 1). In a recent general debate (2008) in the Human Rights Council on the follow-up and implementation of the 1993 Vienna Declaration and Program of Action, for example, *all* States reaffirmed that human rights are universal.[2] Many states where harmful cultural practices are still prevalent have confirmed that they demonstrate 'every respect for the full and effective implementation of international human rights treaties and conventions in all international and domestic forums'.[3]

States no longer cast doubt on the universality of human rights in international fora; they rarely defend cultural or contextual exceptions from universally accepted human rights standards. When such exceptions *are* defended, it is mostly by powerful local ethnic communities at the sub-state level (Section 2). Many states will admittedly defend their own religious and political traditions, but they will typically do so within the bounds set by international human rights law: they may enter reservations to treaties, or invoke treaty clauses that accept restrictions of human rights in certain circumstances. The question then arises what margin of appreciation those states have: at what point do the limitations imposed on the exercise of human rights fall outside the universal human rights framework? (Section 3) In order to solve this conundrum, it is proposed to distinguish between rights *concepts* and multiple rights *conceptions*. Cultural variation is acceptable with respect to the different national or local conceptions of an abstractly defined international human right (concept), as long as the core of the right is not derogated from. In fact, cultural variation should not only be accepted or tolerated, it should also be encouraged. After all, human rights could never be universally realized if they are not translated into the local 'vernacular'. By connecting international human rights with local cultural practices, *change* could also be effected: human rights campaigners should highlight human-rights friendly interpretations of local traditions (*e.g.* the *sharia*) with a view to modifying and eventually eliminating harmful practices (Section 4).

In terms of European foreign policy, this implies that the European Union and European governments (hereinafter called 'Europe') are well-advised to enter into a dialogue with local communities in order to improve the human rights record of foreign states. Respect for cultural

---

[2] Human Rights Council, 7th Session, 25 March 2008, General debate on Agenda Item 8: "Follow-up and implementation of the Vienna Declaration and Programme of Action", pp. 1-2.

[3] *I.e.*, the statement by Egypt in its combined 4th and 5th period reports to the Committee on the Elimination of all forms of Discrimination against Women (CEDAW) (2001).

difference should be a guiding principle of this dialogue, in which criticism has its rightful place in case the target state has exceeded its margin of appreciation (Section 5). Importantly, for a European human rights strategy to be truly effective, Europe may want to take local rights understandings into account. In particular, it may want to reach out to local communities by supporting grassroots initiatives. Grassroots groups know the local vernacular best, could most effectively translate international human rights law into the local cultural language, and draw attention to a culture's potential for change from within. In short, grassroots groups are the single most important contributor to the universalization of human rights (Section 6). At the same time, Europe may want to make sure that its human rights policy is credible and consistent. This implies respecting human rights in Europe to the fullest extent, not using double standards when criticizing foreign nations' human rights records, and contributing to the realization of economic and social rights in the global South (Section 7). Finally, Europe may possibly consider accommodating non-Western traditions *within* Europe, in particular by allowing members belonging to these traditions to live under their own laws, provided that these laws are compatible with national and international human rights standards (Section 8).

1. Ratification and Constitutionalization as Vehicles for Universalization of Human Rights

For an international lawyer, 'universality' of human rights appears as a non-issue. From a legal(istic) perspective indeed, it is observed that a large number of states, some of them with little or no human rights tradition, such as China,[4] have ratified basic international human rights conventions. This testifies to the fact that they recognize the universal character of human rights, and are willing to face the scrutiny of the

---

[4] The concept of human rights is indeed alien to Chinese political thinking. Thus, the idea that there are human rights, even if culture-specific, is revolutionary. Human rights came somewhat to the fore in the early 20th century in China, in a cultural context of emulation of Western ideas and success, yet they completely disappeared from the radar screen after the Chinese revolution in 1949, when a human rights discourse, and legal discourse in general for that matter, was dismissed as bourgeois and useless in a communist state. A very useful overview of China's human rights tradition and the changes it has undergone, is given by S. Deklerck, "Human Rights in China: Tradition, Politics and Change", *Studia Diplomatica* 2003, Vol. 61 No. 6, 53-108.

international human rights bodies – bodies which have not accepted cultural exceptions to justify non-compliance.[5]

Ratification of human rights conventions typically implies duties of periodic reporting to human rights bodies. This in turn requires domestic institutional implementation of human rights norms, and undercuts the persuasiveness of arguments drawn from a discourse that is anathema to human rights.[6] Because treaty ratification leads to institutionalization of human rights, Europe is well-advised to continue to convince states of the added value of ratifying the basic international human rights conventions,[7] and of entering as few reservations as possible upon ratification.[8]

The universality of human rights is not only boosted by treaty ratification, but also by the constitutionalization of rights. The Chinese example is instructive here. After Mao's death in 1976, human rights started to play a more prominent role in official Chinese discourse, which eventually led to the incorporation of a chapter on fundamental rights (and duties) of citizens in Articles 33-56 of the Chinese Constitution of 1982,[9] *i.e.* before China started ratifying human rights conventions. In a bottom-up logic of international law formation, this articulation of

---

[5] *E.g.*, Human Rights Committee, General Comment No. 31, CCPR/C/21/Rev.1/Add.13 (2004), The Nature of the General Legal Obligation Imposed on States Parties to the Covenant, para. 14 ('A failure to comply with [the obligation to take steps to give effect to the Covenant] cannot be justified by reference to political, social, cultural or economic considerations within the State.').

[6] Ratification does of course not imply that all domestic laws will necessarily be in conformity with the provisions of the relevant conventions. *Cf.* CEDAW, General Recommendation No. 21 (1994), paras. 45-46 (noting that 'in some States parties to the Convention that had ratified or acceded without reservation, certain laws, especially those dealing with family, do not actually conform to the provisions of the Convention. ... Their laws still contain many measures which discriminate against women based on norms, customs and socio-cultural practices.').

[7] As of 2008, China had not yet ratified the International Covenant on Civil and Political Rights (ICCPR). During the EU-China Human Rights Dialogue meeting on 15 May 2008, China reiterated its commitment to ratify the ICCPR as soon as appropriate reforms to its judicial system had been put in place. Presidency Press Statement on the EU-China Human Rights Dialogue, Slovenia, 15 May 2008, available at http://www.eu2008.si/en/News_and_Documents/Press_Releases/May/0516MZZ_China_Human_Rights.html (accessed 24 February 2009).

[8] See Section 2 on reservations. Also the human rights bodies have urged states to withdraw (certain) reservations. *E.g.*, CEDAW, General Recommendation No. 21, para. 43.

[9] Admittedly, citizens' rights might be deprived of much of their substance by Article 51 of that document, which provides that '[t]he exercise by citizens of the People's Republic of China of their freedoms and rights may not infringe upon the interests of the state, of society and of the collective, or upon the lawful freedoms and rights of other citizens.'

human rights in domestic legal instruments, even in the absence of strict respect for them in practice or ratification of treaties which embody those rights, contributes to the crystallization of general principles of international human rights law,[10] and thus to their universality. In such a logic, international human rights law is not *imposed* by an international community,[11] but develops organically from national constitutional practice. This of course renders human rights norms more legitimate and palatable.

2. Cultural Arguments

Although the language of human rights is almost universally accepted by now, culture- or context-specific discourses – advocating deviations from universal human rights standards – may still seem to be prevalent. It is observed, however, that by and large, as a result of the trickle-down effect of international human rights law in national legal systems, cultural exceptions are in practice rarely propounded, except by local communities (as opposed to the state that has ratified the relevant human rights treaty), or if they serve the interests of the political or religious establishment.

It is noted in this respect that African states no longer defend such harmful traditional practices as genital mutilation/cutting, domestic violence and child marriage. For one thing, these practices, which are not specifically outlawed in human rights treaties of a universal scope, have been explicitly banned by pan-African conventions. The African Charter on the Rights and Welfare of the Child (1990), which is ratified by 41 African states (out of a total of 53), for instance, provides that states parties 'shall take all appropriate measures to eliminate harmful social and cultural practices affecting the welfare, dignity, normal

---

[10] Compare L. Henkin, "Human Rights and State Sovereignty", *Georgia Journal of International and Comparative Law* 1995-1996, Vol. 25, 31, 40 (terming international human rights law 'non-conventional' or 'constitutional' because it derives from national constitutional rights). See also J. Wouters and C. Ryngaert, "The Impact of Human Rights and International Humanitarian Law on the Process of the Formation of Customary International Law", in M. Kamminga and M. Scheinin (ed.), *The Impact of Human Rights Law on General International Law*, Oxford, Oxford University Press, 2009, 111-131.

[11] In this respect, it may be believed that treaty signature and ratification by non-Western states is the result of stick-and-carrot pressure of Western states. Many states with no human rights tradition, however, such as China, have ratified international human rights treaties without being forced to, economically, politically, or otherwise, by the international community.

growth and development of the child';[12] the more recent Protocol to the African Charter on Human and Peoples' Rights on the Rights of Women in Africa, which has been ratified by 23 (and signed by 43) African states, provides, for its part, that the states parties 'shall prohibit and condemn all forms of harmful practices which negatively affect the human rights of women and which are contrary to recognized international standards'.[13] In addition, political elites typically spurn harmful traditional practices and promise criminal prosecution, while sometimes asking for time to eradicate those practices, given the limited resources of developing states.[14] In so doing, they appeal to a concept familiar to economic, social and cultural rights discourse: progressive realization of rights.

Progressive realization of human rights is not always self-evident in traditional societies. In many states, traditional authorities – who may support harmful practices – may be stronger than the state. In Afghanistan, for instance, as the Special UN Rapporteur on violence against women has pointed out, the 'normative framework governing the lives of most Afghan women, particularly in rural areas, is in fact dictated by

---

[12] OAU Doc. CAB/LEG/24.9/49 (1990), Article 21.
[13] AU Doc., CAB/LEG/66.6 (2000), reprinted in (2000) *African Human Rights Law Journal*, Vol. 1, 40, Article 5.
[14] *E.g.* the statement of Nigeria in the Committee on Economic, Social, and Cultural Rights, Summary record of the 7th meeting: Nigeria. 09/09/98, E/C.12/1998/SR.7, para. 48 ("With regard to domestic violence, traditional African society gave a man the right to administer corporal punishment to his wife, but there again, it was not government policy to encourage such practices, and if the punishment went beyond a certain limit, the man was liable to criminal proceedings for assault and battery. Battered women in Nigeria could file a complaint with the competent department of the Ministry of Women's Affairs, which normally took appropriate action."); also CEDAW, Fifth periodic report of Bangladesh, 31st session (2004).
By the same token, anthropologists no longer defend or tolerate such practices. *Cf.* American Anthropological Association, Committee for Human Rights, Declaration on Anthropology and Human Rights, adopted in June 1999, as available at http://www.aaanet.org/stmts/humanrts.htm (accessed 24 February 2009) ("As a professional organization of anthropologists, the AAA has long been, and should continue to be, concerned whenever human difference is made the basis for a denial of basic human rights, where "human" is understood in its full range of cultural, social, linguistic, psychological, and biological senses. Thus, the AAA founds its approach on anthropological principles of respect for concrete human differences, both collective and individual, rather than the abstract legal uniformity of Western tradition. In practical terms, however, its working definition builds on the Universal Declaration of Human Rights (UDHR), the International Covenants on Civil and Political Rights, and on Social, Economic, and Cultural Rights, the Conventions on Torture, Genocide, and Elimination of All Forms of Discrimination Against Women, and other treaties which bring basic human rights within the parameters of international written and customary law and practice.").

tribal customs'.[15] These customs accept gender-biased practices such as marital rape, sexual assault and other forms of violence against women within the household as a norm.[16] By the same token, traditional local 'power blocks' in Ghana have endorsed such harmful practices as ritual servitude, sexual exploitation of girls, and female genital mutilation, although the state of Ghana has, at the international level at least, spoken out against those practices.[17] It was ominously noted by the Special UN Rapporteur, in her 2008 report on Ghana, that 'local State officials are often unwilling to challenge these chiefs, since the balance of power is often tilted against the State'.[18] Due to the power of local chiefs, human rights bills may sometimes even stall in parliament.[19] Disquietingly, some states dare to argue that it is not their job to change certain cultural traditions of ethnic communities on their territory.[20] The least that one can say is that in states where local or tribal communities wield considerable power, representatives of those communities rather than the state authorities themselves ought to be the primary local interlocutors of a European human rights dialogue.[21]

---

[15] Special UN Rapporteur on violence against women, its causes and consequences, Mission to Afghanistan, 2005, p. 12.
[16] *Id.*, pp. 7-8.
[17] Special UN Rapporteur on violence against women, its causes and consequences, Mission to Ghana, 2008, pp. 14-16.
[18] *Id.*, p. 6.
[19] *E.g.*, CEDAW, combined initial, second and third periodic reports of Benin, 33rd session (2005) (stating that, 'regrettably', bills on such women's rights issues as punishment of rape, punishment of female genital manipulation, and abortion have not been voted by the National Assembly).
[20] *E.g.*, CEDAW, third periodic review Suriname (2007), p. 12 ('Elimination of prejudices is not included in the legislation of Suriname. It is up to NGOs and international organizations to try to change cultural traditions that may be in contravention of the conventions.').
[21] It is noted that also stronger states sometimes condone traditional practices that may appear to conflict with human rights. This typically occurs in a context of legal pluralism in which indigenous communities may exercise substantial judicial powers, as long as they are in accordance with the law of the land and international law. *E.g.*, Article 246 of the 1991 Colombian Constitution on Special Indigenous Jurisdiction ("The authorities among the native peoples may exercise judicial functions within their territorial areas in accordance with their own rules and procedures, which must not be contrary to the Constitution and laws of the Republic."); Colombian Constitutional Court, *Jambalo*, T-523/1997 (ruling that the extent of the physical suffering caused by the whipping of an offender was insufficient to constitute torture). See for an analysis of legal pluralism in Colombia and Bolivia: D.L. Van Cott, "A Political Analysis of Legal Pluralism in Bolivia and Colombia", *Journal of Latin American Studies* 2000, Vol. 32, 207.

When the state itself (as opposed to local or tribal communities) invokes culture, it is mainly *within* the framework of universal human rights protection; statements of non-Western States typically reveal a concern that this framework is *abused* in order to impose *Western* conceptions of human rights.[22] Those conceptions arguably tend to undermine non-Western religious values and beliefs (in particular the Islamic faith).[23] Traditional religious practices have also informed a practice of states, in particular Muslim ones, entering reservations to human rights treaties. Reservations – which are allowed under many human rights conventions – allow states to opt out of certain provisions. They may thus erode the universal protection given by the conventions. Many Muslim states, for instance, have entered (interpretative) declarations and reservations to the Convention on the Elimination of All Forms of Discrimination against Women (CEDAW) and the Convention on the Rights of the Child (CRC). These reservations are typically informed by cultural and religious practices. An example is the perceived incompatibility of the *sharia* with Article 16 of CEDAW, which requires that states 'take all appropriate measures to eliminate discrimination against women in all matters relating to marriage and family relations'.[24] The number of states that have entered reservations to the whole or part of Article 16 is so high that the CEDAW Committee has voiced its serious concern.[25]

---

[22] *E.g.* Human Rights Council, A/HRC/7/L.10, 4 April 2008, Draft report (part two) of the seventh session, statements by Egypt (on behalf of the African group), stating that 'it completely refuses the imposition of a particular value system on others', and by Nigeria, stating 'that the UN should not become a "tool in the hands of a powerful few" to impose their will on others'.

[23] *E.g.* Human Rights Council, 3rd session, 30 November 2006, p. 5, Iran stating 'that the methods of work [of the Human Rights Council] should respect religious beliefs'; Human Rights Council, 7th session, 18 March 2008, Panel on Intercultural Dialogue on Human Rights, Interactive Dialogue, statements on behalf of the Arab Group and the Organization of the Islamic Conference; Human Rights Council, 7th Session, 25 March 2008, General debate on Agenda Item 8: "Follow-up and implementation of the Vienna Declaration and Programme of Action", pp. 5-6 (Pakistan, on behalf of the OIC, cautioning that the Vienna Declaration should be used to combat religious intolerance, especially Islamophobia).

[24] See for an overview: http://www.un.org/womenwatch/daw/cedaw/reservations.htm (CEDAW); http://www2.ohchr.org/english/bodies/ratification/11.htm (CRC) (accessed 24 February 2009). For a defence of such reservations: Egypt, Combined fourth and fifth periodic reports (2001), p. 3 (stating that their purpose is 'ensuring their implementation while at the same time preserving the national particularities of Egyptian society along with those of its historical and cultural customs, characteristics and creeds ...').

[25] CEDAW, General Recommendation No. 21 (1994), para. 41.

Culture- or context-specific arguments are, however, not only based on religion, but are sometimes also drawn from a *political* culture that emphasizes citizens' duties over their rights. They are typically made by those in power rather than the people they are supposed to represent,[26] which is obviously reason for concern. Appeals to a more 'communitarian' discourse may indeed serve to strengthen the power of the state and weaken the rights claims of their citizens. The African Charter on Human and Peoples' Rights, for instance, features, unlike the universal human rights conventions, a chapter on *duties* of the individual.[27] This might justify the rule of the 'big man' to the detriment of the individual. To be fair, however, featuring only three articles, the chapter is far shorter than the chapter on the 'rights of the individual' (26 articles), and it not only concerns duties toward the state, but also toward the family and the society/community.

A state which has placed much emphasis on the duties of the individual *vis-à-vis* the state, and has acted accordingly, is of course China. As is well-known, the Chinese state, being a more centralized, stronger, and controlling state than most of its African counterparts, has made ample practical use of the concept of duties of the individual *vis-à-vis* the state, in ways that strengthen state power and may appear to be in tension with universal human rights standards. China has explicitly linked this concept of duties with its own 'human rights' tradition. In its first white paper on human rights in 1991, the State Council of the People's Republic of China indeed stated that '[a] country's human rights situation cannot be judged in total disregard of its historical and national conditions, nor can it be evaluated according to the preconceived model or standard of another country or region.'[28] It is noted in passing that this view strongly influenced the 1993 United Nations Conference on

---

[26] *Cf.* A. Sen, *Development as Freedom*, Oxford, Oxford University Press, 1999, 246-247 (pointing out that 'the view that Asian values are quintessentially authoritarian has tended to come, in Asia, almost exclusively from spokesman of those in power', and urging the international community to 'listen to the voices of dissent in each society'). See for an outspoken defence of 'Asian values' notably Malaysia, *e.g.*, the Broadcasting Act 1987 (allowing the Minister of Information to revoke the licence of any private company broadcasting material conflict with 'Malaysian values'), as reported (and implicitly criticized) by the Special UN Rapporteur on the promotion and protection of the right to freedom of opinion and expression, Mission to Malaysia, 1998, p. 5.

[27] Part I, Chapter II of the Charter (adopted on 27 June 1981, OAU Doc. CAB/LEG/67/3 rev. 5).

[28] State Council of the People's Republic of China, *Human Rights in China*, Beijing, 1991, p. ii, p. 85.

Human Rights in Vienna, which drew attention to varying contextual and cultural interpretations of universal human rights.[29]

Much of the debate in relation to China's human rights record has centered on Chinese restrictions of the freedom of expression and the freedom of the press. As China is not a party to the International Covenant on Civil and Political Rights (ICCPR), it is technically speaking not bound by Article 19 of the ICCPR, which protects the freedom of expression. That being said, China has proved willing to enter into a dialogue with the international community on the limits of the freedom of expression. It is noted that these limits are incorporated, and circumscribed, in Article 19(3) of the ICCPR. The discussion will thus not abate when China eventually ratifies the ICCPR; instead it will be conducted within the framework of the overlapping consensus of Article 19. This framework is the subject of the next section.

3. Margin of Appreciation

In the previous section, it was pointed out that China tends to justify its restrictions of the freedom of speech by using arguments drawn from universally accepted human rights norms. More generally, a large part of the 'universality versus cultural relativity' debate actually takes place *within* rather than outside a universal human rights discourse. A number of treaty provisions indeed provide that the freedoms which

---

[29] UN General Assembly, Vienna Declaration and Programme of Action, A/CONF.157/23 (1993). In the Bangkok Declaration, the outcome of the Asian regional meeting leading up to the Vienna Conference, where influence of China was particularly strong, it was recognized that 'while human rights are universal in nature, they must be considered in the context of a dynamic and evolving process of international norm-setting, bearing in mind the significance of national and regional particularities and various historical, cultural and religious backgrounds.' Article 8 of the Bangkok Declaration, A/CONF.157/ASRM/8; A/CONF.157/PC/59 (1993). In spite of the attention paid to various cultural manifestations in Vienna, support for universality was strong, however. *E.g.* Article 4 of the Declaration on the Elimination of Violence Against Women (1993), requiring that States condemn violence against women and should not invoke any custom, tradition or religious consideration to avoid their obligations with respect to its elimination.

they protect are subject to restrictions.[30] The freedom of religion (Article 18 ICCPR) and the freedom of expression (Article 19 ICCPR) are the most prominent examples of such freedoms. Article 18 ICCPR, for instance, provides that the '[f]reedom to manifest one's religion or beliefs may be subject only to such limitations as are prescribed by law and are necessary to protect public safety, order, health, or morals or the fundamental rights and freedoms of others'. Article 19 ICCPR, for its part, provides that the exercise of the right to freedom of expression 'carries with it special duties and responsibilities', and that '[i]t may therefore be subject to certain restrictions, but these shall only be such as are provided by law and are necessary: (a) for respect of the rights or reputations of others; (b) for the protection of national security or of public order (*ordre public*), or of public health or morals'. Limitations are often imposed, even in Western states where a legal human rights discourse precisely originated. They are explicitly allowed under the European Convention on Human Rights.[31] Also in Europe, the freedom of speech is curtailed; hate speech is, unlike in the United States, not considered as a good to be protected by the law.[32] The debate over the freedom of speech and the freedom of religion should therefore not be cast in universality vs. cultural relativity terms, but rather in terms of the 'margin of appreciation' left by universal human rights standards to states. Or as the Dutch Advisory Council on International Affairs held in its 1998 report: what is the degree of latitude which a state has in applying human rights, and when has a state exceeded the limits of that latitude?[33]

Therefore, the author cannot entirely agree with pundits who believe that the extended mandate of the UN Special Rapporteur on the

---

[30] It is noted that, even if a right is not subject to restrictions on the basis of the provision specifically protecting the right, it may still be derogated from '[i]n time of public emergency which threatens the life of the nation' (see Article 4.1 ICCPR). Some rights are, however, non-derogable, which means that no derogation whatsoever can be made, under no circumstances (see Article 4.2 ICCPR). The non-derogable rights under the ICCPR include the right to life, the prohibition of torture, the prohibition of slavery, and the freedom of thought, conscience and religion (the latter freedom however being subject to certain restrictions).

[31] Article 9.2 (freedom of religion); Article 10.2 (freedom of expression).

[32] See, *e.g*, the stir caused in the Netherlands by the arrest of the Gregorius Nekschot, a cartoonist which allegedly insulted certain racial and religious groups, in Amsterdam on 13 May 2008. Nekschot may be prosecuted under Article 137c and Article 137d of the Dutch Penal Code (provisions penalizing discrimination respectively incitement to hate).

[33] AIV, report on universality of human rights and cultural diversity, report no. 4, June 1998, p. 15, available at http://www.aiv-advies.nl/ (accessed 24 February 2009).

promotion and protection of the right to freedom of opinion and expression, who is now also to report on the abuse of the freedom of speech for purposes of racial and religious discrimination, epitomizes an encroachment on the universal core of international human rights by culture-relativistic views on human rights. The adoption by the UN Human Rights Council of a resolution on 'Combating defamation of religions' on 28 March 2008, which many European States voted against, is not to be seen as a victory for cultural relativists either. Instead, a search for the desirable limits of the freedom of religion is legitimate and fully consistent with the margin of appreciation left by international human rights law. It is observed here that the questions of defamation of religion and blasphemy have also stirred public debate in Europe. In the Netherlands, for instance, a parliamentary majority has spoken out in favor of the abolition of Article 147 of the Dutch Penal Code, which prohibits blasphemy and allows for its prosecution,[34] while the cabinet, and in particular the Christian parties CDA and ChristenUnie, have taken the stance that religious feelings should be protected, and thus, that the criminalization of blasphemy should not be abolished.[35] In the author's view, it would be a travesty to consider the Dutch cabinet's position as a culture-relativistic one. By the same token, it appears unhelpful to characterize initiatives to study the defamation of religions and possible legal restrictions to the freedom of speech in this context as attempts at undermining the universalist core of human rights.

Following up on the prohibition of blasphemy under Dutch law, it is noted that, somewhat ironically, on the very day of the adoption of the report on the Netherlands of the UN Human Rights Council's Working Group on the Universal Periodic Review (13 May 2008), in which many Muslim nations recommended the taking of legal measures to deal with intolerance, a Dutch public prosecutor had the cartoonist Gregorius Nekschot arrested for his 'intolerant' cartoons... This exact temporal coincidence is obviously accidental, yet it may well be that the Dutch Government has eventually acted as a result of sustained foreign criticism of its liberal freedom of speech climate.

While more government intervention in the freedom of speech is not to be equated to giving in to relativistic demands, it may quite clearly ease the strains in the intercultural dialogue with states that have a more

---

[34] Algemeen overleg Tweede Kamer, 13 March 2008.
[35] At the time of writing of this article, the debate was still going on. It seemed, however, that Article 147 would indeed be abolished, but that the provisions against discrimination would be strengthened. Concerns that the content of Article 147 would implicitly be incorporated in the provisions against discrimination still had to be accommodated.

narrow conception of the freedom of speech. The aim of easing those strains should of course not be an overriding one; it should not cause Europe to abandon its own conception of the freedom of speech, which will inevitably be a wider one than many, if not most, other states. Europe should do its utmost to explain at the international level that reasonable people could reasonably differ over the ideal conception of the concept of the freedom of speech, and that Europe chooses a wide conception of that freedom (*e.g.*, the Dutch public prosecutor does not prosecute the politician Geert Wilders for his Islam-unfriendly movie Fitna on the grounds that the movie, while possibly being insensitive toward Muslims, does not incite to hatred against Muslims, and that criticism of a religion should not be equated to criticism of its adherents).[36] At the same time, Europe should show understanding for states that espouse a narrower conception, but in so doing, remain within the margin of appreciation left by universal human rights law. Europe should not urge those states to replace their own conceptions with European conceptions. As will be elaborated on in the next section, universality of human rights does indeed not imply uniformity of human rights.[37]

---

[36] Dutch Public Prosecutor, Press communiqué, 30 June 2008, available at http://www.om.nl/_nieuws/33558/ (accessed 15 July 2008). The Public Prosecutor relied on case-law of the European Court of Human Rights. Rick Lawson, however, has argued that Article 10 of the European Convention on Human Rights (*i.e.* the provision on the freedom of speech) leaves actually considerable room for the prosecution of politicians for offensive, defamatory or discriminatory statements (margin of appreciation). R. Lawson, "Wild, Wilder, Wildst. Over de ruimte die het EVRM laat voor de vervolging van kwetsende politici", *NJCM-Bulletin* 2008, Vol. 33, 469-484. On appeal, the Court of Amsterdam may have taken his advice to heart, as in early 2009 it ordered the criminal prosecution of Wilders (Gerechtshof Amsterdam, www.rechtspraak.nl (accessed 24 February 2009), LJ nr. BH 0496, 21 January 2009), thereby overruling the Public Prosecutor's decision.

[37] See also the penultimate paragraph of the preamble to the UN Declaration on the Rights of Indigenous Peoples, adopted in September 2007 by the UN General Assembly ('Recognizing also that the situation of indigenous peoples varies from region to region and from country to country and that the significance of national and regional particularities and various historical and cultural backgrounds should be taken into consideration'). UN Doc. A/61/L.67. Also at the level of constitutional law in states with large indigenous communities with their own customary laws, is cultural diversity emphasized. *Cf.* the discussion of relevant case-law of the South African Constitutional Court in W. van Genugten, "The African Move towards the Adoption of the 2007 Declaration on the Rights of Indigenous Peoples: The Substantive Arguments behind the Procedures", March 2008, on file with the author, pp. 16-24, in particular Constitutional Court, judgment, 5 October 2007 in the case CCT 51/06, *MEC for Education: Kwazulu-Natal, Thulani Cele: School Liaison Officer et al. v. Navaneethum Pillay*, para. 65 ('The Constitution thus acknowledges the variability of human beings (genetic and socio-cultural), affirms the right to be different, and celebrates the diversity of the nation.').

4. Universality of Human Rights and Cultural Variation: Distinguishing Concepts and Conceptions

Culture should not be seen as necessarily in tension with universal human rights, or as Indonesia recently stressed in the UN Human Rights Council (2007): 'cultural specificities should not be seen as incompatible with [universal] human rights'.[38] The author strongly believes that, on the contrary, universality, in the sense of universal acceptance of human rights, will be *reinforced* if cultural variation is acknowledged.[39] As universality does not mean uniformity, non-Western cultural manifestations should not be dismissed as necessarily backward.[40]

If, however, the margin of appreciation, which is of course not to be defined solely by Europe (see above), is exceeded,[41] Europe may, and even should, speak out in defense of human rights. In so doing, it could for instance draw attention to existing human rights-friendly interpretations and applications of certain cultural, legal or religious norms within the target country itself. It should be borne in mind in this respect that, as Amartya Sen observed, 'voices have been persistently raised in favor of freedom – in different form – in distant and distinct cultures'.[42] This strategy may immunize Europe against accusations of neo-colonial imposition of alien norms and values.

---

[38] Human Rights Council, 4th session, 20 March 2007, p. 11.

[39] See also Human Rights Council, 7th session, 18 March 2008, Panel on Intercultural Dialogue on Human Rights, Interactive Dialogue, closing statement of the chairman, Professor Malcolm Evans (reaffirming 'that human rights are the product of the shared experience of people and not of only one culture', stating 'that there is no tension between human rights and cultural diversity', and that 'now it is recognised as a necessary component of achieving human rights').

[40] In international law, a bias against non-Western legal practices could indeed be found, at least historically: *cf.* Article 38(1)(c) of the Statute of the International Court of Justice, by virtue of which the Court shall apply, as sources of international law, 'the general principles of law *recognized by civilized nations*'. This expression is currently understood as referring to all independent states, but was historically used to exclude the laws of territories or tribes under colonial subjugation. *Cf.* H. Waldock, "General Course on Public International Law", *Recueil des Cours de l'Académie de Droit International* 1962-II, Vol. 106, 54.

[41] It is noted that in its 1998 report (*supra* n. 33), the AIV held that '[a]lthough the extent of this right will vary from place to place and from time to time owing to existing differences, including religious differences, between cultures and countries, any curtailment most be *as limited as possible*' (at p. 20, emphasis added), but also, on a general note, that '[t]olerance ends where other people's intolerance begins' (at p. 10).

[42] Sen, *supra* n. 26, at 246.

It is an uphill struggle to exactly delimit the contours of the margin of appreciation in the context of the freedom of speech, or other freedoms in relation to which culture-relativistic arguments are often made. Quite clearly, the margin of appreciation is wider at the universal level than at the European level. It is proposed here to draw conceptual inspiration from the work of Jack Donnelly, one of the leading voices in the debate over universality and cultural relativity. Donnelly is an advocate of *relative universality*, a theory pursuant to which '[h]uman rights are (relatively) universal at the level of the *concept*',[43] while '[p]articular rights concepts ... have multiple defensible *conceptions*',[44] and '[a]ny particular conception, in turn, will have many defensible *implementations*'.[45] This distinction implies that, while for instance the freedom of speech is a universally accepted concept, different states and communities could have different conceptions of how the freedom of speech should actually be implemented. While some (Western) conceptions may appear dominant, room should be allowed for limited deviations from those conceptions.[46] Donnelly illustrates this on the basis of the prohibition of apostasy by Muslims. A number of (Islamic) states deny Muslims the right to change their religion,[47] a practice which seems to be at odds with dominant interpretations of the freedom of religion, as enshrined in Article 18 ICCPR. This article provides, amongst others, that '[t]his right shall include freedom to

---

[43] J. Donnelly, "The Relative Universality of Human Rights", *Human Rights Quarterly* 2007, Vol. 29, 281, at 299 (original emphasis).
[44] *Id.* (original emphasis).
[45] *Id.* (original emphasis).
[46] Donnelly speaks of 'limited deviations from international norms'. *Id.*, at 300. Since the abstractly formulated human rights norms are in need of practical implementation, and, legally speaking, states cannot deviate from non-derogatory international human rights norms, it is probably more accurate to state that the norm as such cannot be deviated from, but rather the dominant interpretation which is given to that norm. This allows us to remain within the accepted framework of universal human rights norms.
[47] *E.g.*, the 1991 Criminal Act of Sudan, as cited in the report on the mission to Sudan of the Special UN Rapporteur on the promotion and protection of the right to freedom of opinion and expression, 2000, pp. 19-20. See also the possibly restrictive draft laws of Sri Lanka – not a predominantly Muslim country – ("No person shall convert or attempt to convert, either directly or otherwise, any person from one religion to another by the use of force or by allurement or by any fraudulent means nor shall any person aid or abet any such conversions."), as cited in the report on Sri Lanka of the Special UN Rapporteur on the Freedom of Religion, 2005, para. 62, who voiced concern on the ground that those laws (aimed at protecting Buddhism) 'challenge an aspect of the right to manifest one's religion because they would criminalize certain acts that, according to how restrictively the laws are interpreted, may be part of the right to manifest one's religion.' (para. 74)

have or to adopt a religion or belief of his choice', and might seem to require that states allow individuals to change their religion. It could be argued, however, that, as long as adherents of other religions are allowed to practice their beliefs, and only limited sanctions are imposed on apostates (*e.g.* denial of certain benefits), a state remains within the margin of appreciation offered by universal human rights law.[48]

While the author does not necessarily agree with this conceptualization of apostasy – as it could be argued with equal force that the right to change one's religion belongs to the core of the freedom of the religion, a core which is not subject to a margin of appreciation – the distinction between (universal) concept and (relativist) conceptions may usefully guide the discussion over universality and cultural relativity of human rights, because it draws attention to the different cultural ways in which universal human rights could manifest themselves.[49]

The author wants to reiterate in this respect that cultural diversity is a good to be supported, and not something to be progressively abolished.[50] In this respect, he draws attention to the UNESCO Convention on the Protection and Promotion of the Diversity of Cultural Expressions, signed in Paris in 2005, a convention which all European States may want to become a party to.[51]

Respect, and even celebration, of cultural diversity does not mean that, under the banner of cultural diversity, human rights and fundamental freedoms could be infringed. The UNESCO Convention makes that abundantly clear.[52] Certainly, cultural diversity is sometimes invoked to justify harmful practices. The author, however, like An-Na'im, holds

---

[48] Legally speaking, it could be argued either that the prohibition of apostasy is not covered by Article 18 ICCPR in the first place, or, probably more convincingly, that the prohibition is authorized under Article 18.3 of the ICCPR. This provision allows, amongst others, for the limitation of the freedom to manifest one's religion or beliefs, if this limitation is prescribed by law and is necessary to protect morals.

[49] It is noted that An-Na'im has offered an interesting *internal Islamic* argument *in favour* of the freedom of religion, pointing out that the Qu'ran provides no specific punishment for apostasy and blasphemy, and that no legal consequences are attached to heresy on the grounds that it is not clearly defined in the Qu'ran. *Cf.* A.A. An-Na'im, *Islam and the Secular State*, Cambridge, MA, Harvard University Press, 2008, 121.

[50] See also AIV report 1998, *supra* n. 33, at p. 9 ('cultural diversity can be a source of great dynamism').

[51] See for the status of ratifications of the Convention: http://portal.unesco.org/la/convention.asp?KO=31038&language=E&order=alpha

[52] Article 2.1 of the Convention.

strong views about the dynamic nature of cultures.[53] With the right incentives and support of grassroots activism, an overlapping consensus on the harmful character of such practices could be established, which may in turn lead to their eventual eradication. It is important to realize that change will only occur when it is allowed to occur. Closed societies tend to ossify and to be extremely hostile to change. Therefore, all states, if they take culture seriously, should guarantee the freedom of expression, information and communication.[54] Europe should use the anthropological evidence of the changing nature of culture and tradition to press for more such freedoms.

Precisely the freedom of expression, information, communication, the right to education, and the right to political participation, may allow cultures to change from within, and to incorporate universal human rights values.[55] The potential for change within cultures makes it clear that, as An-Na'im argued, 'the universality of human rights should be seen as a *product of a process* rather than as an established "given" concept and specific determined normative content'.[56] At any one time, the product of this process, facilitated by a number of procedural rights,

---

[53] A.A. An-Na'im, "Global Citizenship and Human Rights: From Muslims in Europe to European Muslims", in M.L.P. Loenen and J.E. Goldschmidt (ed.), *Religious Pluralism and Human rights in Europe: Where to Draw the Line*, Antwerp-Oxford, Intersentia, 2007, 24 ('Since any formulation of Shari'a is the product of human interpretation in a specific time and place, it can change through the same process, over time.').

[54] *Cf.* Article 2.1 of the UNESCO Declaration on Cultural Diversity.

[55] *Cf.* Sen, *supra* n. 26, at 242 (premising an informed choice for cultural diversity on 'such elementary capabilities as reading and writing (through basic education), being well informed and well briefed (through free media), and having realistic chances of participating freely (through elections, referendums and the general use of civil rights'); A.A. An-Na'im, "'Area Expressions' and the Universality of Human Rights", in D.P. Forsythe and P.C. McMahon (ed.), *Human Rights and Diversity: Area Studies Revisited*, Lincoln/London, University of Nebraska Press, 2003, at 8. See on the role of education in eliminate traditional harmful practices, *e.g.*, Article 10 (c) of the Convention on the Elimination of all Forms of Discrimination against Women (CEDAW) (listing as one of the appropriate measures to eliminate discrimination against women: "The elimination of any stereotyped concept of the roles of men and women at all levels and in all forms of education by encouraging coeducation and other types of education which will help to achieve this aim ...").
Philosophical inspiration may be drawn in this context from the work of Jürgen Habermas, in particular his *Theory of Communicative Action* (1981) and *Between Facts and Norms* (1992), in which he espouses a procedural concept of democracy (deliberative politics), pursuant to which the legitimacy of the law is based on a procedure – which allocates rights to citizens – of will-formation that produces communicative power.

[56] An-Na'im, *supra* n. 53, at 2. Also An-Na'im, *supra* n. 49, 138.

is necessarily contingent and temporary. Depending on time, place, and local circumstances, the interpretation of 'universal' human rights will differ,[57] as has also been affirmed by the human rights supervisory bodies.[58] Universality of human rights is, in the final analysis, not a 'one-size-fits-all' concept, but rather one that allows for diversity of interpretations, within the bounds of a margin of appreciation. Respect for, and not merely tolerance of, specific cultural manifestations should pervade the entire universality discourse. This discourse ought to be premised on a constructive dialogue of civilizations, as initiated by the United Nations in 1998.[59] It should be borne in mind that a mindset of 'clashing civilizations', and the attendant human rights absolutism, only leads to 'hedgehog positions' on the part of other civilizations.[60] It does in no way contribute to the universality of human rights, universality being understood as the spread of human rights ideas (which in their modern form admittedly saw the light in the era of Western Enlightenment) to non-Western civilizations through local contextualization.

---

[57] See also B. Oomen, "Mensenrechten zijn nog veel te westers", *de Volkskrant*, 18 February 2006.

[58] *Cf.* CRC General Comment No. 10, CRC/C/GC/10 (2007), Children's rights in Juvenile Justice, p. 16 ("As far as alternatives to deprivation of liberty/institutional care are concerned, there is wide variety of experiences with the use and implementation of such measures. States Parties should benefit from this experience, and develop and implement these alternatives *adjusted to their own culture and tradition*") (emphasis added); CRC General Comment No. 9, CRC/C/GC/9 (2006), The rights of children with disabilities, p. 22, para. 80 ("Programmes and policies [in relation to children with disabilities] must always be *culturally and ethnically sensitive*.") (emphasis added); Committee on the Elimination of Racial Discrimination, General Recommendation No. 31 on the prevention of racial discrimination in the administration and functioning of the criminal justice system (2005), B, C and E.

[59] See for the Framework of Action in this respect of the United Nations University: Dialogue of Civilization: Finding Common Approaches to Promoting Peace and Human Development, available at http://www.unu.edu/dialogue/files/FrameworkForAction.pdf. *Cf.* in particular p. 2 ('respect'): "In order to enter into a meaningful dialogue aimed at better mutual understanding, every individual has to be prepared to exercise tolerance towards other ways of thinking, towards people who base their daily lives on values and experiences other than our own. But tolerance is not enough: equally important is the notion of "respect"- for others as well as for oneself. While tolerance means not to interfere with other's ways of living or thinking, "respect" actually attaches a positive value to what one is or does – respect thus goes beyond mere tolerance."

[60] Compare the statement of the Philippines in the Human Rights Council, 7th session, 18 March 2008, Panel on Intercultural Dialogue on Human Rights, Interactive Dialogue (rejecting the idea of a clash of civilizations).

5. Designing a European Foreign Policy in Relation to 'Cultural Exceptions' to Universal Human Rights

The author understands concerns about a possible erosion of universal human rights standards of freedom of speech through the vehicle of Article 19(3) ICCPR, concerns which have also been raised by the NGO Article 19.[61] It is not excluded that some states pay lip-service to international human rights law, while at the same time construing the authorization to impose restrictions on certain freedoms so broadly as to undermine the entire edifice of human rights. Therefore, the latitude left to states when applying universal human rights should always be a *controlled* one, *i.e.* a latitude subject to international supervision, *e.g.* by international human rights bodies, whether of a political or judicial nature. While this check on state discretion is potentially a powerful one, it should not be forgotten that the system of enforcement and supervision of international human rights law is essentially decentralized, with states and their courts being the primary arbiters of human rights law. The system of supranational supervision is incomplete and weak: while there are supervisory courts in Europe (European Court of Human Rights) and the Americas (Inter-American Court of Human Rights), there is no universal human rights court as we write.[62] In addition, the different human rights bodies have no compulsory jurisdiction over individual complaints, and only quasi-judicial powers.[63] When deciding on individual communications, nonetheless, human rights bodies may set aside reservations to human rights conventions informed by cultural or religious considerations, on the ground that they are incompatible

---

[61] Article 19 – Global Campaign for Freedom of Expression, Press release 31 March 2008, 'UN Human Rights Council Undermines Freedom of Expression', available at http://www.article19.org/pdfs/press/hrc-resolution-passed.pdf (accessed 24 February 2009).

[62] Proposals for the establishment of such a court have been made, however. See *e.g.* M. Nowak, "The Need for a World Court of Human Rights", *Human Rights Law Review* 2007, Vol. 7, 251.

[63] For an overview: W. Vandenhole, *The Procedures Before the UN Human Rights Treaty Bodies: Divergence or Convergence?*, Antwerp, Intersentia, 2004, xx + 331 pp.

with the object and purpose of the convention.[64] Yet so far the human rights bodies have not had the practical opportunity to do so.[65]

Faced with the deficiencies of supranational supervision, individual states may want to develop yardsticks against which other states' restrictions of human rights are to be measured. In its international relations, its bilateral and multilateral dialogues, and its development cooperation, it is legitimate for Europe to use these yardsticks, and on that basis to criticize the human rights records of foreign nations and to aim at improvement of human rights compliance. When unilaterally setting human rights standards and delimiting permissible restrictions on human rights, however, it is important for Europe not to base these standards on its own idiosyncratic view on human rights (which is typically informed by a state's domestic human rights law and practice) lest Europe be accused of (neo-)colonialism or imperialism by the addressee of the standards and of the criticism when the standards are not met.[66] Instead, such standards ought to be informed by an international consensus. Put differently, they ought to be based on widely shared values and convictions in both the global North and the global South. Preferably, these standards could be translated into recognizable norms, practices, and traditions in the target country.

---

[64] *Cf.* Human Rights Committee, General Comment nr. 24 on issues relating to reservations made upon ratification or accession to the Covenant or the Optional Protocols thereto, or in relation to declarations under article 41 of the Covenant, U.N. Doc. CCPR/C/21/Rev.1/Add.6 (1994), para. 18 ("It necessarily falls to the Committee to determine whether a specific reservation is compatible with the object and purpose of the Covenant."); Special Rapporteur of the International Law Commission on 'Reservations to treaties', proposed draft guideline 3.2.1 ('where a treaty establishes a body to monitor application of the treaty, that body shall be competent, for the purpose of discharging the functions entrusted to it, to assess the validity of reservations formulated by a State'), UN Doc. A/CN.4/558/Add. 2.

[65] *E.g.* CEDAW, Working paper no reservations in the context of individual communications, 20 May 2008, UN Doc. CEDAW/C/2008/II/WP.2.

[66] The neo-colonialist card is still played in international human rights fora. See *e.g.* Human Rights Council, right of reply of Sri Lanka, 14 March 2008, available at http://www.lankamission.org/other%20pages/News/2008/March/2008-03-14y.htm (stating, in the context of international criticism of the human rights situation in Sri Lanka, in particular in relation to the conflict with the insurgent group LTTE, that 'this round of debate of the Council has also now been reduced to mere political naming and shaming based on narrow neo-colonial political ambitions being exercised by a small segment of the international community without objectivity and empathy'). See also for the warning against neo-colonialism: Donnelly, *supra* n. 42, at 304 ("The legacy of colonialism demands that Westerners show special caution and sensitivity when advancing arguments of universalism in the face of clashing cultural values. Westerners must also remember the political, economic, and cultural power that lies behind their best intentioned activities.").

They ought to be 'vernacularized', so that they are recognized as part of the own value system by citizens in the target country.[67] Bottom-up or grassroots universality could indeed be part of a more forceful argumentation affirming the universality of human rights. By linking up with the cultural foundations of human rights norms in the target country, the universality of human rights discourse could become more entrenched.[68]

Translation of international human rights standards into the cultural language of the target country may at times require abandoning conceptual rigor. International donors, and Europe is no exception, typically make overseas human rights project financing dependent on specific human rights language in the formulation of proposals. This is understandable, as non-human rights related projects are not to be funded with funds earmarked for human rights capacity-building. Nonetheless, strict adherence to human rights wording of the proposal may exclude from funding valuable projects that avoid references to human rights given the cultural and political context in which the project promoters operate, although those projects in practice do promote human rights. Field research in China, for instance, has demonstrated that many NGOs avoid the term 'human rights' for fear of being harassed by the government, even though in fact, they actively promote such human rights as the rights of the child and of disabled people.[69] Projects that contribute to respect of human rights in China, or any other State for that matter, ought to be funded irrespective of the name-tag given to those projects by local NGOs.

By funding human rights projects that are in line with local cultural understandings and that are not deemed politically sensitive by the government, Europe may create goodwill with the authorities, goodwill which may open the door for a fruitful dialogue on politically more sensitive human rights issues, such as the freedom of speech or the plight of certain minorities. But also in this sensitive dialogue, attention should be devoted to anchoring universal human rights language in traditional values. The dialogue should therefore not only be conducted by legally trained representatives, but also by representatives with an

---

[67] *Cf.* S. Engle Merry, *Human Rights and Gender Violence*, The University of Chicago Press, 2006, 1 ("In order for human rights ideas to be effective ... they need to be translated into local terms and situated within local contexts of power and meaning.").

[68] An-Na`im, *supra* n. 53, p. 9 (advocating a 'strategic construction of the universality of human rights out of the realities of inherent and permanent diversity', and finding it 'necessary to explore which possible foundation or justification is more likely to work in different settings and under which circumstances').

[69] Deklerck, *supra* n. 4, Part 3.D.b.

anthropological or ethnological background, who understand the local cultural system.

One prominent example of a forum for a transnational human rights dialogue could be given here: the EU-China human rights dialogue. Since 1996, 25 rounds of this dialogue, which is preceded by a legal seminar, have already been organized. While the content and outcome of the EU-China human rights dialogue are confidential, it is a public secret that the dialogue has not always been smooth. In May 2007, for instance, the round was cancelled after the Chinese withdrew their delegates in protest at the presence of the NGOs China Labor Bulletin (CLB) and Human Rights in China (HRIC), who were invited to the dialogue by the EU.[70] Good communication and knowledge of (mutual) sensitivities can be said to be key to a successful dialogue. The framework of a 'dialogue' should, however, not prevent Europe from taking China to task over its human rights record. Ideally, the EU-China dialogue may come to mirror the EU-U.S. transatlantic dialogue,[71] where mutual understanding is promoted and solutions to common problems are sought, and the partners reserve the right to take each other to task.

A dialogue does not exclude criticism. While emphasis is to be put on human rights *process* and on respect for other civilizations' views on human rights, criticism has its place in a respectful dialogue, especially when the partner does not live up to its own human rights rhetoric or the promises which it has made, or when a state blatantly exceeds its margin of appreciation in relation to a specific right. States may even have a *duty* to speak out against serious foreign human rights abuses, as part of their moral and legal responsibility to protect vulnerable people from violations of norms of international human rights law, norms in which the international community as a whole has an interest.[72] While

---

[70] China Labour Bulletin, 'Chinese delegation walks out of human rights dialogue meeting with the European Union over the participation of China Labour Bulletin', 29 May 2007, available at http://www.china-labour.org.hk/en/node/44896 (accessed 24 February 2009).

[71] See for the transatlantic dialogues on various topics of common interest: http://ec.europa.eu/external_relations/us/dialogues_en.htm (accessed 24 February 2009).

[72] *Cf.* Article 42 of the International Law Commission's Articles on Responsibility of States for Internationally Wrongful Acts (2001) ('A State is entitled as an injured State to invoke the responsibility of another State if the obligation breached is owed to … (b) … the international community as a whole.'). *Cf.*, at length, T. Meron, *The Humanization of International Law*, The Hague, Martinus Nijhoff, 2006, Chapter 4 ("Humanization of State Responsibility: From Bilateralism to Community Concerns"). See for the ethical argument: M. Walzer, 'Global and Local Justice', The Spinozalens Lecture 2008, 7 April 2008, at p. 6 ('the sight of human suffering, whoever the victims are, brings with it the sense of a duty to respond').

foreign pressure, combined with sanctions, may at times be ineffective or even counterproductive (as it may strengthen the hand of the elite demonizing the West, as is the case in Zimbabwe), it could also be a force for change for the better, as is arguably the case for China. In order to gain more international legitimacy, states may indeed want to burnish their human rights credentials, and act swiftly as a result of sustained human rights criticism from abroad. China, for instance, has allowed free access to the BBC website in China since 2008 (probably subject to some censorship, to be true),[73] quite likely because of the international community's criticism of its press freedom record in the run-up to the 2008 Olympic Games in Beijing, and China's desire to shore up the legitimacy of the Games.

When the target state modifies its human rights policies in a desirable direction, the criticizing state or the international community may obviously want to make sure that the changes are durable and not cosmetic, and internalized by the target state. An effective strategy could be for the critic to congratulate the target state on its progress in the human rights field, while only thereafter making critical observations, supplemented by a proposal to share good practices and technical assistance if need be. Only in extreme circumstances should coercive measures be taken with a view to human rights compliance, since coercion decreases confidence and may even worsen the human rights situation. This mistrust of coercive measures is reflected in the 2000 Cotonou Partnership Agreement between the members of the African, Caribbean, and Pacific group of states (ACP-states) on the one hand, and the European Community and its member states on the other hand: this agreement provides for a regular *political dialogue* on human rights, democracy, and the rule of law, the essential elements of the partnership,[74] for *consultations* if this political dialogue fails,[75] and only ultimately, in case all efforts come to naught, for *dispute settlement* and subsequent *sanctions*.[76]

---

[73] *Cf.* BBC News, 26 March 2008.
[74] Articles 8 and 9 of the Cotonou Agreement.
[75] Article 96 of the Cotonou Agreement.
[76] Article 98 of the Cotonou Agreement.

6. Support for Grassroots Initiatives

It bears emphasis that support for grassroots human rights NGOs and civil society is key to the entrenchment of a universal human rights discourse.[77] Only activists, and not Western states, can act as persuasive intermediaries between international human rights law and local practices,[78] as only activists know the grassroots level thoroughly, while at the same time being part of a transnational network where a universal human rights language is spoken.[79] Those activists may tap the cultural resources of a society where human rights violations are still common, adapt the international legal formulation to the vernacular, and then use this vernacular to effect change and 'push the envelope',[80] *e.g.*, as An-Na'im has argued, by highlighting the transformative potential of the *sharia*.[81] In effect, cultures are not static, but dynamic, also as far

---

[77] See also E. Brems, 'Universele mensenrechten en culturele verscheidenheid', in J. Wouters and C. Ryngaert (ed.), *Mensenrechten. Actuele brandpunten*, Leuven, Acco, 2008, 38 (arguing that 'interventies van (gouvernmentele of niet-gouvernementele) internationale organisaties hebben de meeste kans op succes indien zij verlopen via steun aan plaatselijke initiatieven.').

[78] See also An-Na'im, *supra* n. 49, p. 114, 117 (speaking out against the blind transplantation of Western conceptions of human rights, and arguing that the world could do with a bit less international human rights advocacy, but with more local capacity-building); An-Na'im, *supra* n. 53, pp. 17-18 ('The quality of being a universal norm can ... only be achieved through a global consensus-building process, and neither assumed nor imposed through the hegemony of universalizing claims from one relativist perspective or another. ... Since pressure by external actors is difficult to sustain, and is often counter-productive, it is ultimately up to citizens to hold officials of the state accountable for any violation that may occur.').

[79] *Cf.* Engle Merry, *supra* n. 67, at 15 ('Organizations working at the grassroots are far more aware of the importance of local cultural practices as a resource than are the transnational elites meeting at global conferences.'). *A contrario* Walzer, *supra* n. 72, at p. 15 ('... no-one wants those external supporters to determine what liberation means for this nation – only its own people can (rightly) do that').

[80] *E.g.* Engle Merry, *supra* n. 67, at 25 for a cultural redefinition of violence against women from discipline to abuse.

[81] *Cf.* An-Na'im, *supra* n. 49, pp. 111-112 (arguing that the *sharia* is basically consistent with international human rights law, but that reinterpretation and transformation of *sharia* understanding is required); An-Na'im, *supra* n. 53, p. 21 ("[T]he validity and efficacy of human rights among Muslims must be promoted through an internal transformation of their attitudes about Shari'a in general, and the interpretation of certain principles, especially regarding the rights of women and non-Muslims.").

as human rights are concerned.[82] Cultures may change from within, with some fertilization and transplantation (rather than prodding) from without. The potential for change is also recognized by the human rights supervisory bodies, which have repeatedly called on states to eradicate certain traditional practices.[83] It should obviously not be glossed over that some practices will prove particularly resistant to change, *e.g.*, women's rights,[84] and practices in relation to HIV/AIDS.[85] Changing other traditions, notably those that have been *invented*,[86] or rediscovered,[87] may encounter less resistance. As An-Na`im has noted,

---

[82] AIV report 1998, *supra* n. 33, at p. 9. The changing nature of 'culture' is confirmed in Article 5 of CEDAW ("States Parties shall take all appropriate measures: (a) To *modify* the social and cultural patterns of conduct of men and women, with a view to achieving the elimination of prejudices and customary and all other practices which are based on the idea of the inferiority or the superiority of either of the sexes or on stereotyped roles for men and women ...") (emphasis added).

See also American Anthropological Association (AAA), Committee for Human Rights, Declaration on Anthropology and Human Rights, adopted in June 1999, as available at http://www.aaanet.org/stmts/humanrts.htm (accessed 24 February 2009) ("The AAA definition thus reflects a commitment to human rights consistent with international principles but not limited by them. Human rights is not a static concept. Our understanding of human rights is constantly evolving as we come to know more about the human condition.").

[83] Human Rights Committee, CRC, General Comment No. 28, CCPR/C/21/Rev. 1/Add. 10 (2000), para. 28 ("States parties should eradicated, both through legislation and any other appropriate measures, all cultural or religious practices which jeopardize the freedom and well-being of female children.'); General Comment No. 8, CRC/C/GC/8, (2006), The right of the child to protection from corporal punishment and other cruel or degrading forms of punishment, p. 4, para. 6 (recommending the launching of public information campaigns 'to address cultural acceptance of violence against children').

[84] *E.g.*, Human Rights Committee, General Comment No. 28, CCPR/C/21/Rev. 1/Add. 10 (2000), para. 5 ('Inequality in the enjoyment of rights by women throughout the world is deeply embedded in tradition, history and culture, including religious attitudes.').

[85] *E.g.*, CRC, General Comment No. 4, CRC/GC/2003/4 (2003), Adolescent health and development in the context of the Convention on the Rights of the Child, p. 11, para. 30; CRC, General Comment No. 3, CRC/GC/2003/3 (2003), HIV/AIDS and the rights of the children, pp. 4-5, paras. 11, 13.

[86] *Cf.* E. Hobsbawn and T. Ranger (ed.), *The Invention of Tradition*, Cambridge, Cambridge University Press, 1983, viii + 320 pp. See, *e.g.*, the practice of 'caning' (corporal punishment) of offenders in Singapore, a practice which was actually introduced by the British colonizer.

[87] As CEDAW has noted, in some countries, 'fundamentalist or other extremist views or economic hardships have encourage a return to old values and traditions', as a result of which 'women's place in the family has deteriorated sharply'. CEDAW, General Recommendation No. 21, para. 42.

however, 'all communities must also be willing and able to question and transform their own traditions.'[88]

In order for vernacularization to be successful, it is recommended that Europe disburses funds to grassroots organizations for both local activities *and* international networking. A universal human rights discourse can indeed only trickle down if local organizations link up with international human rights activists, in particular at NGO meetings during international conferences. International human rights networks provide know-how and allow for the exchange of best practices by the participating members. Western donor governments and institutions should see to it, however, that governments in the South are somehow informed of, and involved in the development and financing of projects on their territory. Social and development policy should indeed be primarily set by democratically elected representatives, and it only breeds resentment if Western donors fund their pet grassroots projects in the global South, a strategy which possibly runs counter to the priorities set by the relevant local government.

In its dialogue with grassroots organizations, Europe may want to emphasize that human rights are the ideal vehicle for curbing the excessive or abusive power of the state,[89] and that, after all, this was the appeal of the human rights discourse in 18th century Europe. Europe may nevertheless want to bear in mind that in certain states, *e.g.* apolitical desert societies lacking an urban intelligentsia, a tradition of grassroots organizations has never taken hold, and the prospects of such organizations ever taking hold may be dim.[90] A direct human rights dialogue with the State may prove to be the only alternative for such societies. Such a state-to-state dialogue could follow up on the ratification of human rights treaties by the 'partner'. In the framework of the dialogue, Europe may want to support fledgling institutional structures that protect and support human rights and the rule of law. Although support for grassroots initiatives is crucial to a successful universalization of human rights, it remains no less true that human rights have to be respected, protected, and promoted by the *state*, as it is the *state* which is the addressee of human rights

---

[88] *Cf.* An-Na'im, *supra* n. 53, at 16.
[89] *Cf.* Donnelly, *supra* n. 43, at 286-288; An-Na'im, *supra* n. 53, at 9.
[90] *Cf.* M. Denison on Turkmenistan in *The Economist*, June 28th, 2008 (stating that for these climatological and cultural reasons, 'there is no [human rights] pressure from below'). See also M. Denison, *The Paradox of Personal Rule: Post-Soviet Turkmenistan*, Columbia University Press/Hurst, 2008.

obligations.[91] Building capacity in states with a weak human rights tradition, *e.g.* by providing human rights training to police forces and the judiciary, is necessary if human rights are to be universally respected and protected *on the ground* as well. At the same time, entering into a dialogue with grassroots organizations on the appropriate role of the state in the protection of rights could cause these organizations to demand more far-reaching enforceable rights from the government. It is emphasized again that grassroots demands may carry more legitimacy and have more transformative power than pressure from abroad.

7. Credibility of a European Universal Human Rights Strategy

A successful European human rights strategy is based on respect for cultural diversity, on a process-based dialogue, and on support for grassroots initiatives. Success also depends, however, on strict respect for human rights standards *within* Europe, and on an even-handed approach toward human rights violators worldwide. Using double standards discredits a universal human rights strategy. The use of double standards is indeed typically seized on by states that tend towards a more relativist, anti-Western position, and for whom instances of Western human rights abuses are *gefundenes Fressen* for countering Western criticism of their own human rights record. Member States of the Organization of the Islamic Conference (OIC), for instance, carefully track the human rights records of Western countries, in particular in relation to the position of Muslims, and have drawn the attention of the Human Rights Council to them,[92] in an apparent attempt at deflecting criticism of their own record. In this respect, the Dutch Government is commended for the submission of a report of high quality in the framework of the Universal Periodic Review to the Human Rights

---

[91] *E.g.* Article 2.1 of the International Covenant on Civil and Political Rights ("Each State Party to the present Covenant undertakes to respect and to ensure to all individuals within its territory and subject to its jurisdiction the rights recognized in the present Covenant").

[92] *E.g.*, Iran: Human Rights Council, statement by the Islamic Republic of Iran, 7th session, 14 March 2008; Pakistan, on behalf of the OIC: Human Rights Council, 4th session, 20 March 2007, p. 11, welcoming the report of the Special Rapporteur on Violence Against Women (who pointed to the need to 'reject cultural relativism, the essentialisation of culture, and all oppressive practices justified in the name of culture'), but requesting her 'to focus further on the new patterns of cultural practices... such as gun ownership and the portrayal of women as sexual objects in the media', *i.e.* a hardly concealed criticism of Western practices.

Council in 2008.[93] Predictably, criticism on the Dutch report from states that are considered to tend towards the relativist end of the spectrum mainly related to Dutch tolerance of intolerant speech.[94]

When criticizing the human rights record of states, Europe ought to make sure that all receive their fair share of criticism.[95] Selected criticism, which spares allied states, is fatal to a credible and effective universal human rights strategy. This means that Europe may sometimes have to distance itself from practices of such allied countries as the United States,[96] the U.S. having done a major disservice to the universal appeal of human rights, in the context of the war on terror (Guantanamo, Abu Ghraib, irregular renditions, harsh interrogation techniques …),[97] by refusing to ratify such basic human rights conventions as the Convention on the Rights of the Child and the International Covenant on Economic, Social and Cultural Rights, and by only having ratified 14 out of the 188 Conventions of the International Labour Organization.[98]

As far as credibility is concerned, reference may also be made to the criticism which is often made in the global South that the West emphasizes civil and political rights over economic, social and cultural rights, and collective rights.[99] It is reiterated that all human rights are indi-

---

[93] Dutch report, UN Doc. A/HRC/WG.6/1/NLD/1, 7 March 2008. Many delegations at the Human Rights Council praised The Netherlands for its report and for its frank recognition of the remaining challenges and issues, UN Doc. A/HRC/8/31, 13 May 2008, para. 19.

[94] Many Muslim states recommended that The Netherlands adequately address intolerant opinions. See in particular recommendations nos. 4, 5, 8, 11, 13, 14, 15, 18, 21, 22, 28, 31. Oddly, in view of its own record, Iran also expressed concern over the low presence of women in public and private sectors (para. 40).

[95] See also AIV report 1998, at p. 13 (AIV recommending the Dutch government 'to lay down similar standards in similar cases').

[96] AIV report 1998, at p. 35.

[97] *E.g.* the concern over Guantanamo in the Human Rights Council, 2nd session, Daily Update, 21 September 2006, p. 7.

[98] See generally on U.S. exceptionalism and human rights: M. Ignatieff (ed), *American Exceptionalism and Human Rights* 2005, Princeton University Press, 2005, 353 pp. See for criticism of the U.S. in this respect: An-Na`im, *supra* n. 53, p. 25 (citing the credibility deficit of a U.S. human rights strategy after its invasion of Iraq).

[99] *E.g.* recently the statement of Nigeria in the Human Rights Council, 7th session, 18 March 2008, Panel on Intercultural Dialogue on Human Rights, Interactive Dialogue (stating 'that there should be a better balance between civil and political rights and economic, social and cultural rights'). The AIV has devoted ample attention to this friction in its 1998 report. AIV report 1998, *supra* n. 33, pp. 24-32. See also An-Na`im, *supra* n. 53, at 6 ('Western countries have not shown consistent acceptance of the universality of human rights in their own national policies, particularly in relation to economic, social, and cultural rights. These countries also find it difficult to accept the possibility of protecting any collective or group claim or entitlement as a *human rights* within an existing state …').

visible, interdependent and interrelated, and that international human rights law leaves states some latitude to implement these rights.[100] European human rights strategies that emphasize the indivisibility of human rights are therefore commended.[101] The author praises the Human Rights Council for the adoption, on 18 June 2008, of an Optional Protocol to the International Covenant on Economic, Social and Cultural Rights (ICESCR), which allows individuals to petition the competent supervisory committee about violations of economic, social and cultural rights.

As to the implementation of economic, social and cultural rights, attention is again drawn to the instrument of development cooperation in realizing such rights in the South. It is emphasized that the ICESCR not only requires that each state party realize those rights on its own territory, but also that it 'take steps, individually and *through international assistance and co-operation*, especially economic and technical, to the maximum of its available resources' (Article 2 of the Covenant, emphasis added). This provision may be considered as the legal basis for transnational (or extraterritorial) obligations of the global North *vis-à-vis* the global South in the field of development assistance, trade and investment, and the regulation of transnational corporations.[102] On the basis of the ICESCR, Europe arguably has the duty to provide a reasonable amount of official development assistance in order to reduce poverty in the global South.[103] It may also have a duty to regulate the activities of transnational corporations that violate human rights overseas, but that are incorporated in Europe. In terms of regulation, one

---

[100] See in a children's rights context also CRC, General Comment No. 5, CRC/GC/2003/5 (2003), General measures of implementation for the Convention on the Rights of the Child, pp. 2-3, para. 6.

[101] *E.g.*, Dutch Minister of Foreign Affairs, Human Rights Strategy, 'Naar een menswaardig bestaan. Een mensenrechtenstrategie voor het buitenlands beleid', 6 November 2007, chapter 4.

[102] See in particular the program of the NGO FIAN (FoodFirst Information and Action Network) on extraterritorial state obligations (http://www.fian.org/programs-and-campaigns/extraterritorial-state-obligations). Compare the statement of Nigeria in the Human Rights Council, 7th session, 18 March 2008, Panel on Intercultural Dialogue on Human Rights, Interactive Dialogue (arguing 'that there was further need for greater equity in the distribution of power and resources').

[103] See on such duties M.E. Salomon, *Global Responsibility for Human Rights. World Poverty and the Development of International Law*, Oxford, Oxford University Press, 2007.

could think of providing victims with a forum for litigation in Europe,[104] conditioning export credits or guarantees on respect for human rights, and divesting from listed corporations that are involved in human rights abuses.[105] By regulating transnational corporations, which are often seen in the global South as vehicles for the promotion of Western economic interests, Europe may dispel concerns about double standards for human rights violations. Europe may want to make sure, however, that, when regulating corporate activities, legitimate human rights concerns of the host (developing) state are taken into account. These concerns are often contextual rather than culture-relativistic, and typically relate to the progressive realization of a number of economic and social rights, e.g. labor rights (minimum wages, health and safety standards etc.). Some sensitivity for less far-reaching human rights protection – which may be, in part, the engine of economic growth in the global South – is surely appropriate. Doubtless, in order to gain human rights credibility, Europe may have to walk a fine line between on the one hand, using overly Western interpretations of human rights protection (and then being accused of neo-colonialism and the protection of European industries), and on the other hand, allowing European corporations, and their foreign subsidiaries and suppliers, to go unchecked in weak governance zones in the South, to the detriment of the local population. In terms of universalizing the human rights discourse, at any rate, the importance of regulating (global) business can hardly be overstated. It is precisely the emphasis on the transformative role that a universal human rights discourse can play in regulating the power of (global) markets which makes such a discourse distinctly attractive to every society and its members.[106]

By supporting respect, protection, and promotion of economic, social, and cultural rights in the global South, Western states may undercut *tu quoque* human rights arguments made by developing nations, and thus

---

[104] *Cf.* the recent claim for damages filed by four Nigerian villagers and an environmental group, demanding Shell take responsibility for damage from oil leaks caused by its Nigerian subsidiary. *Associated Press*, 14 May 2008. See for a discussion at the EU level: C. Ryngaert and J. Wouters, "Litigation for Overseas Corporate Human Rights Abuses in the European Union: the Challenge of Jurisdiction", forthcoming in *George Washington International Law Review* 2008-2009.

[105] See for a discussion of regulatory options with respect to corporate violations of international human rights law: C. Ryngaert, *Anders globaliseren. Mensenrechten, milieu en internationale handel*, Leuven, Acco, 2007, 13-75.

[106] *Cf.* Donnelly, *supra* n. 43, 287-288 ("[T]he functional universality of human rights depends on human rights providing attractive remedies for some of the most pressing systemic threats to human dignity", and identifying the rise of the power of the state and the market as those most pressing threats.).

contribute to the universal respect for all human rights. In addition, by strengthening economic and social rights, poverty may be alleviated. And it is poverty, rather than perceived cultural exceptions, that is arguably among the root causes of persistent human rights violations in the global South.[107] The freedom from want – the third of the four freedoms listed by U.S. President Franklin D. Roosevelt in his 1941 State of the Union address to the U.S. Congress –[108] may in turn open up a space for cultural diversity and local justice that is, almost as a matter of necessity, in line with universal human rights standards.[109]

8. Accommodating Non-Western Traditions in Human Rights-Based Western Legal Systems

So far, the author has devoted his attention to the foreign policy dimension of the discussion over the universality of human rights. A similar tension between the universality and particularity of human rights could, however, also be discerned at the *national* level. Many Western states are indeed host to sizable ethnic and religious communities, who all have their own practices, norms, and laws. The question arises how Western law could accommodate these traditions. While it may exceed the scope of this article to thoroughly examine this challenge of accommodation, the author believes that it is useful to point out the analogies between the vernacularization of universal human rights in

---

[107] *Cf.* An-Na`im, *supra* n. 53, at 11 (also listing colonial history and political instability); Human Rights Council, 7th Session, 25 March 2008, General debate on Agenda Item 8: "Follow-up and implementation of the Vienna Declaration and Programme of Action", pp. 5-6 (Pakistan, on behalf of the OIC, stressing 'that poverty alleviation should be at the centre of the human rights machinery if the realization of human rights and fundamental freedoms is to be achieved').

[108] Full text available at the Franklin and Eleanor Roosevelt Institute http://www.feri.org/common/news/details.cfm?QID=2089&clientid=11005 (accessed 24 February 2009).

[109] This is how the ideas of Michael Walzer, winner of the Spinoza Prize 2008, should probably be understood: "If men and women everywhere were protected from the common disasters of nature and social life, if the predatory versions of politics and economics were under control, it seems to me that we could let cultural difference, political struggle, and economic competition work their ways and produce … whatever they produce. … Let there be many pursuits. Let a hundred flowers bloom. It is entirely appropriate (a tribute to human creativity?) that communities, cultures, and religions should have different ideas about the relative value of different social goods and also about the distributive criteria appropriate to each. … [T]he long-term distribution of social goods among people who have been freed from the urgencies of poverty and powerlessness – that should be their own work; that is local justice". See Walzer, *supra* n. 72, at pp. 13-14.

foreign political dialogues, and the accommodation of non-Western traditions by the Western human rights-based legal system.

Like some Muslim states are perceived to cast doubt on the universality of human rights by resorting to cultural and religious exceptions, the accommodation of the Islamic tradition – the *sharia* – by the Western legal system is perceived to be most problematic. This clash may be explained by the universal aspirations shared by both the Western human rights tradition and the *sharia*, and the radically divergent content which their norms seem to have. The author believes that the incompatibility of the *sharia* with Western values is more apparent than real. As has been observed earlier, in its foreign political dialogues, Europe may want to draw attention to more liberal interpretations of cultural traditions, interpretations that are compatible with universal human rights standards. By the same token, European governments may want to support liberal interpretations of the *sharia* by Muslim communities in the West. As Tariq Ramadan has observed, the universal principles of the *sharia* need to be *actualized*, and reason can be active and creative in interpreting those principles.[110] The *sharia* could well be liberally construed in such a way as to both remain within a principled *sharia* framework of reference, and be compatible with universal human rights standards. Such constructions deserve encouragement and support by European governments. Possibly – although the author is aware of the controversial character of such a proposition – this support could translate into allowing communities to live under their own law, at least to some extent, provided that the application of this law is compatible with constitutional and universal human rights standards. This approach, which was recently advocated by the Archbishop of Canterbury,[111] and picked up by the Lord Chief Justice of England and Wales, Lord Phillips,[112] may prove to be a win-win strategy: it may strengthen the universal claims of human rights standards, as these are internalized through local communities' own vernacular – in the case, a liberal interpretation of the *sharia* – while at the same time strengthening the universal claims of the *sharia*.[113]

---

[110] T. Ramadan, *Western Muslims and the Future of Islam*, Oxford, Oxford University Press, 2004, 32.
[111] *Cf.* R. Williams Archbishop of Canterbury, "Civil and Religious Law in England: A Religious Perspective", lecture, 7 February 2008, available at http://www.archbishopofcanterbury.org/1575 (accessed 24 February 2009).
[112] Speech to the London Muslim Council, 3 July 2008, *The Guardian*, 4 July 2008.
[113] *Id.* (citing the opinion of some Muslim scholars that 'an excessively narrow understanding of *sharia* as simply codified rules can have the effect of actually undermining the universal claims of the Qur'an').

9. Concluding Observations

International human rights-based discourses are widely shared in the international community as we write. If the explicit statements of States are anything to go by, human rights indeed seem to have universal appeal. The author has not been able to identify official statements of States, whether within or without the framework of the United Nations, that cast doubt on the universal validity of human rights. By and large, as a result of the trickle-down effect of international human rights law in national legal systems, exceptions to the universality of human rights, whether of a cultural or a contextual nature, are in practice rarely made, except by local communities or if they serve the interests of the political or religious establishment. If they are advanced by States, they are typically made within the legal boundaries set by universal human rights law, although it obviously remains to be seen whether those States in fact remain within those boundaries.

The author nevertheless realizes that there is, at least in some quarters, skepticism towards universal human rights. Those quarters may consider human rights as vehicles of Western arrogance and supremacy that run roughshod over deeply held cultural and religious convictions. Such skepticism demonstrates that human rights are still in a *process of universalization*. Their full realization is an aim to which all States have committed themselves, and which is dependent on (1) domestic political willingness and strong institutions, (2) grassroots support, (3) international assistance, and (4) evenhandedness. In order to further universalize the discourse of human rights, the author proposes that the European Union and European governments (1) support (at times fledgling) state institutions in partner countries, (2) shore up support for local civil society organizations, (3) assist in the realization of economic and social rights in the global South, and (4) ensure that all receive their fair share of deserved criticism.

(1) The government should remain the primary human rights interlocutor of Europe, as it is the *State* which is to ensure respect, protection, and promotion of human rights. Europe may want to engage in a respectful dialogue with states that do not remain within the margin of appreciation left by international human rights law, viz. whose interpretation and implementation of human rights norms cannot by justified by the shared understanding of the scope of those norms. Europe may reserve the right to forcefully speak out in the defense of human rights that are blatantly violated.

(2) While the state may be the primary interlocutor, it is not, and should not be, the only one. It should be borne in mind that genuine universalization of human rights will not occur without the involvement of civil society groups in the target countries. Europe may, for one thing, reach out to powerful non-State opinion-makers, such as religious, tribal and civic leaders, as having those actors on board is, given the influence they have on the population, key to changing ingrained harmful cultural practices. For another, Europe may want to further increase their (financial) support for grassroots human rights NGOs. Those organizations, rather than Western states, can act as particularly persuasive intermediaries between international human rights law and local practices. Knowing the grassroots level thoroughly, while at the same time being part of a transnational network where a universal human rights language is spoken, they may tap the cultural resources of a society where human rights violations are still common, adapt the international legal formulation to the vernacular, and then use this vernacular to effect change and 'push the envelope'.

(3) Europe may want to assist in the realization of economic and social rights in the global South by making credible and adequate commitments to reduce world poverty, in particular through the provision of official development assistance and possibly through the regulation of EU-incorporated but globally active multinationals. This may undercut arguments that Western states are only interested in the realization of Western-style civil and political rights, as opposed to economic and social rights which the global South stands to benefit from.

(4) The author finally wants to emphasize that the credibility of a European human rights strategy aimed at universalizing an international human rights discourse also depends on the evenhanded manner in which Europe takes norm violators to task, and on Europe owning up to a less than perfect human rights record for themselves. Criticizing the human rights situation in foreign States irrespective of the political expediency of such criticism, and improving human rights protection within the own jurisdiction may go a long way to undercut the force of 'double standards' arguments made by states typically coming in for serious human rights criticism. Such an intellectually honest approach towards oneself and allied states may greatly contribute to the continuing universal appeal of international human rights law.

Compromising of Gender Equality Rights – Through the Recognition of Muslim Marriages in South Africa[1]

Rashida Manjoo

Introduction

South Africa's history of colonisation and apartheid included discriminatory laws, policies and practices based on factors including race, sex, gender, culture and religion. The goal was to create a system of legal, social and economic separation of the people of the country. Since 1994, post-apartheid South Africa is a country where many diverse people co-exist in harmony, despite differences based on culture, race, religion etc. The Constitution of South Africa Act 108 of 1996 (hereinafter the Constitution) is viewed by many as an ideal model for multicultural democratic contexts, wherein the right to equality exists with the right to culture, tradition and religion. South Africa is described as a unitary, multicultural, secular democracy that protects individual liberty and freedom through a Bill of Rights, with applicability against both the state and against individuals. The mandate of the new Constitution is transformative justice, which requires positive measures to redress historical injustices and the consequences of past discriminatory laws and policies. The foundational values of the Constitution include non-sexism, non-racism, the right to dignity and also the right to substantive equality.

Under apartheid, despite the limited or non-recognition of other forms of law by the state, there had been widespread observance of both religious as well as African Customary Law. During both the colonial and the apartheid eras, there was limited state recognition and codification of African Customary Laws. As regards Islamic laws and jurisprudence, there was no recognition at all by the state. Marriages conducted by Muslim rites were refused legal recognition on the grounds that they are potentially polygynous, and hence repugnant to good public policy,

---

[1] Copyright of this paper vests in the author. This is an edited version of a paper published as "Making Rights Real: Facing the Challenges of Recognition of Muslim Marriages in South Africa", in *Miller du Toit Family Law Conference Compilation*, Juta Publishers, 2008. Copyright therein is held by the author.

as defined by the white minority ruling class. Such marriages have been denied civil law status and benefits in terms of many laws, including amongst others, the Marriage Act 25 of 1961; the Divorce Act 70 of 1979; Intestate Succession Act 81 of 1987 and the Maintenance of Surviving Spouses Act 27 of 1990. The courts have been used by some people to seek relief against discrimination and disadvantage arising from the non-recognition of their marriages. Cases that have been brought to court include claims for spousal benefits and support; inheritance claims and also actions relating to the determination of the legitimacy of children born of marriages conducted under Muslim rites.

During the apartheid-era, judgements rendered by the courts, clearly reflect an intolerance of diversity, and also the imposition of values of the white minority ruling class on all South Africans. Post-1994, the courts are bound by the spirit, ethos and values of the Constitution which is based on human dignity, freedom and equality. Hence, subsequent judgements reflect these new values and illustrate a rejection of the values articulated in the apartheid-era judgements. A limitation of the judgements in the post-apartheid era is that they largely reflect a focus on the rights and obligations created due to the existence of a de facto monogamous Muslim marriage. Unfortunately, the courts have not recognized Muslim marriages as valid marriages.

Muslims who constitute approximately 1.5% of the population (numbering about 600 000) have been present in South Africa for over 300 years.[2] Their origins, interpretation of Islam, and everyday practices are diverse. They do not constitute a homogenous group, with one approach to personal status or family issues within an Islamic framework. There is no uniform system of personal status laws, either at the formal state level or at the informal community level. In some Muslim communities, the judicial and social welfare divisions of the local *Ulama* Councils (Muslim clergy), informally provide services in the family law area. The dispute resolution function, which is performed by these *Ulama* Councils in the Muslim family law arena, is based on their own subjective interpretations of religious laws and jurisprudence. Thus, matters of marriage divorce, custody, succession and so on are sometimes resolved by these bodies. There is no empirical research on how widespread the use of such forums has been, and also in which geographic region of the country, such usage is most prevalent. Based

---

[2] See generally E. Moosa, "Prospects for Muslim Law in South Africa: A History and Recent Developments", in *Yearbook of Islamic and Middle Eastern Law*, 1996, Vol. 3, 134-137.

on usage in one province in particular (the Western Cape), generalities have been made about the use of such forums.³

The administration of Muslim Personal Laws (hereinafter MPL), by the judicial and welfare sections of the clergy bodies, has been widely criticised. The Commission on Gender Equality (hereinafter CGE), an independent constitutional body, has been involved in numerous activities relating to the problems experienced by women in their interactions with the clergy, as well as problems arising due to legal non-recognition of Muslim marriages. Complaints received by CGE about the handling of family law matters by the clergy bodies, revolve around issues relating to the handling of divorce, polygny, spousal and child support, domestic violence etc. Complaints received by the CGE also clearly indicate that the implementation and practice of religious law, as presently understood and practiced, has resulted in tensions and conflicts between women's right to equality and the right to freedom of religion. Numerous complaints indicate a discriminatory and male-biased approach and interpretation to such issues.

In spite of the above, clergy groups have made persistent efforts, both during apartheid and post-apartheid, to have MPL recognised by the state. The political changes in the 1990s saw the issue of MPL becoming part of larger political discussions about a new, non-discriminatory, non-racist, non-sexist democratic South Africa. The remedial efforts of the current democratic government, is visible in the area of both African Customary Laws and MPL. I confine myself here to discussing the law reform efforts in respect of the recognition of Muslim marriages. The following sections will look at the applicable legal framework; an overview of the law reform effort; and, an analysis of selected provisions of the proposed draft law recognizing Muslim marriages.

Legal Framework

Both the Interim Constitution of 1993 and the Final Constitution of the Republic of South Africa of 1996 contain a Bill of Rights, which guarantees many rights and freedoms, including the freedom of conscience, religion, opinion and belief. The freedom of religion and

---

³ See generally S. Abdullah, *Multicultural Social Interventions and Nation-Building in South Africa: The Role of Islamic Counselling and Psychotherapy*, Unpublished PhD dissertation University of Cape Town, South Africa, 2002.

belief guarantee includes both the right to hold religious belief and to express such a belief in practice. Section 9 of the Constitution of 1996 recognizes the right to equality as a core value and it is formulated both as a command for equal treatment and as a prohibition of unfair discrimination on many grounds, including gender, sex, religion, conscience and belief. The right to dignity (as stated in section 10) has also been used by the Constitutional Court to protect the family and family life. Section 15 (3) permits the State to enact legislation for the recognition and practise of any religious, personal law and family law system and to recognize marriages concluded under any tradition, or a system of religious, personal or family law, subject to such laws being consistent with other provisions of the Constitution. This latter condition means that any laws passed as permitted by Section 15(3), have to comply with the rights and freedoms that are guaranteed in the Bill of Rights, as the Constitution is the supreme law of the land. Section 31 states that everyone has the right to enjoy their culture, practice their religion, use their language, and also to form, join and maintain cultural, religious and linguistic associations, in a manner in keeping with the Bill of Rights.

The Promotion of Equality and Prevention of Unfair Discrimination Act 4 of 2000 (in section 8), forbids customary, religious or other practices which impair the dignity of women and undermines equality between women and men and forbids any policy or conduct that unfairly limits access of women to land rights, finances or other resources. This legislation explicitly forbids systems which prevent and/or disadvantage women from inheriting family property. International and foreign law must also be taken into account by courts when interpreting the Constitution. South Africa has ratified, without reservations, the United Nations Convention on the Elimination of All Forms of Discrimination against Women (CEDAW). Article 16 of the Convention deals with marriage and family life, and the duty on a State, to take all steps to end all discrimination against women in marriage and family life. This is thus an obligation that the South Africa government cannot ignore in its quest to recognise religious marriages.

It is apparent from the above that the political and legislative framework in South Africa is more than adequate to protect both individual and group rights. It is also clear that as a secular, multicultural society with a long history of oppression and discrimination, the framework attempts to accord respect and dignity to different cultures and religions. At the same time it promotes and protects the human rights of all women. There can be no contestation in South Africa that the right to equality, human dignity and freedom have to be respected and protected, as per the Constitution. Religious, cultural and traditional laws are all subject to such rights - both in their content and their implementation. In the following section I set out recent law reform efforts aimed at recognition of Muslim marriages.

Law Reform Efforts by the South African Law Reform Commission

The South African Law Reform Commission (hereinafter SALRC) is a statutory body appointed by Parliament, which had in the 1980s and early 1990s considered the status of the Muslim Personal Law. In 1996 it reconsidered this project with a particular focus on the recognition of Muslim marriages. Due to concerns raised in the past about the representivity of the SALRC project committee on this issue and also the process followed, a new project committee was recommended and subsequently appointed by Parliament in 1999, following a more transparent process of nominations. The mandate of this Project Committee was to investigate Islamic marriages and related matters. An Issue Paper identifying the issues and problems in respect of Islamic Marriages was published in May 2000. A Discussion Paper with a Draft Bill was published in December 2001. After responses were collated, a new Bill was released in October 2002. The final report and a substantially amended draft Muslim Marriages Bill, was released in July 2003 and this has been submitted to the Minister of Justice, but has not been tabled in Parliament to date.

There has been widespread criticism, which included, charges of preferential treatment being given to the clergy, by the SALRC. The Project Committee has asserted that the Draft Bill of 2003 is supported by the majority of the community. This assertion has been maintained despite the committee being notified that the consultation process was flawed; that many women are unaware that the Bill codifies religious law (as opposed to just recognizing Muslim marriages); and, that there is contestation over the schools of interpretation of Islamic law in many of the codified provisions.

The preamble of the Muslim Marriages Bill 2003 sets out the objectives it seeks to achieve. These include: to make provision for the recognition of Muslim marriages; to specify the requirements for a valid Muslim marriage; to regulate the registration of Muslim marriages; to recognise the status and capacity of spouses in Muslim marriages; to regulate the proprietary consequences of Muslim marriages; to regulate the termination of Muslim marriages and the consequences thereof; to provide for the making of regulations; and to provide for matters connected therewith. I set out selected provisions of the Bill below.

Section 1. Definition and Interpretation of the Act. Amongst the numerous definitions, the Bill includes definitions pertaining to different forms of divorce e.g. revocable or irrevocable *talaq; faskh* and *khula*. Broadly the Bill defines *talaq* as the unilateral pronouncement of divorce articulated by a male spouse; *faskh* as a decree of dissolution of marriage on any grounds or basis permitted by Islamic law and by application by either party to the marriage; *khula* as the dissolution of a marriage at the instance of the wife in terms of an agreement reached by the parties. A distinguishing feature of the *khula* is that under this system a wife renounces all financial claims on the husband, especially any unpaid mahr, in order to obtain a divorce.

Section 2. Application of this Act. This law would apply to Muslim marriages entered into after the commencement of this Act where the parties have chosen to be bound by the provisions of this Act. It would apply to Muslim marriages entered into before the commencement of this Act, unless the parties elect not to be bound by the provisions of this Act, and have applied for an exemption. It would also apply in instances where parties are already married under civil law and now elect to have the provisions of this Act apply to their marriage.

Section 3. Status and Capacity of Spouses in Muslim Marriages. This clause states that a wife and husband in a Muslim marriage are equal in human dignity and have equal legal capacity and financial independence. Both parties thus have the capacity to own and acquire assets and to dispose of them; to enter into contracts; and to litigate in their own names. This provision is in accordance with Islamic law and also the Constitution of South Africa.

Section 5. Requirements for a Valid Muslim Marriage. The requirements include consent *i.e.* both parties must consent to the marriage (a woman does not need to consent through a representative); witnesses as required by Islamic law; and also a minimum marriage age of 18 for both parties. This section does not mandate that witnesses must be males.

Section 6. Registration of Muslim Marriages. Marriages entered into before the commencement of this Act (except those parties who have elected not to be bound by the provisions of this Act) have to be registered in the prescribed manner within a period of two years or within a time period determined by the Minister of Justice. Marriages entered into after the commencement of this Act (where parties choose to be bound by the provisions of this Act) must be registered at the time of the conclusion of the marriage. Section 6(3) places obligations on the marriage officer to inform the parties that they are entitled to conclude a contract of their own choice regulating their marital regime or that they may conclude a standard contract. The officer has to present the parties with examples of such contracts and he/she has to ensure that the parties understand the registration procedures.

Section 8. Proprietary Consequences. In terms of this Act, a Muslim marriage shall be deemed to be a marriage out of community of property excluding the accrual system, unless the parties agree to contract into another proprietary system and do so in an anti-nuptial contract. This section also allows for spouses in a Muslim marriage to which this Act is applicable, to jointly apply to court for leave to change their matrimonial property system.

The Bill also recognises and attempts to regulate polygynous marriages. In instances where a husband is in more than one marriage, the law requires that all parties having a sufficient interest in the matter, especially the existing wives (both religious and civil law wives), must be named in, and notified of, any court proceedings relating to a change in marriage contracts. It includes a provision that a husband in a Muslim marriage who intends entering into a further Muslim marriage must make application to court for approval. The court must grant the approval if it is satisfied that the husband is able to maintain equality between the spouses as is prescribed by the Holy Quran. The language in this section is not specific as to what factors the court has to take into account to establish whether equality can be maintained. In terms of normal judicial practice, interpretation is at the discretion of the judge, with reference to the relevant laws and in this instance also any applicable Quranic injunctions. The court may make an order terminating the existing matrimonial property regime and also ordering the immediate division of the estate. All persons having an interest in the matter, in particular the existing wives must be joined in the proceedings. A husband entering into second marriage without the necessary order of court, shall be guilty of an offence and liable on conviction to a fine not exceeding R20 000. Furthermore, it is an offence for a marriage officer to register a second marriage, unless the order of court is furnished by the husband prior to the registration of the subsequent marriage.

Section 9. Termination of Marriages. This section makes reference to existing civil law legislation to assist the process of termination, subject to the grounds and procedures permitted by Islamic law. The section sets out the process governing the different forms of termination including the timeframes for registration of a *talaq* and procedures for the *khula*. The procedures for the division of assets; the custody, access and maintenance of children; and, the issue of a conciliatory gift are also dealt with in this section.

Section 11. Custody of and Access to Minor Children. This clause attempts to introduce the norms of existing legislation as well as those of Islamic law. The Bill attempts to be sensitive to the constitutional protection of children and also to applicable Islamic Law provisions. Hence in custody and access disputes, courts will have to consider the best interests of the child, Islamic Laws, and also any report from the Office of the Family Advocate.

Section 12. Maintenance. This section also attempts to integrate the existing civil law and Islamic Laws. The husband is obliged to maintain the wife during the duration of the Muslim marriage and the father is obliged to maintain his children until they become self supporting (there is no specific age mentioned in the legislation). Maintenance of a child includes the provision of food, clothing, separate accommodation, medical care and education. Upon dissolution by divorce of a Muslim marriage, the husband is obliged to maintain the wife for the mandatory *iddah* period (*i.e.* the mandatory waiting period during which a woman in a Muslim marriage may not marry. This period is applicable to both widows and divorcees and the duration is dependent on the period necessary to establish pregnancy, usually three menstrual cycles); to remunerate the wife where she has custody of the children - including providing a separate residence; and remuneration for breastfeeding for two years from the birth of the child.

Section 13. Compulsory Mediation. Mediation has been included as a compulsory first step towards the dissolution of a marriage. This can be conducted by any accredited mediation agency. Parties to a mediation agreement may apply to a court to have their agreement be made an order of court *i.e.* a legally binding agreement.

Section 14. Arbitration. Spouses in a Muslim marriage may refer a dispute to an arbitrator and the provisions of the Arbitration Act shall apply. The Arbitration Act is currently used in South Africa largely to resolve commercial disputes and it is unclear how it will be used in family law disputes by accredited arbitrators. Courts are not bound by arbitration awards and can thus entertain disputes anew.

Section 15. Courts and Assessors. The Bill proposes that if a dispute is referred to court, that a Muslim judge shall be appointed as presiding officer, failing which a Muslim lawyer of at least ten years' standing shall be appointed as presiding officer. Also, the court shall be assisted by two Muslim assessors (appointed by the Minister of Justice), who shall have requisite knowledge of Islamic Law.

Section 17. Unopposed proceedings. In unopposed matters or matters where the parties have drawn up a settlement agreement, a Muslim judge shall sit without assessors. The reasoning is that in the absence of disputes the judge does not require any additional experts in making the decision to grant the divorce.

Analysis of the Draft Bill

It is acknowledged that the recognition of Muslim marriages requires a legislative intervention, and, that the proposed Muslim Marriages Bill (2003) is but one attempt at resolving the discrimination and disadvantage suffered by people who are members of the Muslim community. Attempts by the courts, post-1994, reflect attempts to ameliorate the constitutional violations that have occurred due to the non-recognition of Muslim marriages.

The Muslim Marriages Bill raises many constitutional concerns including broadly the following: provisions relating to the codification of religious laws in a secular multicultural democracy; the scope of application of such a law; potential violations of women's equality rights both inter-group and intra-group; and issues relating to the achievement of both individual and group equality. The South Africa Constitution does not contain a provision that mandates strict separation of religion and state. The practice by the different organs of state has been to avoid 'entanglement' with religion, which the Bill unfortunately violates.

The Constitution also guarantees freedom of religion and belief and the Bill violates this right both in terms of the interpretations of religious law as found within the codified provisions and also in the provisions relating to state enforcement of such provisions. It is apparent that the Bill represents a compromise to meet constitutional guarantees, and hence, it includes provisions from the different schools of Islam. This is problematic for many as it assumes a common understanding of MPL, and also assumes that the Muslim community in South Africa is a homogenous one. The imposition of one version of religious law to all Muslims is viewed by many as a violation of constitutional rights, as it empowers the state to enforce and control the manner in which people choose to practice their religion and express their faith and belief. Furthermore, the Bill may also be viewed as undermining the autonomy of religious institutions.

In terms of equality between citizens of a nation state, the codification of a religious system which privileges one religious group in a secular democracy may be viewed as violating the equality rights of other groups. This is particularly relevant to the South African context where there are other religious groups whose marriages are not recognized. Furthermore, the provisions relating to the appointment of Muslim judges and assessors to hear disputes brought by Muslim litigants, could also be interpreted as privileging one sector of society and be seen as a violation of the same standard of equality for all citizens, and worse still, as a divisive factor in a context with a history of divisions. The reality in South Africa is one where all judges are bound by the dictates of the Constitution and are expected to use that in their decision-making, whether the litigants are of a different race, sex, cultural or religious group.

Further, as regards intra-group equality norms, the Bill advocates different rules and procedures for people bound by the Muslim Marriages Bill. It treats the proprietary consequences of marriage, divorce rules and procedures, maintenance of spouses, custody of and access to children differently from those that are applicable to citizens using the civil marriage system. One example of this relates to civil law marriages which are automatically in community of property, while marriages under this Bill will be automatically out of community of property. The consequences of a marriage out of community of property excluding the accrual system, is that each party retains assets that they bring into the marriage and also assets that they acquire during the subsistence of the marriage. This effectively works to the disadvantage of the spouse who does not work outside of the home and who may also not inherit family assets.

The provisions relating to compulsory mediation and arbitration are also viewed as problematic, based both on equality arguments as well as ignoring the reality of unequal power relations in many marriages. Furthermore, compulsory mediation is a contradiction in terms, as mediation by its very nature is a voluntary process that parties agree to, with them choosing a neutral third party as a mediator.

In terms of individual rights to gender equality, there are views that the current practice of Muslim Personal Laws cannot be reconciled with the constitutional guarantee of substantive gender equality. This Bill is seen as further entrenching the existing *de facto* inequalities that are faced by many Muslim women, due to the implementation and practices of Islamic law. This view is borne out by the provisions on issues relating to property, spousal support, *iddah* period, divorce rules and procedures and polygyny. For example the proviso relating to post divorce/death waiting periods (iddah) is also viewed as a violation of gender equality, as it is a mandatory obligation imposed on Muslim women only. It is also viewed as illogical as the *de facto* primary purpose behind 'Iddah' is to ascertain the paternity of a child that may be born to her after the death of a husband or the dissolution of a marriage. With technology today, this can be established in a fairly short time and hence the specific time provision in the Bill does not make sense. This a-contextual approach to codification of religious laws is seen as ignoring time, place and scientific developments in the world today. It is also seen as conservative, backward looking and harmful to both the individual and the religion.

Another example of potential violation of individual equality rights relates to provisions in the Bill which recognise and sanction the practice of polygyny, while at the same time providing some legislative protective measures. This raises two crucial issues in the context of the entrenched right to equality, both in general terms as well as with regard to sexual equality. There is no provision in the Bill for a woman's right to enter into multiple marriages and this begs the question of whether the right to religion is overriding the right to equality in this instance. The Bill also ignores economic factors and unequal power relationships which force women into polygynous marriages. By legislating to regulate polygyny through the courts, the inequality/discrimination defect is not necessarily cured. Further, there is no requirement for the wife's consent prior to her husband's entering into of a subsequent marriage. Debates have ensued as to whether court regulation of polygyny is practically possible, in modern social and economic conditions, and also, whether men will follow the prescribed court process — particularly in a context where there is a lack of acceptance of the state's right to intervene in the religious domain.

Conclusion

In light of the abovementioned problems, the Parliamentary Office of the Commission on Gender Equality after numerous interventions, decided to exercise its mandate and to draft a secular law which recognises all religious marriages. This draft legislation is a generic law of general application and does not codify any aspects of any religion. The CGE legislation was tabled with the relevant state officials in 2005, but to date it has not been disclosed to the public, by the relevant state department. The lack of attention to the crucial constitutional issue of discrimination against people belonging to the Muslim community is of concern to many. A Constitutional Court challenge, to force the legislature to take the necessary remedial steps to address the violation resulting from non-recognition of religious marriages, has been launched. Judgement is pending herein.

As noted above, the reality is that South Africa is a secular country, that has also constitutionally entrenched the right to freedom of religion, belief, conscience and opinion. The protection of minority group rights whether based on religion or culture is constitutionally guaranteed in broad terms. The question of interpretation of the supremacy of constitutional guarantees of gender equality and religion or culture, is also now clear after the seminal Bhe case in the Constitutional Court. The Bhe case concerned the resolution of a conflict between gender equality rights and cultural rights. The issue that faced the court was one that related to inheritance rights of girl-children under African Customary Law. The court in this case struck down the discriminatory customary law practice which precluded women and girl-children from inheriting family property. This judgement affirmed clearly that where equality rights clash with rights to culture, the equality right will override the right to culture. Based on this judgement, an inference can be made that the same approach will be adopted when a clash arises between equality rights and religious rights.

The legislative process will reveal whether the protection of minority group rights includes the right to use a legal system which is in conflict with the Constitution and its fundamental protection of the principle and practice of equality of all citizens. The court processes will reveal whether an obligation to enforce an unconstitutional system, which violates individual rights, will be sanctioned by the courts. The hope by many is that the substantive equality rights of women will trump over the inclusion of archaic and discriminatory provisions which violate women's right to both equality and religion. What is needed is a remedy that does not force women to choose between gender equality and religion.

References

Abdullah, S., *Multicultural Social Interventions and Nation-Building in South Africa: The Role of Islamic Counselling and Psychotherapy*, Unpublished PhD dissertation, University of Cape Town, South Africa, 2002.
Cachalia, F., *Legal Pluralism and Constitutional Change in South Africa: The Special Case of Muslim Family Laws*, Unpublished paper, University of Cape Town, 1991.
Constitution of the Republic of South Africa, Act 108 of 1996.
Manjoo, R. (ed.), *The Recognition of Muslim Personal Laws in South Africa: Implications for Women's Human Rights*, working paper, Human Rights Program at Harvard Law School, 2007.
Moosa, E., "Prospects for Muslim Law in South Africa: A History and Recent Developments", in *Yearbook of Islamic and Middle Eastern Law*, 1996, Vol. 3, 134-137.
Muslim Youth Movement Gender Desk (2003) *Response to the Proposed Draft Bill, Islamic Marriages Act...of 20...*, unpublished paper.
South African Law Reform Commission, *Muslim Marriages Act... of 20...*, published draft Bill, 2003.
South African Law Reform Commission, *Islamic Marriages and Related Matters, Project 106,* published report, 2003.
Bhe and Others v. Magistrate of Khayelitsha and Others 2005 (1) BCLR 1 (CC).

Islam and the Democratic State under the Rule of Law – And Never the Twain Shall Meet?

Mathias Rohe

Abstract

It goes without saying that neither secular democratic states nor Islam as a religion could be perceived to be homogeneous and immutable in time and space. This paper will firstly focus on misunderstandings relating to secularity and democracy: Contrary to the widespread understanding of secularity among Muslims, secular states open broad space not only for the private exercise of religion, but also for its public practice and appearance. As to democracy, Muslim traditionalists use to juxtapose its mechanisms to the 'eternal provisions of God-given Sharia'. It will be briefly demonstrated that every norm, being derived from God or a human sovereign, has to be interpreted and implemented by fallible human beings. In addition to that, democracy alone describes only a part of 'Western' legal orders: The basic rights and values of these orders, summarized by the 'Rule of Law' in the sense of an order protecting and promoting human rights, are not subdue to majority decision, since a major function of such rights is to protect minorities against the force of the majority; the individual to this respect is the smallest possible minority. Thus, the premises of political and of traditional Islam seem to fundamentally misunderstand the mechanisms of such legal orders. But are there other, more flexible approaches within Sharia? The last part will focus on models of European Muslims' attitudes towards Western legal orders (pragmatism, rejection of (traditional) Islam, Islamism, traditionalism, civic entrenchment) and a possible search and definition of common ground.

Introduction: The Concept of Democracy under the Rule of Law and Islamic Norms

Abdullahi An-Na`im, in whose honour this paper was presented at the Catholic University of Leuven, has intensely researched and published on ways and modes to reconcile the religion of Islam with the ideas underlying the secular state. His recent book on Islam and the secular state is a most inspiring fundament for my following reflections. Indeed, the democratic state under the rule of law, which is the current state model in Europe and other parts of the world, is much more than democratic alone. It would be simply wrong to reduce its mechanisms to 'the rule of the majority' choosing its representatives in free elections. To the contrary, the rule of law is a powerful means to restrict the will of the majority for the sake of the protection of individuals and minorities: The basic rights granted by the UN Convention on Human Rights, the European Convention on Human Rights and national constitutions are inviolable and thus not subject to any majority decision (Rohe 2009, forthcoming).

Freedom of religion for all kinds of religions is guaranteed in Europe by the European and national constitutional provisions like art. 9 of the European Convention on Human Rights (ECHR) providing for the freedom of religion. The scope of these rules is not restricted to private worship, but also grants an adequate (not an unlimited) protection of religious needs in various aspects of public law (from building mosques up to social security issues) or private labour law (*cf.* Rohe 2007). Nevertheless, there are some differences in the application between several European countries. This is due to differing convictions regarding the desirable degree of distance between the state's activities and religions.[1] The European Court of Human Rights accepts such differences according to various decisions: *E.g.*, it refused to take the ban of teachers (Dahlab/Switzerland 2001) or students (Sahin/Turkey 2006) wearing headscarves in schools or universities as a violation of article 9 ECHR. Thus, the ECHR would grant a – very considerable – European common minimum standard of rights, whereas some national constitutions including the German one open even broader space.

In Germany, the most important provision to regulate religious affairs is art. 4 sections 1 and 2 of the German Constitution.[2] This article is not limited to the private religious conviction. It also grants the public manifestation of belief and the state is obliged to care that this right is not unduly limited. Of course there are legal limits for rights whatsoever including religious ones. Nobody would be allowed to threaten others on religious grounds, to name but one example. Nevertheless, the German

---

[1] For an overview *cf.* Potz and Wieshaider (2004); European Parliament (2007); Rohe and Elster 2006.

[2] The wording is as follows: Art. 4 [Freedom of faith, conscience, and creed]. (1) Freedom of faith and conscience, and freedom to profess a religious or philosophical creed, shall be inviolable. (2) The undisturbed practice of religion shall be guaranteed.

legal system provides a far reaching freedom of religion. This freedom is, according to the unanimous opinion among legal experts and the German government and administration, not restricted to established religions like Christianity and Judaism, but also applies to Islam. Furthermore, art. 3 sect. 3 of the German Constitution prescribes that no-one may be discriminated against, or given preferential treatment, for reasons of their religious belief.[3]

In sum, the secular legal orders in Europe do not refuse religion; they are not at all anti-religious ('lā-dīnī') as it is sometimes wrongly understood.[4] To the contrary they open a broad space for religious belief and life, including the establishment of religious organizations, places of worship or private schools, not to mention religious instruction in public schools according to the German educational system, social security payments for religious burials and other rites for those in need.[5] It is only that the state itself has to be neutral and is prevented from interference into religious affairs. The most important result of this legal secularism is the equivalence of religions including the freedom not to adhere to a religion or the freedom to change it.[6] According to a unanimous understanding in European law this neutrality is a prerequisite for true religious freedom, which cannot be dispensed with. A prominent French Muslim accordingly calls this system to be of 'positive neutrality' (*i.e.* towards religions) (Bencheikh 1998, 57).

Thus, the question for Muslims arises whether a non-Islamic state granting far reaching religious freedom to everybody is acceptable or even 'Islamic' in the sense that Islamic values are accorded by it. A possible approach could be found in common ground, in the search for an overlapping consensus between the human rights-orientated secular state and the religion of Islam. Taking the human rights claim to universality seriously will necessarily lead to the worldwide search for an overlapping consensus with respect to contents of human rights. In Islamic tradition, a possible basic link can be found in the concept of fundamental rights protected by Sharia rules.

Sharia is far from being a legal textbook. In fact, it is a highly complex system of rules for deriving and applying Islamic norms in a particular context in time and space. The relevant literature, formulated over a period of nearly 1400 years, is as various and colourful as the history

---

[3] For practical examples *cf.* Rohe (2009, forthcoming, p. 82).
[4] *Cf.* Bielefeldt (2003, p. 60) for critical Muslim voices.
[5] For details concerning several European states *cf.* Aluffi and Zincone 2004.
[6] For the intrinsic connection between full religious freedom and secularism *cf.* Bielefeldt (2003, p. 15).

and culture of Islam itself. Islamic law in its different Sunni and Shiite forms as well as the handling of religious norms rely on interpretation and conclusion, thus on human thinking and arguing.[7] Since the early times of Islam experts have not confined themselves to merely applying norms in their strict verbal sense, but asked for the (more or less clear) sense and the aims of these norms (Arab. 'illa). Abū Ishāq al-Shātibī (d. 1388) and others defined basic goods to form these fundamental rights. If these basic goods are taken as a point of departure, existing interpretations of Sharia norms are no longer immutable. Al-Shātibī has explicitly raised the question for the so called 'maqāsid al-sharī'a', the last goals of Islamic normativity.[8] He found these goals in the protection of five goods (Arab. darūrīyāt, necessities) accepted among all peoples, namely religion, life, offspring, property and reason. According to him, these protective aims are absolute and not open to abrogation, but only mutable in single aspects to preserve the very protective aim (al-Shātibī 1421/2000, Vol. 3, 77). Acting under Sharia rules is not an aim in itself: If the superficial circumstances for an act are given, but still the act would not be in accordance with the protective aim, the act would then violate the norm, because the norm was valid only for a certain aim (al-Shātibī 1421/2000, Vol. 2, 285). Those claiming that these aims could not be understood – reproaching the co called bātinīya[9] with this point of view – would destroy Sharia (al-Shātibī 1421/2000, Vol. 2, 291). The norms (Arab. adilla, 'signs') of Sharia were unable to contradict reason, because the ability to understand them by means of reason is the prerequisite for their binding effect (Arab. taklīf) (al-Shātibī 1421/2000, Vol. 3, 16). Only the religious ritual obligations (Arab. 'ibādāt) were beyond human reason, while all other norms were accessible to it.[10] Such approaches have nowadays become the fundament for many reformist interpretations of Sharia rules.[11]

---

[7] Very clear in this respect are Osman (2001, p. 34); Öztürk (2003, p. 103). Cf. also the basic work of Krawietz 2002.
[8] al-Shātibī (1421/2000, Vol. 2, pp. 8, 39 et al.); cf. al-Raysuni (1426/2005, esp. p. 137); Kamali (1999, esp. p. 400). For the present reception of his thought cf. Masud (2001, p. 8 f.); Ibrahim (2007, p. 6); Ibn 'Abdarrahmān 1423/2002; Johnston (2007, pp. 149, 157).
[9] This was a specific term used for the Shiite Ismailis, but also in a broader sense for those rejecting a worldly understanding of texts preferring the 'inner' (Ar. bātin) meaning of it; cf. the article 'baÔiniyya' in EI², Vol. 1 (M.G.S. Hodgson).
[10] al-Shātibī (1421/2000, Vol. 2, pp. 294 et al.). A valuable compilation of his core ideas is presented by al-Raysuni (1426/2005, p. 317).
[11] Cf. only Engineer (1996, pp. 11 ss., 61, 89); Engineer (2003, p. 90); Al 'Alwani (2002, pp. 37, 48); Balić (1984, p. 184); Borrmans (1999, p. 89); Bagby (1985, p. 6); Krämer (1999, p. 177).

Thus, the repeatedly formulated idea of God being the sole legislator[12] is nothing more than an idea without practical content in worldly matters. Since the early times of Islam it has been human beings who interpreted these norms according to their (fallible) human capacities and developed the rules for applying these norms. Moreover, no norm whatsoever would be applicable without any interpretation, at least with respect to its applicability in time and space and regarding the concrete persons bound by it. Such interpretations are dependent on the personalities of their interpreters and the circumstances they are applied in and thus subdue to constant change. The far reaching pluralism among Muslims from the very beginning may be the best proof for that. The range of possible interpretations is not endless, but extremely broad. The Jordanian prince al-Hasan Bin Talāl has described Sharia to be a never ending process.[13] The most difficult 'basic good' to deal with will certainly be 'religion' because traditionally it was the religion of Islam alone to be taken into account. Thus, the principal equality of religions and convictions in public space to be granted in secular states will be the most challenging topic for modern Muslim theology and law. If 'religion' in this sense might be interpreted as 'the common good' irrespective of the particular religious affiliation, the gap could be bridged.

Indeed there are efforts to derive equal rights of religions from Islamic principles. With respect to the participation of religious minorities, the Indian scholar 'Ubaid Allāh Sindhī, who was educated in Deoband (d. 1944) developed a far reaching approach.[14] He demanded a new sight of formulating consensus (ijmā'), including non-Muslims and only aiming at issues of common human interest. According to Muhammad Qasim Zaman this approach may be traced back to the Indian reformist thinker Shāh Walī Allāh (d. 1762) and to the medieval mystic Ibn 'Arabī (d. 1240) and his core idea of unity of creation (wahdat al-wujūd) (Zaman 2006, 153, 167). On this basis the adherents to different religions are able to formulate a common consensus on the basis of their respective religion. It is remarkable that Sindhī published at the time of the Indian independence movement, enabling by his

---

[12] *Cf.* only al-Zuhailī (1997, pp. 651, 657) and the respective statements in the judgment of the Supreme Court of Abu Dhabi, no. 748/1991 of November 15, 1991, quoted in Hammādī (1419/1998, p. 30): According to this decision, legislation is bound by the divine norms of Sharia, thus in cases of conflicts between positive law and Sharia norms the judge has to apply the latter.

[13] During his keynote speech in a conference on religion and the rule of law in Amman (February 27, 2008).

[14] Information about him and his work in Zaman (2006, pp. 153, 162).

theories to build a common identity of Hindus, Muslims and others – this consensus obviously overcomes the limits of the 'religions of the book'.

In a similar way, the Egyptian scholar Fathi Osman demands equal rights for non-Muslims instead of mere tolerance towards them. Their status as 'dhimmis', protected people enjoying only minor rights, is rooted in history, but not in immutable norms. According to him modern Islamic states are institutions founded on firm legal rules. Non-Muslims are a part of these states enjoying full and equal rights (Osman 2001, 42 s., 48 s.). His compatriot Fahmī Huwaidī, who is taken to belong to a moderate Islamist spectrum, published a book under the title of 'Compatriots, not Dhimmis'.[15] He explains, for example, that the poll tax (jizya) was not specifically Islamic, but a Persian heritage (Huwaidī 1999, 128). Its reason was the lack of contributions to the state's defence by these groups. But this has changed nowadays, and all citizens are now paying the same taxes to the state, being then entitled to support according to their needs.

On the other side, western legal orders exclude human rights from any democratic majority rule trying to restrict or abolish them. The German development after the end of the Nazi regime may serve as a particularly fitting example: It was in this country that the state itself turned into a fundamentally anti-human rights legislator and administrator. Thus, how to give human rights a 'secular' foundation while the modern state as the very institution of secularism is not necessarily reliable in granting them? The German reaction was to implement 'human dignity', which can be understood as the very sum of human rights, to be inviolable and protected by the state (cf. only Jarass and Pieroth 2007, art. 1 n. 1). According to art. 79 sect. 3 of the constitution, this provision cannot be changed by any legislative majority whatsoever. The scholarly debate on the foundation of this provision has not come to an end. In any case, art. 1 tries to implement the idea of natural law (whether founded religiously or on mere 'reason') into a normative text, thus creating a 'positive order of natural law'.[16] A former philosophical/moral concept is thereby coined as an enforceable right in practice, unifying the human rights concept of the US Declaration of Independence with the French constitutional approach in the Declaration of 1789 (Sachs and Höfling 2009, art. 1 n. 2).

---

[15] Huwaidī 1999; cf. also Müller (1996, p. 163). For a comparable view An-Na'im (1992, pp. 465, 489, 508).

[16] Sachs and Höfling (2009), art. 1 n. 1 s. with further references; critical of this 'metaphysical' approach Dürig and Herdegen (2003), art. 1 n. 17.

Islam and the Democratic State under the Rule of Law

Thus, it is clear that the secular democratic state under the rule of law is the only model in sight to implement human rights efficiently, and only if the rights of the individual are superior to any state's claim to total control. In this sense the transcendent foundation of human rights is the basis for using them against dictatorial regimes.

This leads some Muslim scholars to reject any 'additional' religious foundation of the human rights-concept. *E.g.*, the French scholar Ghaleb Bencheikh[17] considers all kinds of additional religious reasoning to endanger the fundaments of the secular human rights order. The price to pay for this approach would be the alienation of a considerable number of Muslims seeking a reconciliation of religious and secular concepts, thus being enabled to be both 'good Muslims' and 'good citizens' of a democratic state under the rule of law. Therefore, others like the Iranian Nobel peace prize winner Shirin Ebadi, who was the first woman in Iran to preside over a court before the 'Islamic Revolution', or the Egyptian scholar Nasr Hamid Abu Zaid (Abu Zaid 2001, 68), who suffered from severe prosecution in Egypt (*cf. e.g.* Thielmann 2003) for his reformist religious convictions, try to reconcile the two concepts, not by artificially compromising conflicting issues, but by 'explaining' or 'translating' the concept of human rights into broadly accepted terms of the Islamic culture, thus 'entrenching' and re-tracing it to similarly accepted internal value systems. Amina Wadud simply rejects the idea to leave the definition of the meanings of Islam to neo-conservative extremists (Wadud 2006, 191).

This approach deserves respect in my opinion: One of the major obstacles for reforms in the Islamic world in more than a century was the suspicions against reformers to be collaborators of western dominance and colonial occupiers. If the concept of human rights, which in its formulation (not necessarily in its content) are indeed a western creation, shall be accepted beyond comparatively small minorities of intellectuals or deeply secularized parts of the population, such efforts of entrenchment are the only visible means to achieve this goal in the middle range. In Yemen, for instance, a secular women's organization called Women's Forum for Research and Training began to cooperate with open-minded, reformist Muslim theologians; in their seminars, Qur'anic provisions and international human rights documents are

---

[17] Statement during a conference organized by the Konrad Adenauer Foundation, the Heinrich Böll Foundation and the Bundeszentrale für Politische Bildung on 'Muslime als Staatsbürger' (Muslims as Citizens) in Berlin on February 9, 2007; *cf.* also the discussion mentioned by Wadud (2006, p. 191).

compared to figure out common values *e.g.* with regard to democracy and equal rights for men and women (*cf.* the report of Sabra 2003).

Muslim thought in Europe to this respect deserves particular attention, since there is open space for a free discourse without political claims of power to be involved into the debate.

Muslim Positions and Attitudes Towards the European Secular Democratic State Under the Rule of Law

In sum, there are five models of attitudes among Muslims with respect to the given legal and social framework. These patterns certainly do not describe individuals, but typical approaches among considerable groups respectively. In terms of quantification it is a very tentative approach, because there are still only few empirically reliable data from European countries. Actual research in this field is done.

The 'Muddling Through' Approach (Pragmatics)

A considerable number of Muslims simply do not care about the issue for several reasons (rejection of 'orthodox' rules and positions; preference for mystic ways). They are simply accepting the European legal and social framework in their daily lives without any further theoretical reflections on that topic. Certainly, they are facing several problems, but usually for reasons of a weak economic or educational standing. Some of them would also complain to be prevented from political participation in their countries of domicile, as long as they do not obtain the respective citizenship. Several polls *e.g.* in Austria indicate that they form the largest group of Muslims in Europe. According to polls in Germany among Turks and Germans of Turkish origin (*cf.* von Wilamowitz-Moellendorff 2001, 7), a vast majority would accept democracy to be the best political regime available in our days and actively support it. A new study among Muslims in Germany in general supports this view, while showing that there is a significant minority of c. 10-12% open for radicalization (*cf.* Brettfeld and Wetzels 2007, 492). One should not forget that a considerable number among them has more or less lost relations to religion and religious practice in daily life. From a religious point of view, there is no bar whatsoever among this group to actively participating in a democratic secular state and its society.

The 'Ex-Muslim' Approach

In recent years, some individuals have formulated extremely critical positions towards Islam as such, obviously due to very negative personal experience ('the faction of the angry women'), like Ayaan Hirsi Ali in the Netherlands or Necla Kelek in Germany. In Germany, the 'Central Council of Ex-Muslims' was established, which follows a harsh anti-religious path. Their concepts range from demands for a fundamental reform of Islam to the statement that Islam is not prepared to any reform whatsoever, and that therefore the choice between the secular democratic state and the adherence to Islam is inevitable. As Kelek (2007, Z 1, Z 2) puts it: "For me Islam as a Weltanschauung and a system of values cannot be integrated into the European societies (…) It lacks the institutional, structural and theological prerequisites for that (…). Islam is not capable for integration, whereas the single Muslim as a citizen is. He may preserve his belief and his identity in our society, as the European tolerance of enlightenment perceives the members of all religions to have equal rights." This is an approach obviously aiming at an entire assimilation to secular concepts while abandoning religion as such in total.

Exclusivist Approaches

Among those interested in normative issues concerning the relation between Islamic norms and European orders, there is a small, but dangerous group of extremists rejecting European orders and demanding the supremacy of Islamic norms as a whole. They denounce European legal orders to consist of weak and arbitrary man-made laws in fundamental contrast to the law of God as they perceive it, and European societies to lack any moral standards. Only a small number of them are ready to use violence in promoting their goals; the vast majority would restrict itself to argumentative activities, but creating thereby an atmosphere of structural rejection of the surrounding society, which could enable further radicalization.

Groups like Khilavet Devleti, Hizb al-Tahrir or Murabitun are to be mentioned in this context as well as individual preachers of hatred.[18] The last chairman of Khilavet Devleti for instance openly refused to accept German penal courts when he was accused (and later sentenced) of murder of a rival 'caliph' in Germany. But also organizations like

---

[18] For details cf. e.g. Rohe (2006, pp. 120, 131 ss.).

Tablighi Jamaat cannot be omitted here: Despite their – at least verbal – rejection of violence, their ideology is based on the anti-colonial approach of the Indian Deoband school. It adheres to a massively anti-western and anti-Christian ideology. Even in the Bavarian countryside there were such activities, *e.g.* by disturbing the procession held on Palm Sunday in 2006 in the Franconian village of Pappenheim. I am particularly worried of the fact that such groups – often run or supported by itinerant preachers – obviously try to influence those newly immigrated who are living in especially unstable conditions at that time.

One of the few voices publicly demanding the introduction of Islamic law and Muslim arbitration in Germany is the extremist founder of an Islamic centre in Berlin. In a book on *The Rules of Personal Status of Muslims in the West* (al-Rāfi'ī 2001, *cf.* Rohe 2005, 98, 109 s.), he constantly declares non-Muslims to be infidels and rejects German legal rules and judgments as 'rules of infidelity' (Sālim 2001, 618). Consequently, he urges Muslims in Germany to maintain the rules of traditional Islamic family law. He even argues that the traditional punishment for adultery – flogging or stoning to death – should be applied to Muslim women in Germany (!) who are married to a non-Muslim, even if they are unaware of the 'applicability' of these rules in their cases.[19] He denounces the German system of social security to be evil, because it grants wives independence from their husband's maintenance payments and thus enables them to 'disobey' their husbands (Sālim 2001, 79).

Last not least we have to mention extremist literature spread in many western countries (*cf. e.g.* Rohe 2008, 459, 495 and ss.), heavily funded *e.g.* by Saudi Arabian organizations. This literature is extremely traditionalistic at best, and often even extremist in its attitudes towards non-Muslims and western societies as a whole. Those who follow such concepts seek to live in far reaching segregation from 'non-believers' around them. It is not by accident that the book of the above mentioned extremist was published in Riyadh.

---

[19] Sālim (2001, p. 394). *Cf.* also the results of an essay competition among Muslims in Britain on issues concerning penal law (Mohammed 1995, pp. 14, 37): The winner is quoting a Muslim author saying that Europeans are afraid of the application of Islamic penal norms (ordering harsh corporal punishments which are contradicting human rights) because they have a criminal nature and wish to commit unjustifiable crimes.

Traditionalistic Approaches

Those following traditionalistic approaches usually would heavily reject the extremist ideology mentioned above as far as it concerns the use of violence or the attempts to gain political power as such. On the other hand, there are remarkable similarities between them and the Islamists with respect to 'social norms' concerning gender issues. According to my experience they do not represent the majority of Muslims in Europe, but are the best organized group particularly in mosques.

Traditionalists mostly intend to co-operate with non-Muslims and are ready to integrate into the given order, but maintain a very traditional position towards gender-related issues and in matters of orthopraxy. Insofar they would follow the concept of preserving religious identity in a structurally 'alien' environment. In general they use traditional mediaeval sources without considering modern approaches of reinterpreting the sources according to time and place, which is part of Islamic tradition, too.

A defensive stance of this approach towards the 'preferable Muslim life in Muslim societies' is characteristic of its European adherents. Typically they would base the necessary adaptations of their religious practice to the given conditions to be justified by the principle of necessity (darūra). Thus, they perceive themselves to live in a permanent state of religious emergency. This position is based on the mediaeval Islamic concept of the two worlds – dār al-Islām, house of Islam, and dār al-harb, house of war – in confrontation, but with a zone connected to the Islamic world by (temporary) peace treaties (dār al-'ahd[20]) where Muslims can live in security and therefore are obliged to respect the prevalent law of the land. Nevertheless, in the past many Muslim lawyers advised against long stays abroad (outside the dār al-Islām), fearing that this could prevent Muslims from fulfilling their religious duties.[21] This fear is obviously due to historical events and experiences during the Reconquista (cf. only Dressendörfer 1971), the crusades and later hostile encounters between Christian European and Islamic powers. It is not by accident that the concept of the fundamental distinction between two opposite houses was mainly elaborated in these times. Similar points of view can still be found today among very

---

[20] Cf. article 'dār al-'ahd' in Wizārat al-awqāf wa l-shu'ūn al-islāmīya 1990; 'Abd al-Qādir (1419/1998, p. 59) as well as the references in EI², Leiden 1991 under 'dār al-Òulî' (Macdonald).

[21] Cf. Ibn Rushd (1325/1907, Vol. 2, p. 286); even stricter statements in al-Qairawānī (1994, p. 486); Khoury (1985, p. 128); cf. also Miller (2000, p. 258).

traditional, sometimes extremely anti-western lawyers.[22] The central point always seems to be the fear that the Islamic world may be weakened by migration. However, this obviously does not correspond with our present reality: according to a new survey one third of all Muslims live outside Islamic states, many of them by their own choice.[23]

Thus, the concept of dār al-'ahd may serve as a fundament for a peaceful co-existence in a diaspora situation, since it obliges Muslims not to break the law of the land as an equivalent for being granted personal security and protection by the state of residence. However, it is doubtful whether the self-definition of a 'diaspora' would be very helpful for actively being part of and contributing to society as a whole.

Nevertheless, some Muslims are developing a so called 'fiqh al-aqallīyāt', a system of rules for Muslim minorities based on the traditional concepts: According to this system, Muslims are entitled to live in European states, are obliged to accept the prevalent law and may find viable solutions in practicing their belief as a minority. But within this system, Muslims structurally define themselves to remain 'foreigners' in European societies. Some would try to maintain or to promote the application of Islamic legal norms to the broadest possible extent in European states.

In sum, traditionalistic views enable Muslims to justify a peaceful co-existence, but in a comparatively far reaching distance to society as a whole. This attitude will certainly create problems in situations requiring more than a mere acceptance of the law of the land, *e.g.* in cases of obtaining citizenship or administrative functions. In these cases, it is a necessary requirement to actively support the core rules of secular democratic states granting human rights. Besides that, it would be problematic to educate future generations in structural distance, *i.e.* the conviction that, while the law of the land has to be accepted as a matter of fact, it should be replaced by a non-secular order in the future.

Religious Positions of Civic Entrenchment and Their Historical Burden

The fifth way is based on the idea of substantial integration into European societies, to fully accept and contribute to their leading principles and laws while preserving Muslim identity within the given frame of far reaching freedom of religion.

---

[22] See Ibn Baz and al-Uthaymeen (1998, in particular p. 71); The Fiqh Council of the Muslim World League on its 16th session in Mecca (1422/2002, pp. 8, 11).
[23] Kettani (1986, p. 18); also see Abedin (1990, p. 1).

For instance, the Bosnian Muslim lawyer Enes Karić, who teaches at the Islamic Faculty in Sarajevo, explicitly states that the caliphate is not a part of the religion of Islam.[24] Instead, his approach to states legislation and administration is solely looking at contents. His starting point is his interpretation of Sharia to be a set of rules with moral goals. According to his understanding, a state which is willing to provide a sufficient social structure, e.g. funds for students or pensions, which intends to establish economic and social justice, which respects and promotes human rights, is an Islamic state in this sense (according to the proverb he cited ''adl al-dawlati īmānuhā, zulm al-dawlati kufruhā' – justice is the belief of a state, injustice is its unbelief). Finally he describes the European secular democratic state under the rule of law to fulfil these demands and concludes: 'Therefore, we don't need a double system'.[25] He perceives the concept of citizenship to be a major European achievement. At the same conference Mustafa Ef. Klanco, the Bosnian chief imam of Germany, formulated that the sooner Muslims in Europe are ready to leave diaspora-thinking behind them, the better the necessary state of integration will be achieved. At the same time he is blaming the installation of imams being sent to the country ill-prepared and only for a few years for major deficiencies to this respect. On a more theoretical level, a Muslim participant[26] in a public discussion in Vienna on the secular state's need for religion pointed out that it is a task for Muslims to adopt the states public order, namely the concepts of tolerance, acceptance of the law, readiness to contribute and bear responsibility, and solidarity. He demanded to internalize, to 'theologize' these indispensable values.[27] This approach would mean to value the principles of the democratic secular state granting human rights from a religious point of view rather than to substantiate the system by religious norms.

The French imam Tareq Oubrou has stated that a concept of Sharia should be developed which replaces the legal mechanisms of Sharia by those of the prevalent French law (1998, 28). Concerning *fatwas* given in Europe, Oubrou demands that the mufti has to keep in mind that

---

[24] *Cf.* also Enes Karić, 20th Century Islamic Thought in Bosnia and Hercegovina, to appear in 2009 quoting the author E.N. Bulbulović, who dealt with the caliphate issue in the 1920s.

[25] Lecture held during a conference in Sarajevo organized by the German Friedrich Ebert Foundation on November 19, 2007.

[26] He is teaching at the Vienna academy for the education of teachers in Islamic instruction.

[27] Report by Prof. Andreas Khol (2007, p. 37), the former president of the Austrian national Assembly.

the application of the *fatwa* has to fit into the ruling legal framework. Therefore, the mufti has to know this framework and its interpretation (*ibid.*, 39). Positions of this kind would enable Muslims to actively participate in society.

Thus, more and more Muslim thinkers are seeking new approaches to defining Islamic life as a part of the given legal and societal conditions of life in Europe. They reject the former division between dār al-Islām and dār al-harb, saying that in our days earth is simply 'one house' for mankind as a whole, and that every Muslim is entitled to live in any part of the world and is responsible for the sake of the society he/she is living in. They stress that there is no support for the classical view, neither in the Qur'an nor in the sunna, and that it is no more than an invention of the classical lawyers.[28] Instead of that, intense international co-operation and common legal rules and values are creating completely different conditions that do not allow a concept of general hostility, as developed in the past in Europe and in the Islamic world alike to be maintained. According to them, the entire world nowadays constitutes one single camp ('dār wāhida'), one all-embracing 'dār al-'ahd'.[29]

At the same time, the above-mentioned French imam Tareq Oubrou (1998) presented an 'Introduction théorique à la charî'a de minorité', in which he proposes the removal of mere cultural 'foreign influences' associated with Islam which hinder integration in France (*ibid.*, 28). His approach is strongly supported by Muslim women organizations and intellectuals who are for example searching for a renewed Islamic understanding of equality of sexes, criticizing widespread phenomena of oppression and assaults against girls and women[30] and cautiously distinguishing religious commands from cultural phenomena which

---

[28] *E.g.* Zakaria (1989, p. 54); Oubrou (2003, pp. 193, 197); "Graz Declaration" of a conference of leaders of Islamic centers and imams in Europe in Graz/Austria, June 13-15, 2003: "The medieval distinction between opposite 'dar al-Islam' and 'dar al-harb' has to be objected. It is based neither in the Qur'an nor in the sunna, and has no relevance whatsoever nowadays, being a historical phenomenon which is outdated since a very long time" (author's translation from the German version). The declaration is published on the homepage of the Islamic Community in Austria http://www.derislam.at/islam.php?name=Themen&pa=showpage&pid=66; also see the references in Shadid and van Koningsveld (1995, para. 3.2).

[29] At the ISESCO conference in Frankfurt am Main/Germany on September 29 and 30, 2003 on "Dialogue among Civilizations: Diversity within complementarity" the Muslim participants from all over the Islamic world and Europe unanimously agreed on this concept.

[30] *Cf.* Badawi (1995, pp. 73, 75 s. and 79); Sheriff 2003, p. 11; Abdul-Rauf (1995, p. 120); Mahmoud (1995, p. 76); Çileli 1999; AG Korbach (2003), p. 335.

influence daily life sometimes much more than the former.³¹ This new approach opens a broad space for the harmonization of the European legal framework with Islamic life in Europe.

Such harmonization may be achieved by the search for common grounds in the respective intentions of secular and religious norms.

According to my experience a huge number of Muslims does not share the restrictive traditionalist view and would support a more integrative approach, that is, to define Europe to be the 'home' of European Muslims. Muslim thinkers like Fathi Osman stress that "permanently living in a country, and in many cases acquiring its citizenship, implies a commitment to observing its laws and caring for its interest and that fulfilling this commitment is a moral and legal obligation in Islam".³² Let me conclude here with the words of a prominent French Muslim, who acted as an imam in the city of Marseille and enjoys a high reputation among liberal Muslims in France and Europe as a whole (while others heavily criticize him):

> The presence of Islam in France gives Muslims the unexpected opportunity for experiments and to develop the theology of a minority among other minorities. This opportunity is not only due to the fact that France has a cosmopolitan society containing a strong Muslim community. It is mainly based on France being a laicist state and realizing this laicism by the neutrality of its official authority towards religious issues whatsoever. This lack of state intervention, in combination with the lack of social pressure, which is known in Muslim societies, permits the creation of reformist and liberal tendencies for the sake of Islam. This theology of minorities is not only interesting and beneficial for the Muslims in France, by ensuring their peaceful and brotherly co-existence with the other communities. A great interest also consists in the fact that it is transferable to the Islamic world itself. If Islam does not wish to be excluded from the new international order to be seen on the horizon, it has to prepare itself to the Universal, also internally, and has to accept that it represents a minority among others in a global perspective, a contributing partner and not an aggressive enemy. Nowadays human rights, the freedom of belief and conscience and laicism are the most consented principles and are solely in

---

³¹ *Cf.* Karmi (1996, pp. 69 ss.); Engineer (1996, p. 11); Barlas 2002; al-Mughni (2001, p. 184); Osman (1996, p. 20).
³² Osman (2001, pp. 27, 33); Osman quotes Qu'ran surahs 5:1; 16:91-6; 17:34 to support his opinion.

the position to conduct the human society, which is so pluralistic. These principles are free of an ideology, which would contradict the ruling ideologies or would contravene one of them. They do not demand to respect one single ideology or confession; they demand to respect other human beings, all of them, whatsoever might be his convictions or belief. This is the 'ma'rūf' of our days. These ethics, well known and recognized in mankind as a whole, will have to lead the initiatives of every interpreter willing to fill the Holy Qur'an with life here and now. (Bencheikh 1998, 188, author's translation from French)

This position will enable Muslims in Europe not only to accept the ruling ideas and laws concerning democracy, the rule of law and the protection of human rights including the equality of sexes and religions in a sense of 'bearing' them, while maintaining the self-definition to be a permanent minority alien to the majority society, but to actively participate in developing the society they are part of.

Concluding Remarks

Two or three decades ago, the issue I was discussing here would have been mere fiction. In most of the European societies except some regions on the Balkans, there were only few numbers of Muslims living there permanently or for a longer time. In others, like France and the UK, the kind of relations dating from colonial times was more or less maintained concerning Muslims living in the mainland. Hardly anybody cared about a 'Muslim identity in Europe'. After having realized that there will be a stable Muslim presence in Europe, the question of such a Muslim identity arose among many Muslims here. Some of them appear to formulate a defense for Muslim existence in Europe against demands to refrain from living there. Others plead for a more intense self-engagement in the existing political parties, NGOs or other initiatives, refuse the idea of creating specific Muslim organizations and consider the formulation of a theological framework for Muslims in Europe to be useless[33] or even harmful: According to them, it would submit the system

---

[33] Statement of Dr. Hasni Abidi, Director of the Centre for Studies and Research in the Arab World and the Mediterranean, Geneva, at the ISESCO conference in Frankfurt am Main on September 29 and 30, 2003.

Islam and the Democratic State under the Rule of Law

of the secular democratic state under religious supervision.[34] Some of them focus on practical problems concerning daily life, while others try to create a theoretical, theologically well-funded framework for Muslim life and self-definition in a mainly non-Muslim environment. Until now these initiatives are rare, but are increasing in number and intensity. This might be due to the fact that Muslims now are convinced to stay in Europe permanently, and to the increasing number of well-educated Muslims dealing with these issues. In the latter sense, Sharia in Europe would mean to define Sharia rules for Muslims here in accordance with the indispensable values of democracy, human rights and the rule of law governing European legal orders. Within the framework of these orders, Muslims have to be enabled to practice their belief not only in a theoretical position, but in daily life. Insofar all Europeans should remember that freedom of religion and therefore religious pluralism is an integral part of the liberal European constitutions, and that everybody who is willing to respect the rule of the land should enjoy this freedom. The ECHR would grant a – very considerable - European minimum standard of rights, whereas some national constitutions including the German one open even broader space.

In sum, the secular legal orders in Europe don't refuse religion; they are not at all anti-religious.[35] To the contrary, in general they open a broad space for religious belief and life regardless of whether the religion of the majority or of smaller groups is at stake. There is sound reason for an optimistic view, given the fact that there are stable majorities in Western societies among Muslims and non-Muslims interested in a peaceful co-existence and accepting individual perspectives of living within the balanced legal orders of necessary unity and far reaching diversity under the common basic rules, rights and duties.[36]

---

[34] In this sense Ghaleb Bencheikh at a conference in Berlin on February 9, 2007 by the Konrad Adenauer Foundation, the Heinrich Böll Foundation and the Bundeszentrale für Politische Bildung on the issue of 'Muslime als Staatsbürger' (Muslims as Citizens).

[35] *Cf.* Bielefeldt (2003, p. 60) for critical Muslim voices.

[36] *Cf.* the words of the former president of the European Commission Romano Prodi concerning the dialogue of cultures: "It is not the matter just to passively experience events and to accept a cultural uniformity within which the values and the will of the strongest would be imposed on the rest. The European Union, a singular example of democratic constitution and integration of different cultures, can prove that there is an alternative formula to cultural uniformity or domination: a dialogue which respects different cultures and their representatives, as long as these different cultures are ready to respect the fundamental values of man." "Valoriser l'héritage culturel commun!", *Le Figaro* 2002, April 4, p. 14.

References

'Abd al-Qādir, K. (1419/1998), *Fiqh al-aqallīyāt al-muslima*, Beirut, Dār al-Īmān.
Abdul-Rauf, M., *Women and the Family* (3rd ed.), Alexandria, VA, Al-Saadawi, 1995.
Abedin, S.Z., "Muslim Minority Communities in the World Today", *Islamochristiana* 1990, Vol. 16, 1-14.
Abu Zaid, N.H., *Ein Leben mit dem Islam*, Freiburg im Breisgau, Herder, 2001 AG Korbach, "Beschluss vom 23.01.2003. 7 F 996/02", *Familie, Partnerschaft, Recht (FPR)* 2003, 334.
Al 'Alwani, T.J., " Für ein korrektes Verständnis der Sunnah", in T.J. al 'Alwani and 'I. al D. Khalil (ed.), *Der Koran und die Sunnah. Raum Zeit Faktor*, Köln, GMSG, 2002.
Aluffi, R. and Zincone, G. (ed.), *The Legal Treatment of Islamic Minorities in Europe*, Leuven, Peeters, 2004.
Badawi, Z., "Muslim Justice in a Secular State", in M. King (ed.), *God's Law versus State Law*, London, Grey Seal, 1995.
Bagby, I.A., "The Issue of MaÒlaÎa in Classical Islamic Legal Theory", *International Journal of Islamic and Arabic Studies* 1985, Vol. 2, No. 2, 1-11.
Balić, S., *Ruf vom Minarett* (3rd ed.), Hamburg, EB-Verlag Rissen, 1984.
Barlas, A., *'Believing Women' in Islam. Unreading Patriarchal Interpretations of the Qur'an*, Austin, University of Texas Press, 2002.
Bencheikh, S., *Marianne et le Prophète – L'Islam dans la France laïque*, Paris, Grasset, 1998.
Bielefeldt, H., *Muslime im säkularen Rechtsstaat* (Transcript), Bielefeld, 2003.
Borrmans, M., "Cultural Dialogue and 'Islamic Specificity'", in G.M. Muñoz (ed.), *Islam, Modernism and the West. Cultural and Political Relations at the End of the Millennium*, London, Tauris, 1999.
Brettfeld, K. and Wetzels, P.,"Muslime in Deutschland – Integration, Integrationsbarrieren, Religion sowie Einstellungen zu Demokratie, Rechtsstaat und politisch-religiös motivierter Gewalt", in Bundesministerium des Innern (ed.), *Ergebnisse von Befragungen im Rahmen einer multizentrischen Studie in städtischen Lebensräumen*, Hamburg, 2007.
Çileli, S., *Wir sind Eure Töchter, nicht Eure Ehr"*, Michelstadt, Neuthor-Verlag, 1999.

Dahlab/Switzerland, "Entscheidung vom 25.02.2001", *Neue Zeitschrift für Verwaltungsrecht (NVwZ)* 2001, 1389.
Dressendörfer, P., *Islam unter der Inquisition. Die Morisco-Prozesse in Toledo 1575-1610*, Wiesbaden, Steiner, 1971.
Dürig, G. and Herdegen, M., *Grundgesetz. Kommentierung der Artikel 1 und 2 Grundgesetz* (special issue), Munich, Beck Juristischer Verlag, 2003.
Encyclopaedia of Islam (EI²) (2nd ed.), Leiden, Brill, 1986-2002.
Engineer, A.A., *The Rights of Women in Islam*, New York, St. Martin's Press, 1996.
Engineer, A.A., *On Developing Theology of Peace in Islam*, New Delhi, Sterling, 2003.
European Parliament, Directorate General for Internal Policies of the Union, *Islam in the European Union: What's at Stake in the Future?*, 2007.
The Fiqh Council of the Muslim World League on its 16th session in Mecca (1422/2002), reported in "A message from Muslim scholars to Muslim Minorities in the West", *Daawah*, No. 4.
Hammādī, H. (1419/1998), *Qadā' al-hudūd wa l-qisās wa l-diya, majmū'at al-mabādi' allatī qarrarathā al-mahkama al-ittihādīya al-'ulyā mundhu inshā'ihā wa hattā l-ān*, Abu Dhabi.
Huwaidī, F., *Muwātinūn la dhimmīyūn* (3rd ed.), Cairo, Dār ash-Shurūq, 1999.
Ibn 'Abdarrahmān, 'A. (1423/2002), *'Ilm maqāsid al-shāri'*, Jāmi'at al-Imām Muhammad bin Sa'ūd al-Islāmīya, Riyadh.
Ibn Baz, A. and al-Uthaymeen, M. S., *Muslim Minorities – Fatawa Regarding Muslims Living as Minorities, Message of Islam*, Hounslow, 1998.
Ibn Rushd (1325/1907), *al-Muqaddima al-mumahhida*, Vol. 2, Cairo.
Ibrahim, M., *Maqāsid al Šarī'a. Islamische Šarī'a versus Menschenrechte?*, Darmstadt, 2007.
Islamische Glaubensgemeinschaft in Österreich (ed.), *Die Grazer Erklärung der europäischen „Imamekonferenz" vom Juni 2003*, available at http://www.derislam.at/islam.php?name=Themen&pa=showpage&pid=66 (accessed 30 March 2009).
Jarass, H.D. and Pieroth, B., *Grundgesetz für die Bundesrepublik Deutschland. Kommentar* (9th ed.), Munich, Beck Juristischer Verlag, 2007.
Johnston, D., "MaqāÒid al Sharī'a: Epistemology and Hermeneutics of Muslim Theologies of Human Rights", *Die Welt des Islams* 2007, Vol. 47 No. 2, 149-187.

Kamali, M.H., *Principles of Islamic Jurisprudence* (2nd ed.), Petaling Jaya, Ilmiah Publishers, 1999.
Karmi, G., "Women, Islam and Patriarchalism", in M. Yamani (ed.), *Feminism and Islam*, New York, Ithaca Press, 1996.
Kelek, N., "Freiheit, die ich meine", *Frankfurter Allgemeine Zeitung* 2007, 15 Dec., pp. Z 1, Z 2.
Kettani, M.A., *Muslim Minorities in the World Today*, London, Mansell, 1986.
Khol, A., "In Gottes Namen", *Die Presse* 2007, 17 Nov., p. 37.
Khoury, A.T., *Islamische Minderheiten in der Diaspora*, Mainz, Grünewald, 1985.
Krämer, G., "Techniques and Values: Contemporary Muslim Debates on Islam and Democracy", in G.M. Muñoz (ed.), *Islam, Modernism and the West. Cultural and Political Relations at the End of the Millennium*, London, Tauris, 1999.
Krawietz, B., *Hierarchie der Rechtsquellen im tradierten sunnitischen Islam*, Berlin, Duncker & Humblot, 2002.
Mahmood, T., *Uniform Civil Code. Fictions and Facts*, Delhi, India and Islam Research Council, 1995.
Masud, M.K., *Muslim Jurists' Quest for the Normative Basis of Shari'a*, Inaugural Lecture, Leiden, ISIM, 2001.
Miller, K.A., "Muslim Minorities and the Obligation to Emigrate to Islamic Territory", *Islamic Law and Society* 2000, Vol. 7, 256-288.
Mohammed, A., [no title], in *Essays on Islam. Essay Competition. Winning Entries* (ed.), Leicester, The Federation of Student Islamic Societies, 1995.
al-Mughni, H., *Women in Kuwait. The Politics of Gender*, London, Saqi Books, 2001.
Müller, L., *Islam und Menschenrechte. Sunnitische Muslime zwischen Islamismus, Säkularismus und Modernismus*, Hamburg, Deutsches Orient-Institut, 1996.
An-Na`im, A., "Religious Freedom in Egypt: Under the Shadow of the Islamic Dhimma System", in L. Swidler (ed.), *Muslims in Dialogue*, New York, E. Mellen Press 1992.
Osman, F., *The Children of Adam. An Islamic Perspective on Pluralism*, Washington D.C., Center for Muslim-Christian Understanding, History and International Affairs, 1996.
Osman, F., "Islam and Human Rights", in A. El-Affendi (ed.), *Rethinking Islam and Modernity. Essays in Honour of Fathi Osman*, Leicester, The Islamic Foundation, 2001.

Oubrou, T., "Introduction théorique à la charî'a de minorité", *Islam de France* 1998, Vol. 2, 27-41.
Oubrou, T., "Die 'Minderheits-Scharia' in Frankreich: Reflexionen zu einer rechtlichen Integration des Islam", in A. Escudier (ed.), *Der Islam in Europa. Der Umgang mit dem Islam in Frankreich und Deutschland*, Göttingen, Wallstein, 2003.
Öztürk, Y.N., "Die Zeit nach den Propheten. Der Koran fordert Demokratie. Wer islamische Despotien verteidigt, fälscht Gottes Wort", *Die Zeit* 2003, No. 9, available at http://www.zeit.de/2003/09/Essay__85zt_9frk (accessed 30 March 2009).
Potz, R. and Wieshaider, W. (ed.), *Islam and the European Union*, Leuven, Peeters, 2004.
al-Qairawānī, A.M., *Kitāb al-jihād min kitāb al-nawādir wa l-ziyādāt* (M. von Bredow, co-author), Stuttgart, Franz Steiner Verlag, 1994.
al-Rāfi'ī, S., *Ahkām al-ahwāl al-shakhsīya li l-muslimīn fī l-gharb*, Riyadh, Dār al-Watan, 2001.
al-Raysuni, A. (1426/2005), *Imam al-Shatibi's Theory of the Higher Objectives and Intents of Islamic Law*, London, International Institute of Islamic Thought.
Rohe, M., "Islamisten und Schari'a", in *Islamismus – Berlin, Diskussion eines vielschichtigen Phänomens* (ed.), Berlin, Senatsverwaltung für Inneres, 2005.
Rohe, M., "Islamismus und Schari'a", in *Integration und Islam* (ed.), Nuremberg, Bundesamt für Migration und Flüchtlinge, 2006.
Rohe, M., *Muslim Minorities and the Law in Europe. Chances and Challenges*, Delhi Global Media Publications, 2007.
Rohe, M., "Muslimische Identität und Recht in Kanada", *RabelsZ* 2008, Vol. 72, 459-512.
Rohe, M. *Islam and the Foundations of Human Rights*, lecture held in Radboud University Nijmegen, 2009 (forthcoming).
Rohe, M. and Elster, S., "Zur öffentlichrechtlichen Situation von Muslimen in ausgewählten europäischen Ländern", in *Perspektiven und Herausforderungen in der Integration muslimischer Mitbürger-Innen in Österreich* (ed.), Vienna, Bundesministerium des Inneren Wien/Sicherheitsakademie, 2006, available at http://www.bmi.gv.at/downloadarea/asyl_fremdenwesen/Perspektiven_Herausforderungen.pdf (accessed 30 March 2009).
Sabra, M., "Working Together against Legal Discrimination and Male Violence", *Qantara.de* 2003, available at http://www.qantara.de/webcom/show_article.php/_c-478/_nr-21/_p-1/i.html (accessed 30 March 2009).

Sachs, M. and Höfling, W., *Grundgesetz. Kommentar* (5th ed.), Beck Juristischer Verlag, Munich, 2009.

Sahin, L, "Urteil vom 10.11.2005", *Neue Zeitschrift für Verwaltungsrecht (NVwZ)* 2006, 1389.

Shadid, W. and van Koningsveld, P.S., *Religious Freedom and the Position of Islam in Western Europe*, Kampen, Kok Pharos, 1995.

al-Shātibī, A.I. (1421/2000), *al-Muwāfaqāt fī usūl al-sharī'a* (4 vols), Muhammad 'Abd al-Qādir al-Fādilī (ed.), Beirut, al-Maktaba al-'Asrīya.

Sheriff, S., "Forced marriage", *Muslim News* 2001, 29 Aug., No. 172, p. 11.

Thielmann, J., *Naṣr Ḥāmid Abū Zaid und die wiedererfundene Ḥisba*, Würzburg, Ergon, 2003.

von Wilamowitz-Moellendorff, U., *Türken in Deutschland – Einstellungen zu Staat und Gesellschaft* (Arbeitspapier No. 53), in Konrad-Adenauer-Stiftung (ed.), 2001.

Wadud, A., *Inside the Gender Jihad. Women's Reform in Islam*, Oxford, Oneworld, 2006.

Wizārat al-awqāf wa l-shu'ūn al-islāmīya (ed.), *al-Mawsū'a al-fiqhīya*, Vol. 20, 2nd ed., Kuwait, 1990.

Zakaria, R., *Is Islam Secular?*, Aligarh, Sir Syed Academy, Aligarh Muslim University, 1989.

Zaman, M.Q., "Consensus and Religious Authority in Modern Islam", in G. Krämer and S. Schmidtke (ed.), *Speaking for Islam. Religious Authorities in Muslim Societies*, Leiden Brill, 2006.

al-Zuhailī, W., al-Fiqh al-islāmī wa-adillatuhu (Vol. 6), Damascus, Dār al-Fikr, 1997.

TOWARD THE TRIUMPH OF REASON

Mohammed Benzakour

These days I tend to see my friends in terms of their attitude toward the downtrodden. If they concede but a millimetre to honouring the circus heroes of global capital, under the guise of an – at best two-faced – proclamation of 'western' achievements such as freedom and democracy, then I stop considering them as friends; it seems that the mask of culture behind which they used to hide was nothing but a thin veneer. People can debate whether Berlusconi, Bush, Blair, Sarkozy, Merkel or Balkenende are clever politicians or good leaders, but to regard them even for a moment as defenders of Civilisation is proof that our highly acclaimed 'Reason' is in need of a good overhaul.

According to a common conception, the Islamic world has no 'separation of church and state', and in the final analysis this identification of religious and political power is considered the chief obstacle to a secularisation of Islamic societies. Quite apart from the fact that it was only in the days of Muhammad's leadership that secular and religious power coincided, it is unreasonable to strive for this ideal now, since it was only in that period that the faith community was led by someone who had access to divine revelation – Muhammad. Moreover, this argument unfortunately overlooks the crucial tenet (one that I am very fond of) that in Islam all believers are equal, since all Muslims have the same direct, irreplaceable, *individual* relationship to God (something that the Reformed Church, with its predestination, and the Catholic Church with its papal authority approach a bit differently). It is this highly individual relationship that makes me averse to imposed dogmas, firmly drawn principles, forms and rites, since they say nothing about the *essence* of the divine. The divine is something I encounter at times on a snow-capped mountain top, and sometimes in the inkwell, but even more often in the small hours of the night, when by candlelight a tender woman softly caresses my ear with the tip of her tongue.

Be that as it may, to each his or her own conception of God, live and let live, but we must never allow a reality shaped by the spirit of the age to blind us to the proper configuration of Cause & Effect. Anyone who maliciously reverses that configuration or presents it in a one-sided fashion does violence not only to history but first and foremost to humanity itself. Therefore it is good to recall that movements which (as in the prophetic era) sought to unite worldly and religious power (also known as 'Islamists') found their source and inspiration in historical social circumstances more than in holy writ (which is seen by many neo-conservative populists as 'instructions for terrorism').

It is a moving story, but the great impetus for these political movements came more or less after the collapse of the Ottoman Empire, during the First World War (1914-1918), when England and France created mandates and protectorates (fancy words for shameless exploitation) in Syria, Lebanon, Iraq and Palestine. Thus Islam as a whole, which until the rise of the modern West had been the greatest power in the world, was reduced to as series of separate, dependent entities. Whereas in Europe and America, modernity had led to a completely new independence, in the Islamic world it came hand in hand with a humiliating dependence. Muslims would not be human if this did not bother them. The colonial powers treated the natives with great disdain, and it was not long before Muslims discovered that their new overlords had nothing but deep contempt for their religious traditions, or rather: their *identity*. The Europeans may have brought numerous improvements to their colonies in the fields of medicine, education and the physical infrastructure (which according to V.S. Naipaul was insufficient, since colonialism had promised to bring civilisation but failed miserably in doing so), but those improvements did not always lead to unqualified satisfaction. Thus the Suez Canal (an initiative of the French consul Ferdinand de Lesseps) was a disaster for Egypt (which, it is no coincidence, was the cradle of Islamism). It seemed that Egypt had to provide all the money, labour and materials and, what is more, give up an area of five hundred square kilometres – while the shares in the Suez Canal company were exclusively in the hands of Europeans! Partly because of these immense expenditures, Egypt went bankrupt, giving England the excuse in 1882 for a military occupation in order to protect the interests of its shareholders. Of course, railways and paved roads were built in the colonies, but the local population seldom benefited. The infrastructure was intended primarily for the advancement of the colonists themselves. The mission schools, which often taught children to look down on their own culture, gave the local population an unmistakable sense that on the one hand they were held in contempt by the West, while on the other hand they were no better off with the tyrannical elites who ruled the roost. One of the most damaging consequences of colonialism was the gulf that (unconsciously?) opened up between people with a western-style education and everyone else; the latter constituted a mass of people who remained inevitably stuck in a pre-modern status quo, with all the domestic clashes and the inability to understand them that continues to this day.

Thus, in Iran, a revolution took place led by a coalition of freethinking Iranians and reform-minded ulamas. This revolution led to the introduction of a parliament and a constitution, but the English, after discovering oil in Iran, wanted to set up a protectorate and continually fiddled with the elections. From 1921 onwards, the Pahlawi shahs - with the support first of England and later of America - established dictatorships in which no parliamentary opposition was possible.

After the Second World War, England and France became secondrate powers and the United States became the leader of the western world. Although Islamic countries may no longer have been colonies and were independent in name, yet America continued to hold their fate in its hands. During the Cold War, the United States sought allies in the region by lending support to unsavoury governments and unpopular leaders. A truly disastrous example occurred in 1953, after Shah Mohammed Reza Pahlawi was ousted and forced to leave Iran. He was returned to the throne thanks to a bloody coup d'état devised by the British intelligence services and the CIA. Later, Saddam Hussein, who became president of Iraq in 1979, enjoyed the protection of the United States, who allowed him to plunder and murder with impunity – even when in a single afternoon he gassed 5000 Kurds. Only after the invasion of Kuwait did Hussein become the target of America's wrath and enmity. The motives behind this about-face are not difficult to guess.

Intellectuals who omit to consider this historical dimension when they turn to speak of the rise of 'political Islam' are pulling the wool over people's eyes. For while the Arab battlefields are still soaked with blood, millions of ordinary Muslim citizens are feeling more betrayed, abandoned and helpless than ever. When we talk to them, a deep sorrow glistens in their eyes: 'we are prisoners in our own country'. And the fact that in a disaster (the earthquakes in Turkey, Egypt and Morocco, for instance), the government services regularly reach the affected areas 24 hours later than the Islamic charitable organisations reinforces citizens' conviction that 'faith in Allah' is their last hope in a 'country that is corrupt from top to bottom'.

In short: the protest against Western elements that is formulated in Islamist terms is, in the end, not a moral protest against a modernisation that is happening 'too fast'; no, it is rather a reaction to a development process that *is not going fast enough*. The political scientist Nazih Ayubi put it strikingly: 'the Islamists are not angry because the airplane has replaced the camel: they are angry because they could board the plane.'

Back to the Qur'an. Although this holy book emphasises that war is justified only as self-defence, the Islamists consider that America and Israel are the natural aggressors. What their hearts and their eyes tell them is that since the foundation of Israel, tens of thousands of their Muslim brethren in Palestine have seen their houses daily attacked by American grenades; that in Afghanistan over ten thousand citizens have been killed; that the bankruptcy of Iraq – once the Islamic cradle of civilization and art – is the result not only of the lust for oil rather than for 'democracy' but also of the economic sanctions led by the Americans that had already caused the death of a hundred thousand Iraqis, including many children. About the sanctions, former American Secretary of State Madeleine Albright had drily noted that 'this is a very hard choice, but the price is worth it'.

Let us draw our conclusions. What lessons did the world's most powerful nation learn from September 11th? 9/11 led to a hundred times the number of deaths in the Twin Towers, and the recent massacres in the Gaza Strip are but the continuation of a policy launched by Ben Gurion. The 'War against Terrorism' is a noble struggle in theory, but in practice it is looking more and more like a 'War of Terrorism'. This should not come as a surprise, for it is a well-known law of nature: the more fanatically one struggles against something, the more one begins to resemble that which is being fought. When a war is presented as a battle between Good and Evil, then essentially there is no reason to look for the roots of the violence, for in such cases, it is pointless to seek a fundamental understanding.

But that is dangerous and foolish. For if we do our best to cut through the religious language of Bin Laden or of the leaders of Hamas, we hear something else: a pattern of deep hurt and frustration with a long and bloody background – something that has for quite some time now been part of the repertoire of all sorts of anti-imperialist groups in the Third World.

In J.M. Coetzee's novel *The Lives of Animals*, the main character, Elizabeth Costello, asks herself the question: "If I can think my way into the existence of a being who never existed, then I can think my way into the existence of a bat or a chimpanzee." I in turn would ask the question: if we can feel empathy with fictional characters, and now even with animals (a few years ago, a Party for the Animals was founded in the Netherlands), why do we have so much difficulty empathising with real people, with mortals with whom we share the substrate of life?

Empathy is a form of tolerance and of pain. It takes intellectual curiosity and frenetic literary energy to understand why someone acts as he or she does. Even a person who decides to blow himself up in a bus. The willingness to think deeply about this complex, existential question – that would be a true step along the way toward the triumph of Reason.

List of contributors

Ahmed Aboutaleb grew up as a son of an imam in a small Moroccan village in the Rif region. Together with his mother and brothers he moved to the Netherlands in 1976 at the age of 15. Aboutaleb" then studied telecommunications at different schools up to the "Hogere Technische School where he obtained a Bachelor of Engineering degree. After graduating he found work as reporter first for radio Veronica and subsequently for NOS-radio and *RTL Nieuws*. He also worked at the public relations department of the Dutch health ministry. He was State Secretary for Social Affairs and Employment from February 22, 2007 until December 12, 2008 in the Cabinet Balkenende IV, and is Mayor of Rotterdam since 2009.

Durre S. Ahmed taught from 1975-2009 at the National College of Arts, Pakistan's premier arts institution. She was Professor of Psychology and Communication and Director, Graduate Program in Communication and Cultural Studies She is the author of *Masculinity, Rationality and Religion: A Feminist Perspective* and editor and contributing author of *Gendering the Spirit: Women, Religion and the Post-colonial Response*. Presently she is Chairperson and Senior Research Fellow at the Center for the Study of Gender and Culture, Lahore. Since 1995 she has been engaged in issues of dialogue, interculturality and Muslims in Europe, particularly in Belgium, at various educational and public institutions. She is one of 9 jurors worldwide for the annual multimillion dollar Templeton Prize for Progress in Religion (2009-2011). Dr. Durre S. Ahmed has Master's degrees in Psychology (Pb); Sociology (Columbia); Communication (Columbia), Education(Columbia) and a Doctorate in Communication and Education (Columbia). She is also a practicing psychotherapist.

Abdullahi Ahmed An-Na`im is *Charles Howard Candler Professor of Law at Emory University*. Abduh, as he is called by his family, friends and students, studied law at the University of Khartoum, in his native Sudan, and Cambridge, England and earned his Ph.D. from the University of Edinburgh, Scotland. He taught law since 1976, first in Sudan, and then USA, Canada, Sweden, and did research work in many parts of Africa and Southeast Asia. An-Na`im is the author of *Islam and the Secular State* (2008); *African Constitutionalism and the Role of Islam* (2006); and *Toward an Islamic Reformation: Civil liberties, Human Rights and International Law* (1990). His edited books include

List of Contributors

Human Rights under African Constitutions (2003); *Islamic Family Law in a Changing World: A Global Resource Book* (2002); *Cultural Transformation and Human Rights in Africa* (2002); *The Cultural Dimensions of Human Rights in the Arab World* (in Arabic, 1994); *Human Rights in Cross-Cultural Perspectives: Quest for consensus* (1992). He has also published more than sixty articles and book chapters on human rights, constitutionalism, Islamic law and politics. Websites of his research projects at Emory Law School include Women and Land in Africa, Islamic Family Law and Islam and human rights are all linked to his homepage at www.law.emory.edu/aannaim. His current project on the Future of Shari`a (Islamic Law) can be viewed at http://sharia.law.emory.edu

Shaheen Sardar Ali is Professor of Law at the University of Warwick in the United Kingdom, Professor II at the University of Oslo, Norway and Vice-Chair, United Nations Working Group on Arbitrary Detention. Formerly she was Professor of Law at the University of Peshawar, Pakistan. She has served as Chair of the National Commission on the Status of Women of Pakistan and cabinet Minister for Health, Population Welfare and Women Development in the north west frontier province of Pakistan. Her research interests include International Law of Human Rights, Women's Human Rights, Children's Rights, Public International Law, Islamic Law and Jurisprudence, Gender and the Law, Constitutional Theory and Alternate Dispute Resolution. She has written more than sixty articles and chapters for books, authored five books and edited two, the most widely read of which is *Gender and Human Rights in Islam and International Law: Equal Before Allah, Unequal Before Man?* She was awarded the British Muslims Annual honours achievement plaque in the House of Lords in May 2002 and the Asian Woman of Achievement Award in the Public Sector in 2005.

Mohammed Benzakour was born in the Reef mountains. He came to Holland as a child. During his sociology and public administration studies he became a councillor in the Zwijndrecht town council for the Dutch labour party. After brief excursions in the Dutch parliament and the civil service he discovered his writing talent when in 1998 NRC Handelsblad published his first article. The columns that followed in, among others, *Contrast* and the *Volkskrant* regularly caused controversy and later appeared in Benzakour's collected columns, *Osama's Cave: Allah, Holland and me* (2005) and *Stinking Surgeons* (2008). He received the ASN Media Prize in 1999 and the Silver Zebra in 2001 for insights in a 'society in motion' He also won the Peace Prize for Journalism.

Jean-Yves Carlier is professor at the Université catholique de Louvain (UCL), the Université de Liège and avocat (Belgium). He is or was visiting professor in different universities (Paris 2, Caen, Genève, Montréal, Liège, Ouagadougou, Cotonou, Bujumbura). He is president of the *Centre Charles De Visscher pour le droit international et européen* (CeDIE, UCL). He teaches International Private Law, European Law and Human Rights. Among his publications: *Autonomie de la volonté et statut personnel,*(Bruylant, 1992); *Europe and refugees: A Challenge?*, (ed. with Dirk Vanheule, Kluwer, 1997); *Who is a Refugee?* (with K. Hulhmann, C. Peña Galiano and D. Vanheule, Kluwer, 1997); *The Free Movement of Persons Living with HIV/AIDS*, (Official Publication of the European Community, 2000); *La Charte des droits fondamentaux de l'Union européenne* (ed. with O. De Schutter, Bruylant, 2002); *Droit des étrangers et nationalité* (ed. with S. Saroléa, Larcier, 2005); *Le Code marocain de la famille. Incidences au regard du droit international privé en Europe* (with M.-C. Foblets, Bruylant, 2005); *L'avenir de la libre circulation des personnes dans l'U.E./The Future of Free Movement of Persons in the EU* (ed. with E. Guild, Bruylant, 2006); *La condition des personnes dans l'Union européenne* (Larcier, 2007); *The Status of Persons in the European Union,* Casebook (Bruylant, 2008); Droit d'asile et des réfugiés, De la protection aux droits, *Recueil des cours, Académie de droit international, La Haye,* 2008, t. 332 (2007), pp. 9-354. More: http://www.uclouvain.be/169115.html

Marie-Claire Foblets is professor of Law and of Anthropology at the Universities of Leuven (Louvain) and Antwerp. She actually chairs the Institute for Migration Law and Legal Anthropology at the Law Faculty in Louvain (Leuven). Her research focuses on migration law, including citizenship/nationality laws, compulsory integration, anti-racism and non-discrimination. In the field of anthropology of law, her research focuses on cultural diversity and legal practice with a particular interest in the application of Islamic family laws in Europe, and more recently in accommodation of cultural and religious diversity under State law (i.a.: M.-C. Foblets, *Les familles maghrébines et la justice en Belgique. Anthropologie juridique et immigration*, Paris, Karthala, 1994; M.-C. Foblets (ed.), *Familles – Islam – Europe. Le droit confronté au changement*, Paris, L'Harmattan, 1996 (coll. Musulmans d'Europe); M.-C. Foblets (ed.), *Femmes marocaines et conflits familiaux en* *immigration. Quelles solutions juridiques appropriées?*, Antwerp, Maklu, 1998; M.-C. Foblets and J.Y. Carlier, *Le nouveau Code marocain de la famille. Son application en Europe* [The Family Code in Morocco. Its Application in Europe], Brussels, Bruylant, 2005; M.-C Foblets, *Recht op maat. Culturen in de rechtbank* [Culture(s) in the court room. Justice made to measure], Antwerp, Maklu (forthcoming).

Ziba Mir-Hosseini is an independent consultant, researcher and writer on Middle Eastern issues, based at the London Middle East Institute and the Centre for Middle Eastern and Islamic Law, both at SOAS, University of London. She specializes in gender, family relations, Islamic law and development. She has a BA in Sociology from Tehran University (1974) and PhD in Social Anthropology from University of Cambridge (1980), and has held numerous research fellowships and visiting professorships; she has been Hauser Global Law Visiting Professor at New York University since 2002. She is a founding member of Musawah Global Movement for Equality and Justice in the Muslim Family. Her publications include *Marriage on Trial: A Study of Islamic Family Law in Iran and Morocco* (I.B. Tauris, 1993, 2002), *Islam and Gender: The Religious Debate in Contemporary Iran* (Princeton University Press, 1999), and (with Richard Tapper) *Islam and Democracy in Iran: Eshkevari and the Quest for Reform* (I.B. Tauris, 2006). She has also directed (with Kim Longinotto) two award-winning feature-length documentary films on contemporary issues in Iran: *Divorce Iranian Style* (1998) and *Runaway* (2001).

Fouad Laroui is an economist of Moroccan origin and writer. After his studies in the Lycée Lyautey (Casablanca), he joined the prestigious École Nationale des Ponts et Chaussées (Paris, France), where he studied engineering. Later he obtained a PhD in economics and moved to the Netherlands where he is currently teaching econometrics and environmental science at the VU Universiteit Amsterdam. He became a Dutch citizen in 1995. He is a most successful writer and was awarded several times for his publications. One may remember: *Les dents du topographe* (Prix Découverte Albert-Camus) (1996); *Vreemdeling: aangenaam* (2001); *Verbannen woorden* (2002; in this same year he received the E. du Perronprijs for his whole work); *Chroniques des temps déraisonnables* (2002); *L'Oued et le Consul; Et autres nouvelles* (2002); *Tu n'as rien compris à Hassan II* (2004); *De l'islamisme. Une réfutation personnelle du totalitarisme religieux* (2006).

List of Contributors

Bettina Leysen is currently gynaecologist-consultant at the Universitair Ziekenhuis Antwerpen and lecturer in the field of "Culture and Health" at Cimic (Center for Intercultural Management and International Communication) at the Katholieke Hogeschool Mechelen. She has been the driving force behind the A. & A. Leysen Forum.

Rashida Manjoo is the UN Special Rapporteur on Violence against Women. Most recently, she has served as the Des Lee Distinguished Visiting Professor at Webster University, USA where she has taught courses in human rights with a particular focus on women's human rights and also transitional justice. She is also a Professor in the Department of Public Law at the University of Cape Town, South Africa where she collaborates on research relating to culture, religion and women's human rights. She is an Advocate of the High Court of South Africa and a former commissioner of the Commission on Gender Equality (CGE), a constitutional body mandated to oversee the promotion and protection of gender equality. She was the Eleanor Roosevelt Fellow with the Human Rights Program at Harvard Law School (2006-07) and also a clinical instructor in the program in 2005-2006.

Bhikhu Parekh is Emeritus Professor of Political Philosophy at the Universities of Hull and Westminster, and was until recently Centennial Professor at the Centre for Global Governance at the London School of Economics. He is the author of several widely acclaimed books in political philosophy, the latest being *A New Politics of Identity* published by Macmillan in 2008. He has been a Visiting Professor at several universities including McGill, Harvard and University of Pennsylvania. He has received many academic awards including Isaiah Berlin Prize for Lifetime Contribution to Political Philosophy. He is a Fellow of the British Academy, of the European Academy, and of the Royal Society of Arts.

Mathias Rohe (born 1959 in Stuttgart/Germany) studied law and Islamic sciences in Tuebingen and Damascus. He holds the chair for Civil Law, Private International Law and Comparative Law at the University of Erlangen-Nuremberg (Germany). After having served as a judge at the Court of Appeals of Nuremberg for a number of years, he is now in charge as the founding director of the Erlangen Center for Islam and the Law in Europe at his university. He has published intensely on Islamic law and on legal issues related to Muslims in the West (e.g.: *Das islamische Recht: Geschichte und Gegenwart*, 1st and

List of Contributors

2nd eds. Munich 2009, C.H. Beck – to be translated into English due to an award given by the German Ministry of Foreign Affairs and others; *Muslims and the Law in Europe: Chances and Challenges*, New Delhi 2007, Global Media Publications). He works as an advisor for several German and European governments and is a member of the German Islam Konferenz.

Cedric Ryngaert is Assistant Professor of International Law at Leuven University and Utrecht University. He is a BOF research fellow at Leuven University, and a member of the Leuven Centre for Global Governance Studies and the Dutch Research School of Human Rights. He has published mainly in the fields of the law of jurisdiction, immunity, international criminal justice, human rights, and non-state actors in international law. In 2008, he conducted a study for the Advisory Council of International Affairs of the Dutch Ministry of Foreign Affairs on the universality of human rights. This study formed the basis for his contribution to this volume.

Prakash Shah is currently Senior Lecturer at the School of Law, Queen Mary, University of London. His specialist areas include ethnic minorities and diasporas in law, religion and law, immigration, refugee and nationality law and comparative law and legal pluralism. He has previously taught at the School of Oriental and African Studies and the University of Kent at Canterbury in the UK, and at the International Institute for the Sociology of Law, Oñati, Spain. He is editor of a book series with Ashgate on Cultural Diversity and Law and managing editor of the *Journal of Immigration, Asylum and Nationality Law*. Some of his recent publications include: *Legal Practice and Cultural Diversity* (Aldershot, Ashgate, 2009, joint editor), *Law and Ethnic Plurality: Socio-Legal Perspectives* (Leiden and Boston, Martinus Nijhoff, 2007, editor), *Migration, Diasporas and Legal Systems in Europe* (London, RoutledgeCavendish, 2006, editor with Werner F. Menski), *The Challenge of Asylum to Legal Systems* (London, Cavendish, 2005, editor), and *Legal Pluralism in Conflict: Coping with Cultural Diversity in Law* (London, Glass House, 2005, sole authored).

www.ingramcontent.com/pod-product-compliance
Ingram Content Group UK Ltd.
Pitfield, Milton Keynes, MK11 3LW, UK
UKHW041914140426
5217IPUK00013B/154